Boom Bust

Boom Bust

HOUSE PRICES, BANKING AND
THE DEPRESSION
OF
2010

Fred Harrison

SHEPHEARD-WALWYN (PUBLISHERS) LTD

First published in 2005 by
Shepheard-Walwyn (Publishers) Ltd
15 Alder Road
London SW14 8ER
Reprinted 2005
Paperback reprint 2007
2nd edition November 2007

British Library Cataloguing in Publication Data
A catalogue record of this book
is available from the British Library

ISBN-13: 978-0-85683-254-3
ISBN-10: 0-85683-254-5

Typeset by Alacrity,
Chesterfield, Sandford, Somerset
Printed and bound in the United Kingdom by
Bookforce

Contents

Acknowledgements   vii

Preface to the Second Edition   ix

Prologue   xiii

PART I
AS SAFE AS HOUSES?

1   Britain's Housing and the Business Cycle   3

2   Banking on Failure   21

3   The American State of Virtual Reality   38

4   The Incredible Alan Greenspan   54

PART II
GENESIS OF THE BOOM-BUST CYCLE

5   Rent and the 18-Year Cycle   73

6   The Patterns of History   '   100

7   The Alchemy of Land Speculation   119

8   The End of Boom Bust?   135

PART III
ANATOMY OF THE FIRST GLOBAL CYCLE

9   The New Economy: Selling an Anglo-American
     Myth   155

10   Launched in the USA   168

11   Gordon Brown's Magic Mantra   185

PART IV
THE AUTOMATIC STABILISER

12   Counter-Cyclical Action   207

13   Australia: The Pathology of Taxation   226

14   Dividends from Democratised Finance   246

PART V
THE RECKONING

15   2007: From Peak to Downwave   265

Index   274

Acknowledgements

IT IS WITH PLEASURE that I take this opportunity to thank those who helped me to bring *Boom Bust* to fruition. In particular, my gratitude is extended to Mason Gaffney and Ron Banks for their wise counsel over the years; Ed. Dodson (USA) and Bryan Kavanagh (Australia) who generously shared with me the results of research in their countries; and Don Riley for stepping in with material support at a time when I most needed it. My publisher Anthony Werner has been a relentless source of constructive criticisms, and Anne Morrell bore with fortitude the tedium of correcting what seemed like an endless stream of revisions. No words, however, can adequately express the debt I owe to my wife, Rita, whose moral support and editing skills were indispensable in bringing this volume to a conclusion.

To Rita

Preface to the Second Edition

I T WAS with mixed feelings that I witnessed the end of the housing boom in the United States in 2006. I was sad, because the real estate downturn confirmed my prediction, made two years ago, that the global economy was on track for a major slump. Millions of pensioners and home buyers will lose billions of dollars. With cheap credit, those families had borrowed their way into the great American Dream. They were encouraged to assume that rising house prices would provide adequate collateral for their homes, furniture, car and vacations. Those dreams will now be crushed by the brutal mathematics of property speculation.

But I was also angry, because it could have been avoided. The financial 'products' that were used by the banks to raise further loans had locked families and pensioners into a trap. Rising interest rates caused sub-prime householders to default, which precipitated the fall in house prices. This, in turn, undermined the value of the collateralised products that banks traded among themselves. And that was why the credit chain snapped.

I had predicted this outcome. But when *Boom Bust* was published in 2005, economists told me that it was fanciful to believe that we would live through another depression. Central banks around the world, I was assured, had learnt the lessons of the 1930s.

So why was I standing in a queue with hundreds of depositors, many of them pensioners, at dawn on Monday, September 18, 2007, outside the locked doors of the Northern Rock? As Britain's fifth largest mortgage lender, this was supposed to be a secure home for their life's savings. But they wanted their money out – causing a run on the bank, a classic feature of the 1929 crash in America that led to the Great Depression.

I wanted to know why the savers did not accept the reassurances of the Bank of England, which offered bail-out money. They were not willing to take the word of the government that it would guarantee their deposits. This loss of trust was the most disturbing feature of the credit crisis. People voted with their feet to tell the politicians that their guarantees were not worth anything.

I should not have been surprised at this absence of trust. The depositors could not be expected to read the Northern Rock's balance sheet and work out whether it was solvent. After all, even the bankers of Wall Street and the City of London were caught unawares as credit began to dry up in August. When it came to the crunch, *the banks did not trust each other!* They were unwilling to lend money between themselves, so people's instincts – to reclaim their cash from Northern Rock – appeared to make sense. Their bank was the most exposed to the credit crunch in Britain.

There was a deep irony about the plight of Northern Rock. For me, it symbolised the cynicism of a financial sector that had grown fat on bonuses. Did that explain why they were not interested when I sounded the alarm bell? A senior executive from Northern Rock inadvertently revealed the attitude of the moneymen. It happened at a meeting in London. I was invited to brief a group of high-powered financiers. As we were departing, the man from Northern Rock said: 'At least we will still be here' – meaning, if there was a housing-led recession, his bank would survive the turmoil that I was forecasting.[1] Little did he know that Northern Rock would become the first big league victim in Britain. Four weeks after the credit crunch began in the US, Northern Rock was For Sale.[2]

Over four days, depositors removed an estimated £3bn from the bank's vaults. They panicked because they were not familiar with the fine detail of the crisis that originated with the multi-billion dollar payments for assets that were of dubious value. The bankers had invented a new game of Money Musical Chairs. Now the music had stopped. The problem was that many of the losers left standing could not be identified. Some of them held financial instruments that were worthless; but balance sheets did not reveal who held them.

One man who should have given sufficient warning to the banks was Alan Greenspan, when he was Chairman of the US Federal Reserve. He failed to do so, and after retiring in 2006 he invented a new school of thought that we will call *psychonomics*. House price bubbles, he claims in *The Age of Turbulence*, were rooted in the human psyche and people's euphoria-to-fear mood swings. This mystification of the science of economics enabled him to blame the credit crisis on 'human nature'. He also claims that no one could have forecasted the crisis. But a year before he retired, the first edition of *Boom Bust* warned (on page 181) of the exotic financial devices that were created in the speculative phase of the cycle, which concealed bad debts.

The regulatory authorities lost track of this debt mountain, because it was quickly repackaged in new financial instruments and sold to institutions.

Mortgages were wrapped up in collateralised debt obligations (CDOs) and sold to others to 'spread the risk'. Reckless lenders mixed poor quality loans (to borrowers who purchased houses built on sand in Florida, for example) with secure mortgages on properties in high-value locations in New England. Then they off-loaded the packages and pocketed the proceeds. So the credit merry-go-round whirled on the back of house prices that were soaring towards what I called the 'Winners' Curse' phase of the business cycle (see page 89). I warned that, instead of 'a clean-out of the debt, the excesses ... were concealed in opaque accounting practices and laundered through the world's financial markets'.

No one, anywhere in the world, was immune. People who did not engage in real estate speculation on a socially significant scale, like Germans, were exposed to the virus that was incubated in the US money markets. Germany was infected because her banks invested in financial instruments that contained mortgaged properties from as far afield as San Diego in Southern California, where house prices rose by 22% in 2002 alone. The warning of the clear and present danger went out with the first edition of *Boom Bust*:

> The banks transferred the risks to others; and that, ultimately, meant it was carried by working people through a reduction in the quality of the investments held by their pension funds.

As home-owners defaulted, the implications of the bad debts dawned on the bankers. Stock markets panicked as investors tried to get their money back. Bill Gross, head of the world's largest bond fund (the California-based Pacific Investment Management Company), appealed to President George W. Bush to 'write some cheques' to 'prevent destructive housing deflation'. A 10% drop in house prices, he warned, would represent the sharpest drop in asset prices since the Great Depression of the 1930s. In some regional markets, the drop exceeded 10%.

For the UK, I predicted that house prices would achieve double-digit growth in 2007. I was correct (see Table 1 below). I also forecast that Britain's housing market would stall at its peak when the ratio of average house prices to average earnings hit 6.5 (see page 6, Table 1:1). That ratio was achieved in the summer of 2007.[3]

TABLE I

House Price Increases at 2007^{Q_1} (%)

	1 year change	2 year change	5 year change
UK	13	30	90
Australia	9	13	54
Canada	10	24	36
USA	-1.3	18	36

Source: Halifax; Datastream.

The financial trauma of 2007 need not have happened, but that is not what Alan Greenspan wants to hear. He has a legacy to protect as 'the world's greatest central banker'. So referring to the cycles of boom/busts, he asserts: 'There's no way of altering the pattern'.[4] But thanks to the policy failures of people like Greenspan, patterns *will* now be altered. For in the upswing of the next business cycle, cash-flush, resource-rich nations will no longer be in awe of the acumen of Wall Street and the City of London. The consequences for geo-political power will be profound. Yesterday's underdogs – in China and India, in Russia and the Middle East – will watch in horror as millions of people in the Anglo-American countries lose their homes. This will be interpreted as the betrayal of the trust on which moneymen depend for their business. A weakened Western economy – the crises com-pounded by the failure of President Bush's foreign policies (notably, in the Near East) – will suffer the fragmentation of its financial centres in favour of Shanghai, Mumbai and Dubai. The degree to which the West will be able to recover to meet this challenge depends on the willingness of its leaders to adopt the counter-cyclical policy that I describe in Part IV.

London
November 2007

REFERENCES

1 Because the meeting was sponsored under Chatham House rule (everything said would remain confidential), I cannot disclose the identity of the host organisation, one of Britain's leading financial institutions.
2 Lloyds TSB was reported to have been invited by Northern Rock to launch a rescue takeover, which the Bank of England vetoed. John Waples and Grant Ringshaw, 'Northern Rock takeover blocked', *Sunday Times Business*, September 16, 2007.
3 The Halifax Rural Housing Review reported that the ratio hit 7.1 in the country-side and 6.2 in towns.
4 Edmund Conway, 'You cannot end cycles of boom and bust – it's human nature', *The Daily Telegraph*, September 17, 2007. This was an interview with Greenspan, to promote his memoirs.

Prologue

NASA is the US Government's space-probing agency. American taxpayers have funded its scientific research and manned missions with hundreds of billions of dollars. No expense is spared to gather the best brains to devise the most sensitive instruments to deepen our knowledge of the physics affecting Earth. And yet, NASA failed to alert us to an emerging danger, one that has the potential to destroy life itself. The hole in the ozone layer, an earth-scorching opening of the curtain that screens us from ultraviolet radiation, was not identified. It remained nature's secret until Joseph Farman and his colleagues of the British Antarctic Survey discovered it in 1985.

Why did NASA fail? Actually, it did not miss the changes. The agency's sophisticated equipment logged the data. 'Their instruments had recorded the losses [of ozone],' reported *Business Week* (July 22, 1991, p.10), 'but the computer interpreting the results had been programmed to ignore readings that deviated so far from normal.' Computers are as intelligent as the intelligence that is fed into them. The problem was with the way NASA applied its knowledge. The scientists chose to ignore as unimportant the numbers that were too far from what they regarded as the norm. Because the readings on the instruments were abnormal, they could be dismissed as aberration.

A similar problem arises with the way social scientists apply their knowledge of the working mechanisms of capitalism. The instruments employed by governments are far from perfect, but they *do* collate alarming evidence that should trigger the red warning lights. But like NASA, government goes into sleep mode when the statistics on inflation deviate from the expected norm (anywhere between 2% and 10%) to alarmingly high (20% increases in house prices) to shattering annual price rises of up to 60% in the land market. Conventional economic wisdom excludes the numbers that deviate too far from the officially sanctioned norm.

As a result, the 'hole' in the capitalist economy – the cyclical recessions that play havoc with the finances of households and the budgets of nations – remains a mystery. The problem is with the way that the data is interpreted. The representatives of the people fail to *comprehend* what we can see with our eyes. We walk all over the facts, but we cannot make sense of them. Despite the best brains at the disposal of governments, despite the vast amounts of money devoted to research in our universities, we continue to disregard the earth-bound realities.

In this study, I level the charge of negligence against Tony Blair's finance minister, Gordon Brown, and American central banker Alan Greenspan. But this study is not a party political attack. It diagnoses the problem with the philosophy at the heart of government economic policy. Aspects of that philosophy which ought to be challenged are silently accepted by all parties. Thus, while I partly characterise the problems in Britain and the USA in terms of the biographies of a few influential men, we have to remember that finance ministers and central bankers come and go; the booms and busts that destabilise our societies, however, are the product of some of the laws and institutions that underpin our communities.

My argument with the people in authority is that they ought to know better. Central bankers have a duty to speak plain English, to offer a comprehensive account of the financial workings of the economy so that we may take control of our destinies. But Greenspan turned his knack of disguising the meaning of his words into a joke. Irwin Stelzer, a close observer of the US economy, noted that Greenspan 'is famous for his ability to use language in such a way that it ceases to be a means of communication'.[1] As for politicians, they have a duty of leadership to the people who trusted them with their votes of confidence, so they ought to offer decisive plans for change rather than compromising for fear of losing votes. They would lose those votes only if they failed to explain the reasons why it is necessary to reform some of our key practices in the realms of public finance and property rights.

Self-censorship has damaged governance to the point where central bankers and finance ministers have imposed on us a crude tool of economic management – the rate of interest, the cost of borrowing money. Monetary policy – as it is currently administered – exacts a heavy price on people who work for their living. Economists call that price the 'sacrifice ratio' – the cumulative loss of output that results from action to reduce inflation.[2] They cannot agree on the scale of those losses. If the policy moderated the booms and busts, the price might be worth paying. It doesn't. Monetary policy is forced to carry too great a burden of responsibility for the excesses of those who can exploit the weaknesses in the structure of the capitalist economy. Monetary policy affords the appearance of action for the people in authority, but it cannot ultimately challenge the powerful forces that periodically cause economic activity to slump.

If there were no remedy to the cycles of booms and busts we might tolerate the charade. There is therapeutic value to be derived from engagement in acts of symbolic gestures. We may not actually be able to exclude the evil spirits from our communities, but the chants and rituals that warn them may make some people *feel* more secure. But I claim that a remedy for booms and busts does exist.

If I am correct, what are the implications? We would need to reinterpret the significance of the central bankers' conclaves. When they meet to judge whether to raise or lower the interest rate, they participate in a psychodrama that has more to do with appearances than with reality. Do we feel better for this ritual? When the bankers emerge to pronounce on how much we will have to pay to borrow money, the collateral consequences of their decisions are damaging for the enterprise economy. The negative impacts apply whether the interest rate is raised or lowered. Either way, a malfunctioning economy is further impaired, not stabilised, in a financial onslaught that transmits negative effects on the way people work, save and invest.

In the course of my interrogation of the evidence, I challenge Gordon Brown with the accusation that his analysis is fatally flawed. He appeals to 200 years of history to endorse his management of the UK economy – a claim promoted by Tony Blair's government in the general election of 2005. I draw on 400 years of evidence to demonstrate that the decisions he took when coming to power in 1997 would make little difference to boom-bust cycles.

Everyone needs shelter. And yet, for three centuries, working people have found it difficult to provide decent homes for themselves. Either we have to blame nature as being niggardly (in which case, nature is curiously selective in the way it bestows its favours), or the foundations of our laws and institutions are seriously defective. I refute the claim that we can hold nature responsible. The Industrial Revolution provided us with the compressed power to deliver all the material goods that we could possibly want. And yet, many people are denied the dwellings they need at prices they can afford. From the agricultural 18th century through the heyday of industrialism in the 19th and 20th centuries to the so-called 'New Economy' of the 21st century, the same pattern may be traced: the same social processes that deprive people of that most basic of needs, the shelter that is supposed to be the family nest.

I take as representative of the conventional views the words and deeds of the Governor of the Bank of England and the Chairman of the US Federal Reserve. They believe that the rate of interest can be manipulated to iron out the business cycle. I will explain why this is based on a fundamentally deficient understanding of the internal mechanisms of the market economy. *As it is at present structured, capitalism is congenitally incapable of balanced growth.* Manipulation of interest rates will not alter that fact; on the contrary, it exacerbates the turbulence in the markets that are supposed to order people's labour and their savings.

If I am correct, if my explanation provides a robust account of the causes of booms and busts, the implications are profound. It becomes possible for people to plan with greater confidence, to time the purchase of their homes and the amount they must save to meet the needs of their children and their retirement years.

If I am correct, the onus is placed on people to take control of their fate. The booms and busts over three centuries have slipped through the sophisticated financial and organisational defences invented by the most ingenious of entrepreneurs, they have overwhelmed the most powerful of governments and defeated the collaborative efforts of people working in partnership through organisations such as trade unions and co-operative societies. But these failures arose because people were not equipped with the knowledge that would enable them to trace so many of their problems to the root cause. That knowledge is now at their disposal.

If I am correct, the time has come to declare a democratic war on taxation. The public's finances have been transformed into a divisive tool in what are supposed to be democracies of the people. I shall explain why the home-owner, in particular, bears a heavy responsibility. For many reasons, the people who hold the title deeds to their properties ought to take the initiative and lead a campaign of reform to change the way we pay for the services that we share.

Now, armed with the insights that I offer, it is no longer possible to resign ourselves to the inevitability of feverish booms and ruinous busts. We must cease to demonise the hate-figures of history, notably the landlords. Socialists continue to fight the wars of obsolete doctrines. The *New Statesman*, for examples, the voice of the British Left, in a cover story (September 20, 2004), shrieked: 'Hands off our land! How millions are deprived of a home by a few aristocrats'. While we continue to wage ideological war on the enemies of yesterday, millions of people will continue to suffer exclusion from their birthrights and labour rights. Political philosophy needs to move on to the realities of today, because *we the people* have become part of the problem. We cannot honestly continue to blame others for the repeated breakdowns in the economy.

We, the property-owning people, have the democratic power to insist on changes to those laws and institutions that conspire to defeat the legitimate aspirations of all of us. But the temptations to remain silent are great. Homeowners, in particular, have been enriched beyond their wildest dreams by the injustices that are built into the principles of governance. The increase in the equity in their homes, however, has its dark side: the escalation of debt that hangs around the necks of millions of people. As we see from the table below, the debt burden in Britain accelerated during the housing boom at the beginning of the century. Professor Peter Ambrose estimates that housing debt between 1980 and 2004 ought to have increased to about £155bn, allowing for inflation and the increase in home ownership.[3] In fact, debt rose to more than £800bn (2004). For those cashing in their equity, the housing market looks like a sure-fire bet. For those who need homes, the housing market means a lifetime of bondage.

TABLE I

UK Housing Debt & GDP: £bn

	1980	1985	1990	1995	2000	2002
Housing debt outstanding	53	127	295	390	536	671
Gross Domestic Product	231	355	557	719	950	1037
Debt as % of GDP	23	36	53	54	56	65

Source: Steve Wilcox, *UK Housing Review 2003/2004*, Coventry: Chartered Institute of Housing, 2003, Table 45, p.131.

This pathological state of affairs cannot be blamed on the psychological failings of individuals. Economic instability is primarily due to tax-and-tenure laws that institutionalise booms and busts, for which governments are responsible. Two examples from the run-up to the Depression of 2010 illustrate the failure of politics.

- **In the USA,** investors uncovered an old tax law that enabled them to buy commercial property without paying capital gains tax. Speculators created Tenants in Common Associations and rushed into 'the fastest-growing property ownership strategy since the Oklahoma land rushes of the 1890s'.[4]
- **In the UK,** Gordon Brown opened a yawning gap in the tax laws to foster speculation in property from April 2006. Under his new pension rules, investors could channel pension funds into real

estate and reduce their tax liabilities – their money matched by donations from the public purse.[5]

In both cases, the privileged treatment of real estate (i) pushes prices above realistic levels, and (ii) transfers tax revenue paid by low-income wage-earners to high-income owners of land. Thus, fiscal policy – working through the land market – redistributes income from the poor to the rich; fostering windfall gains for a minority and a lifetime's indebtedness for the poor.

In the course of my investigation into the pathological conditions that foster this indebtedness, I shall accuse some of our policy-makers and social scientists of failing in their duties as stewards of the nation's interests. They presume to organise people's lives by manipulating the cost of borrowing money, but their decisions are ultimately grounded in wilful ignorance. The Bank of England's Monetary Policy Committee (MPC) is a case in point. In 2004, it raised interest rates without a full understanding of the impact on the housing market. Its economists did not know what the consequences would be on people's consumption decisions or the direction in which house prices would move. It was no comfort to be told by Mervyn King, the Governor of the Bank of England:

> I do not know where house prices are going – but I also know that no-one else does either.[6]

People who are handsomely paid to know the answers may be ignorant, but the reader of this book will now gain a deeper understanding of the vital trends without having to rely on the experts. And that is how it should be, for the ultimate responsibility for our common wealth, our personal prosperity and the welfare of our communities resides in the hearts and minds of each and every one of us.

REFERENCES

1   Irwin Stelzer, 'Fed's Greenspan faces a tricky balancing act', *Sunday Times*, January 9, 2005.
2   Ed Balls and Gus O'Donnell, *Reforming Britain's Economic and Financial Policy*, Basingstoke: Palgrave, 2002, pp.78-80.
3   Peter Ambrose, 'British Housing', mimeo, Filling the Vacuum Conference, London, October 15, 2004.
4   Jim Pickard, '1031 trend takes off in the US', *Financial Times*, January 4, 2005.
5   Kathryn Cooper, 'Buy-to-let investors get £4bn tax boost', *Sunday Times Money*, January 9, 2005.
6   Scheherazade Daneshkhu, 'After signs of slow down, which "path to equilibrium" will house prices take?' *Financial Times*, September 25, 2004.

PART I

As Safe as Houses?

I

Britain's Housing
and the Business Cycle

§1 A Budget for Boom Bust

MARCH 17, 2004, 12.30 pm: the dispatch box of the House of
Commons. Gordon Brown rose from the green bench occupied by
ministers of Her Majesty's Government. This was his eighth budget,
and the last day on which he could announce a remedy for the looming boom bust. Would he vindicate his claim to be the prudent
Chancellor of the Exchequer who had balanced the nation's books and
steered Britain around the recession of 2001? Or would he fail the test
that he had set for himself as head of the Treasury? The contents of
Brown's speech would determine Britain's economic fate for a decade.
He had left it to the last minute. By my calculations, he had three years
in which to introduce legislation and implement a pre-emptive strike
against the violent beasts that lurk inside the capitalist economy – the
booms and busts.

Twice before, in 1909 and 1931, Brown's predecessors had legislated
changes to taxes that laid the foundations for sustained growth. But
the reforms were expunged from the law books because of the
implacable opposition of the peers of the realm. This time, it could be
different. Tony Blair's government had a majority in the Commons of
159 MPs. And he had dismantled the blood-line buttresses that protected the privileges of the House of Lords. All that the government
now needed was for Gordon Brown to act as a tough-minded chancellor to reform public finances in a way that would finally shift real
power to the people.

The chancellor knew where to look for the vulnerable points in the
economy. A year earlier, he correctly identified the issue that defeated
his predecessors. They had strained to deliver full employment, but
were repeatedly thwarted by activity in the housing market. When
Brown stepped into the Treasury building in Parliament Street, at the

bottom of Whitehall, in 1997, he was determined not to suffer that ignominy. He asked his civil servants to analyse and learn from the business cycles that terminated in recessions. He revealed their findings in his budget speech on April 9, 2003. Brown compared Britain's record with countries like France and Germany, and drew this conclusion:

> Most stop-go problems that Britain has suffered in the last 50 years have been led or influenced by the more highly cyclical and often more volatile nature of our housing market.

Politically, this diagnosis helped Brown to defer a decision on an awkward problem. He used the housing cycle as a reason to delay the announcement on whether Britain should abandon sterling in favour of the European Union's currency, the euro. Britain needed to synchronise itself into the continent's housing markets, which were less prone to violent price swings. Then Britain could contemplate locking herself into Europe's monetary system. But the decision to use the housing market to stall on the euro exposed the void in Brown's policies. Now, he would have to explain how he would prevent the next housing boom bust. With prices at the beginning of the decade rising at annual rates of 20% or more, the housing market was 'overheated'. What could be done to prevent similar price rises at the end of the decade, prices that would initiate a wild spending spree and the downturn in the years from 2008 into the trough of 2010? To search for solutions and buy more time, Brown commissioned reports from two eminent economists on the financing and supply of residential property. The results of those enquiries were in his hands when he stood up to address the House of Commons on March 17, 2004.

The parliamentary sketch writers in the Press Gallery were preoccupied by the sub-text of the budget speech. Gordon Brown was pitching for the top job in government. He wanted to move into No. 10 Downing Street lock, stock and barrel. He already lived in the small apartment above No. 10, by agreement with Tony Blair. But he also wanted to occupy the Prime Minister's office. Practically everything that he had done during the seven years of his chancellorship was weighed in terms of whether they would affect his prospects of becoming Premier. Brown's political future was bound up with the health of the economy.

His first task was to establish – and advertise – his credentials as the master craftsman of economic management. Since 1945, he told the law-makers who packed the Commons, Britain had repeatedly lapsed into recession, moving from boom to bust.

> But I can report that since 1997 Britain has sustained growth
> not just through one economic cycle but through two economic
> cycles, without suffering the old British disease of stop go –
> with overall growth since 2000 almost twice that of Europe and
> higher even than that of the United States.

The Presbyterian Scotsman was not averse to singing his own praises. He was triumphant as he pronounced his willingness to confront the 'tough decisions' head-on. As a result, he had entered the history books as the architect of a strategy that would deliver prosperity uninterrupted by the downturns that had caused misery for millions in the past.

But there was more to come. Gordon Brown's achievements were even more awesome.

> Having asked the Treasury to investigate in greater historical
> detail, I can now report that Britain is enjoying its longest
> period of sustained economic growth for more than 200 years
> ... the longest period of sustained growth since the beginning of
> the Industrial Revolution.

Here was a claim of historic significance. Earlier generations of economists and finance ministers had struggled to find the secret of sustainable growth. The formula had eluded them. And then along came Gordon Brown, the heir apparent to the New Labour throne, and the magical formula was pulled out of the red ministerial briefcase.

It was all an illusion. Gordon Brown had not introduced the reforms that could neutralise the propensity of the economy to surge to the peaks that terminate in a valley of tears. Having failed to set in place the preventive measures, the Brown boom bust of 2005-10 would go down in the history books as yet another dismal failure in the quest for sustainable growth.

But that outcome was not on the minds of the journalists who gathered to hear the chancellor. Most of them were willing to declare him a competent master of the art of economic management. The challenge for Brown was to maintain that illusion. How would he perform his sleight of hand? The eagle-eyed politicians on the benches of Her Majesty's Opposition failed to spot the crafty juggling that lulled the nation into thinking that it was in safe hands. The financiers in the City of London also failed to realise that Brown's micro-management techniques had fostered the formative stages of the most traumatic phase in the business cycle.

To expose the interior flaws in the policy edifice that he constructed with meticulous care, we will apply Brown's own tests.

● A government that permits volatility in house prices is locked into
  the stop/go cycle.
● Two hundred years of historical evidence affords the evidence for
  exposing the fatal weaknesses in the foundations of capitalism.

We will push the evidence even further back, and scrutinise
Brown's stewardship by examining 400 years of economic history. In
doing so, we will reveal that Gordon Brown, by his acts and omissions,
allowed the gnawing virus at the base of the industrial economy to
flourish. *He failed to stop people from speculating in the capital gains
that could be captured in the housing market.* The downturn in economic
activity that would follow from this frenzied activity would drive large
swathes of the middle classes into financial crises on an unprecedented
scale.

This happened twice within living memory. Two Tory chancellors,
Anthony Barber in 1970 and Nigel Lawson in 1983, also thought they
could defeat the logic of the business cycle. In fact, they entered
the Treasury as hostages to a historical process which – if it was not
neutralised – would irrevocably associate their names with severe economic volatility (Table 1:1). In each of the post-World War II housing
boom busts, house prices became so unaffordable that they had to
plummet – dragging the rest of the economy down with them.

TABLE 1:1

UK Housing-Driven Boom Busts

Chancellor of the Exchequer	House price peaks	Bust: business cycle's trough	Peak ratio of house prices to earnings	House price falls: %[1]
Anthony Barber (1970-4)	1973/4	1974/5	4.7	33
Nigel Lawson (1983-9)	1988/9	1991/2	5.0	23
Gordon Brown (1997-)	2007/8	2010	[6.5][2]	[20][2]

1 From price peak back to long-run equilibrium; in real terms.
2 Author's forecasts.

The drop in the real value of houses in the mid-'70s was camouflaged. Superficially, the problems began when the Heath government decided to liberalise the financial system in the Competition and Credit Control reforms of September 1971. Record level wage settlements funded by a pliable credit-creating system meant that mortgages and other loans could be eroded away by roaring inflation. But disguising the drop in the real value of people's homes did nothing to moderate the pain felt by those working people who, having struggled to buy their homes, were thrown onto the dole queues.

This ought not to have happened in the 1980s. Margaret Thatcher and her finance ministers were hard-line monetarists. They would not countenance Anthony Barber's profligate pump-priming policies. And yet, they did preside over a classic housing-fuelled consumer boom. Nigel Lawson took the blame. He did, after all, have sufficient time in the Treasury to propose remedial measures. This time, however, the freefall outcome was not so well disguised by inflation: as prices crashed, the homes of hundreds of thousands of families were repossessed because they could not afford to maintain mortgage payments. John Muellbauer, an economist at Nuffield College, Oxford, was one of the few who tried to sound the alarm bells. The house price/consumer debt nexus could be read in the statistical record, but there was something more specific about the nature of the problem that he felt ought to be highlighted.

> Land speculation plays its part too; as prices rise, some land is held back in the hope of being able to sell at a higher price later. After the peak, land prices fall sharply as owners try to sell while prices are still high. The 1971-73 boom followed by the 1974-76 slump was a classic instance of instability.[1]

The third postwar boom bust will be irrevocably associated with the presiding New Labour chancellor, Gordon Brown. In the reported agreement he had with Tony Blair, in return for not competing for the leadership of the Labour Party he would be responsible for domestic policies when and if they came to power. Whatever the truth about that deal, Brown did, indeed, through his control of the public purse, preside over the domestic political agenda. One result was the boom in house prices which priced low-income first-time buyers out of the market in 2002. They were replaced by middle income speculators who invested in buy-to-let apartments. When the property market paused in late 2004 they, in turn, were replaced by relatively rich buyers of property. Thus began the elevation of the ratio of house prices to earnings towards new records. Symbolically leading the rush upwards was Tony Blair and his wife Cherie. When they bought a house in Bayswater in September 2004 for £3.6m, City Editor Robert Peston calculated that 'they are borrowing about six times their combined income'.[2] Others would emulate the Blair family's willingness to go deep into debt to the point where, when the collapse came, many of them would be bankrupt.

This outcome could have been avoided. Gordon Brown, if he did not wish to join the list of failed chancellors, had a maximum of seven years in which to implement the remedies that could reshape the housing market. In opposition, he methodically planned the party's economic strategy to the finest detail. Nothing could be left to chance if Labour wanted to return to power. At the election in 1997, the voters decided to give the Blair team its chance. And Gordon Brown's first act on arriving at the Treasury was to announce the independence of the Bank of England. There would be no political tampering with the money supply. In future, interest rates would be set by a Monetary Policy Committee (MPC) composed of eminent economists. Brown set the target inflation rate: 2.5%. The central bank just had to keep inflation at, or close to, this level, and expansions of the money supply of the kind that fuelled the Barber and Lawson booms would be consigned to history.

But that 2.5% target – which had to be met 'at all times'[3] – was defined by Gordon Brown to *exclude mortgage interest payments* on houses. The official definition of inflation included the *de*preciation of the bricks and mortar but ignored the *app*reciation in the value of land beneath the buildings. Here was a puzzle. House prices, which determine the size of people's mortgage debt, are not independent of inflation. Stephen Nickell, a professor at the London School of Economics who served as a member of the MPC, explained the connection.

> House prices in Britain are currently [2002] rising extremely rapidly. This house price boom has had, and is having, an impact on monetary policy and interest rates because house prices impact directly on consumption and aggregate demand, and hence on future inflation prospects.[4]

If the Bank of England had been legally obliged to include all the information on house prices in the target rate of inflation, it would have been confronted with a terrible dilemma. For as Nickell stressed: 'Setting interest rates to control house prices could easily push both inflation and the economy off course'. Thus, the Bank warned the public that, when it set interest rates, it was *not* targeting house prices.

Following its decisions at one monthly meeting, it declared that 'it would be important for the Committee to make clear that this did not imply that it was targeting house price inflation, or any other asset price'.[5]

Gordon Brown failed to deal with two realities when he established his monetary policy.

- House prices have a life of their own. They are ignored by governments at their peril.
- If the Bank of England was not directly responsible for curbing volatile house prices, responsibility reverted to the Treasury. The chancellor would have to use fiscal tools to orchestrate stability.

Despite relinquishing authority over monetary policy to the Bank of England, *the responsibility for prices in'the housing market did remain firmly in Brown's hands.* But he did not adopt the remedial tools that could have delivered a sustainable supply of homes at prices that people could afford. His last chance to take decisive action was the budget of 2004, for it would take three years to erect the ramparts against the boom that was due to peak in 2008. He failed to act. That left the business cycle on-course for its termination and the drop into the trough in 2010. But there was one curious detour along the way: a little hitch in the business cycle that we need to unravel.

§2 Mystery of the Missing Recession

HOW DID Britain avoid the 2001 recession that ensnared other countries? Recessions *followed* after each of the post-war periods when real house prices rose above the level of real household disposable income – in 1972, 1979 and 1987.[6]

Britain's manufacturers *did* suffer a recession. Total output of the economy rose by over 5% from the end of 2000 to the end of 2003, but manufacturers had a different story to tell. They suffered a fall in output of over 5% in that period. The 6.7% rate of return on their capital (2001) was the lowest since the trough of the recession nine years earlier, in 1992. How did Gordon Brown guide Britain through the global turbulence of these years to avoid the embarrassment of a formal recession for the whole economy? His achievement provided him with a political narrative which he put to good use. One week before his 2004 budget he told the New Labour Party faithful at their spring conference:

When I present my budget next week the first, the central and
most important theme ... will [be] for hard working families, to
lock in economic stability ... not just for a year or two, not just
for an economic cycle. Our aim should be to lock in stability for
a generation ... we will take no risks with inflation.[7]

Inflation, that is, *excluding a large slice of the costs that people incur when
they buy their homes.* According to the official definition of inflation, the
one on which the Bank of England had to focus, Britain had enjoyed
stable prices. But so, indeed, had the rest of the world. Japan's prices
declined for a decade. Germany also appeared close to deflation. In
other countries, inflation was moderate as retailers slashed prices to
attract customers and producers competed for shares in the increasingly cut-throat global markets.

How, then, do we account for Britain's missing recession? Had
Gordon Brown, the editor of unremittingly socialist tracts during his
early political career, changed the rules of the capitalist economy? The
clues are to be found in the financial sector. *Gordon Brown sponsored a
classic Keynesian pump-priming operation.* This time, however, there was
one peculiar difference. Instead of accepting responsibility for managing the economy, he shifted the burden on to ordinary families.

According to the wisdom passed down through the decades since
Keynes wrote his *General Theory* in 1936, governments could counter-
attack the prospect of a recession by employing offsetting measures.
Unemployment was supposed to be due to a shortfall in the money
people spent in the markets. So if government increased public spending, this would compensate for declines in private consumption and
investment.

Brown stood this doctrine on its head. Instead of accepting the
political obligation to maintain full employment, he silently shifted
responsibility onto Britain's households. Instead of increasing taxes
and/or public debt, to finance investment in infrastructure (to create
jobs and sustain growth), he presided over the growth of a record level
of personal indebtedness. By July 2004 that debt reached a staggering
£1 trillion. To underpin this indebtedness, a blind eye had to be turned
to inflation in the housing market. If the business cycle had played out
in the way that we would have predicted on the basis of historical
trends, the price of houses would have deflated in 2001-2. I will explain
in Chapters 5 and 6 that this would have been the outcome
of a mid-cycle recession. Instead, under Gordon Brown's stewardship, the residential sector was allowed to bubble. This set new bench-
marks for prices: the next housing bubble would have to inflate to

stupendous levels before finally collapsing and driving the economy into the Depression of 2010.

But in the meantime, Britain's consumers were on a spending spree. They borrowed like there was no tomorrow to finance the purchase of luxury goods, holidays in exotic locations, new cars, and improvements to their homes. Following the election of New Labour in 1997, consumption grew faster than output, with retailers sucking in imported goods to make up the difference. Between 1999 and 2001, consumption grew exactly twice as fast as Gross Domestic Product (GDP). Unsecured consumer debt rose at an annual average rate of nearly 11% over the five years to 2004. While Gordon Brown preened himself with declarations about his virtuous 'prudence' in handling the nation's public finances, he sanctioned private bingeing that undermined the culture of thrift. *Britain's consumers would Spend, Spend, Spend the economy out of the recession before anyone noticed!* They spent more on their credit cards than the rest of Europe put together. By 2003 those credit cards were loaded with a debt of £120bn. Shoppers in the other 14 nations of the European Union (EU) spent just £45bn between them.[8]

The financial and psychological key to the spending spree was an out-of-control housing market. With every percentage increase in the capital gain on their homes, owners felt wealthier if not wiser. They withdrew equity at record rates so that they could buy the luxury goods that created the trade imbalance between Britain and the rest of the world. They also borrowed more to 'trade up' to more valuable properties – the home-owner's way of speculating in the capital gains of the future.

The hothouse finances of the nation were devastating for industry. They drove up the value of sterling relative to other currencies. Britain imported cheap goods from the Far East while her manufacturers suffered a collapse in orders. As Gordon Brown directed people's attention to the 2.5% target inflation rate, house prices were soaring ten times faster.

The Financial Services Authority (FSA) rang the alarm bells in January 2003. It described as 'unsustainable' the escalation in mortgage debt. And what was the Treasury doing about the borrowing binge? Gordon Brown failed to take effective action against the inflationary pressures coming from the one asset that mattered in his campaign to deliver stability. The official outcome was the appearance of inflation under control. This was a statistical illusion that was exploited for political gain by the chancellor. The UK economy escaped a formal recession in 2001 because Gordon Brown had imprudently allowed the population to neglect the need to save and invest.

The nation's savings ratio sagged. It was over 10% of income when New Labour was elected in 1997, and it dropped to 4% in 2000; recovering a little, but dropping to under 5% in 2004. Savings are crucial for at least two reasons. Money needs to be set aside in the form of pensions, if people do not wish to live on the breadline in their years of retirement. Secondly, the formation of capital equipment with which to compete in the global economy was crucial if the UK was not to be left behind by its competitors. It was incumbent on Gordon Brown to ensure that savings were sufficient to meet the needs of the nation.

Strangely, the chancellor was silent on the prudential need to save. In March 2004, a coalition of six investment organisations launched a campaign to try and stir interest in the Treasury on the need to save if the nation was to meet the challenges of the 21st century. The financiers were pessimistic, for 'Mr. Brown has not used the word saving in a Budget or pre-Budget report since 2001'.[9] The Association of British Insurers noted that saving was not one of the government's top five issues, and its members were concerned that the government did not have a co-ordinated strategy for filling a huge hole in the nation's finances.

The low savings rate aroused anxieties in the financial sector, but it made sense for the Treasury. It was bound by the rules of prudential management invented by Gordon Brown and his economic adviser, Ed Balls, a Harvard-educated journalist. Their way to avoid a formal recession was for the nation to deplete its savings, the reciprocal of which was for people to sink into debt. So responsibility for the economy was covertly shifted away from the Treasury. Families were left to prime the financial pumps and keep the credit flowing so that the economy would not suffer six consecutive months of negative economic growth – the formal definition of a recession.

Brown's role in disturbing people's willingness to save was criticised by Sir Richard Sykes, an adviser to the government and Rector of Imperial College, London.[10] But the criticism came too late to moderate the Treasury's priorities. The price of Brown's financial negligence would be a terrible one. For the best part of three years, beginning in the summer of 2001, the increase in financial liabilities of Britain's households exceeded the increase in assets.[11] People were dangerously exposed to the vagaries of a world economy that was contracting. If unemployment in the UK had suddenly turned upwards, tens of thousands of families would be bankrupted, many of them forced to yield their homes to pay their debts. That this did not happen was not due to prudential management; quite the reverse. The economy stayed afloat because households sank into debt.

§3 The House Price Test

ACCORDING TO Gordon Brown's test, for Britain to sustain growth, it was vital to avoid increases in house prices that exceeded the trends in other countries. Historically, Britain's house prices rose *far faster* than prices on the continent. Table 1:2 shows that, over a period of three decades, the average price of houses in Britain escalated at a rate that eclipsed those in other European countries. Ireland and Spain were the only two countries with comparable increases. Germany experienced virtually no increase in the real price of accommodation, which helps to explain the post-war economic 'miracle' that it enjoyed.

TABLE 1:2

Real House Price Rises, 1971-2001

	Average[1]
UK	3.3
Germany	0.1
France	1.2
Italy	1.5
Spain	3.3
Netherlands	2.8
Belgium	2.1
Ireland	3.1
Sweden	0.0
Finland	0.7
Denmark	1.3
Average	*1.8*

1 Geometric Mean
Source: Kate Barker, *Securing our Future Housing Needs: Interim Report – Analysis*, London: HMSO, December 2003, p.17, Table 1.1.

These trends continued at the turn into the 21st century under the stewardship of Gordon Brown. Germany and France enjoyed stable house prices. Britain returned to annual increases of 20% or more. So in 2004, the UK economy was dangerously lopsided. Had the UK gone into recession in 2001, as it was destined to do, the rise in unemployment would have put a brake on house prices. Instead, thanks to the private pump-priming, prices continued to escalate. Without a pause, they escalated to the point where the average house price to average earnings ratio reached 5.8. So when the market finally exhausts itself in the peak of 2007-8, the ratio is likely to be an extraordinary 6.5 (Table 1:1).

By the end of the decade, homeowners will be critically exposed to debt as never before. They were able to finance their debts in the four years to 2004 because interest rates were at historically low levels. But the chickens will come home to roost. The rise in interest rates began in late 2003. With the price peak, in 2007, families will begin to default on their mortgages.

When will the collapse occur? The experts were of little help to those consumers who tried to make rational decisions about how much debt they could carry, and for how long. We summarise the prognoses offered by a selection of analysts in Table 1:3. These were published in April and May 2004. They provide a snapshot of the assessments offered to people who needed information on when to buy and sell their homes. The range of views is bewildering. They were expressed by financial institutions that influence public policies and economists whose expertise shapes the behaviour of the public. The prognoses stretch the full width of the colour spectrum, from black to white.

Gordon Brown did not appreciate the warning from the International Monetary Fund (IMF) that 'an abrupt correction' in the housing market posed the main risk to the UK, and he rejected the comparison with the crash of the early 1990s. As house prices raced up by 20% a year, the chancellor claimed that the UK was on-course for 'balanced growth'.

Music to Brown's ears was the view represented by the chief economist of the Paris-based Organisation for Economic Cooperation and Development (OECD). Jean-Philippe Cotis pronounced: 'I don't see a house price crash but rather a gentle slowdown because monetary policy is taking action on this with a pre-emptive tightening'. The OECD shared the view of the Bank of England, whose best forecast was that the rise in house prices would grind to a halt in 2006.

The scariest predictions were expressed by a minority of analysts. City fund manager Tony Dye was known as Dr Doom because in the late 1990s he warned that American share prices were dangerously high. He claimed that house prices in 2009 would be 30% lower than in 2004. That prediction was not much help to home-owners or investors, however. '[T]he skill, as Dye should know by now, lies in getting the timing right. He talks of the market being near the end of the boom, but then gives a prediction of a 30% decline in real terms over the next five years.'[12]

TABLE 1:3

UK House Prices:
prognoses offered in the 12 months to May 2004

Forecaster	Risk of price crash: experts' predictions
International Monetary Fund[1]	'Possibility of an abrupt correction'
Gordon Brown[2]	No repeat of the 1980s crash
OECD[3]	'A gentle slowdown'
Bank of England[4]	Zero price increase by 2006
CEBR[5]	'Soft landing is perfectly possible'
Goldman Sachs[6]	10-15% fall (2004-6)
NIESR[7]	50/50 chance of crash
Capital Economics[8]	20% drop (2004-7)
Citigroup[9]	Price drop in 2005
Kate Barker[10]	'Risk not critical'
Tony Dye[11]	30% drop (2005-9)
Martin Wolf[12]	'Nobody knows, but it will happen'
Henry Tricks[13]	'Easter 2004 marked the peak'
The Economist[14]	Bubble to burst 'within next year or so' [i.e., by May 2004]

1 Ashley Seager, 'House crash would derail economy, warns IMF', *The Guardian*, April 22, 2004.
2 Ed Crooks and Andrew Balls, 'Brown tries to calm IMF's housing fears', *Financial Times*, April 26, 2004.
3 Ashley Seager, 'House prices to slow, not crash', *The Guardian*, May 12, 2004.
4 Various Minutes of the Bank of England's Monetary Policy Committee meetings.
5 Douglas McWilliams, 'Collapse will start from substantially higher prices', Letter, *Financial Times*, April 20, 2004.
6 Scheherazade Daneshkhu, 'House prices could fall by 15%, warns bank expert', *Financial Times*, April 15, 2004.
7 Anna Fifield and Ed Crooks, 'Price rise risk to homes market', *Financial Times*, April 30, 2004.
8 Rupert Jones, 'Official data show house prices falling', *The Guardian*, April 14, 2004. Eighteen months previously, Capital Economics had forecast a 30% fall (Kevin Brown, 'Housing crash: another story', *Financial Times*, April 17, 2004).
9 Faisal Islam, 'City bull warns of fall in housing market', *The Observer*, April 25, 2004.
10 Ashley Seager, 'Rate setter says house price bubble can stay intact', *The Guardian*, April 29, 2004.
11 Jim Pickard, 'House prices are about to crash, says "Dr Doom"', *Financial Times*, April 13, 2004.
12 Martin Wolf, 'A housing market collapse draws nearer', *Financial Times*, April 16, 2004.
13 Henry Tricks, 'Has the housing boom hit a peak?', *Financial Times Weekend*, May 22, 2004.
14 Pam Woodall, 'House of cards', Survey: Property, *The Economist*, May 29, 2003.

According to Dye, the pause in prices in late 2004 would not be followed by a revival. In his view, 'The slump could last until 2009'.[13] An economist at Deutsche Bank agreed: 'The bad news is that house prices could stagnate for more than five years'.[14] These predictions would take the UK economy into a grave crisis in 2010 *without* an intervening boom phase of the kind which I claim is the pre-condition for recession.

The problem with turning points, according to Martin Wolf, the *Financial Times'* chief economics commentator, was that they could not be predicted: 'Nobody knows when the bust will come. But come, I believe, it will'.[15] When it came, the crash would be of the order of 30% according to Andrew Oswald, professor of economics at Warwick University. He was certain that prices would drop by 30% between the summer of 2003 and the end of 2005. So confident was he that, in January 2003, he boldly advised readers of *The Times:*

> Sell your home by May. Then go away. Over the next two years there is going to be blood on estate agents' carpets from Thurso to Torquay ... [M]y professional advice is that you should put your home up for sale as soon as possible ... Take my tip: move into rented accommodation in time for summer sunshine.[16]

An owner whose home was worth the national average, who took that advice, would have lost a capital gain of around £40,000 over the period of the professor's forecast. Prices rose by around 20% a year (much more in the north of England and Wales). Home owners in Merthyr Tydfil who took the professor's advice would have been particularly aggrieved. In the 12 months to October 2004 the average price of houses in their Welsh town surged by 53%! Neighbouring towns enjoyed similar windfall gains: Neath (43%) and Port Talbot (42%). For Wales as a whole, the Halifax registered an increase of 37.5%.[17] A year after offering his expert advice, Oswald grudgingly apologised to the readers of *The Times* for misleading them.[18] His credibility as a forecaster was tarnished, but perhaps by not as much as the forecaster who publicised the prediction that 'The late 1980s was extreme and we won't have anything like that for another hundred years'.[19]

Investment bankers Goldman Sachs believed that a bust was unlikely. That was also the view of the London-based Centre for Economic and Business Research (CEBR) which, armed with its 'housing futures model', concluded that the chances of a house price collapse were well below 50%. Tim Congdon, chief economist at Lombard Street Research, offered a similar view. A slow-down in the rate of increase of house prices, he wrote, was not the same as a crash, and 'the boom-bust cycles of the 1970s and 1980s ought not to be repeated'.[20] Hedging its bet was the prestigious National Institute of Economic and Social Research (NIESR), which claimed that the chance of a housing crash was 50/50.

Starting from a shared theory of the market economy, world-class economists and commentators, armed with the best available data and supported by batteries of analysts, arrived at opposite conclusions. TV programmers were free to turn the housing market into a branch of show-business, with 'reality' shows galore on how to make money out of property speculation, some from second homes in exotic locations.

Home-owners could be forgiven for being confused. There is one conclusion only that can be drawn with confidence about the prognoses: the experts do not know what they are talking about. By this, I mean that they are just as likely to be correct if they *guessed* the prospects for Britain's housing market, as if they relied on a methodical examination of the evidence. That appears to be the conclusion of one property market commentator, Henry Tricks of the *Financial Times*. Tricks, in reporting that Britain's estate agents were split 2:1 over the prospects of a crash before the end of 2005, was led by the flow of information from the property market to report that he would not be surprised if Britain had already passed the peak of the house-price cycle (Easter 2004). Three months later, now bewildered by the resilience of house prices, Tricks announced: 'I am hanging up my columnist boots and throwing my estate agents' brochures in the bin. Why? Because I can no longer claim to have a clue what's going on in the housing markets ... The one dismal truth about house price commentators is that we peddle unsound data'.[21]

Economists also confessed that they did not know what to make of the housing market. One of them was Kate Barker, a member of the Bank of England's MPC. She admitted that 'in common with many other commentators I have been very surprised by how sustained the period of strong house price growth has proved to be'. Nevertheless, she had this comforting message about house prices to offer:

> [I]t is however increasingly likely that at some point they may fall back, but it is still by no means certain either that they will necessarily fall significantly, or that any decline will be abrupt.[22]

Barker was not alone in this fog of incomprehension. Another of her colleagues on the MPC, Marian Bell, admitted that house price increases had been 'amazing'. But she was absolutely clear on the role of the Bank of England: it was not to prevent a housing bubble, but to clear up the mess afterwards.[23] If influential economists in the Bank of England are nonplussed, is it surprising that we can bank on failure when it comes to managing the economy?

As a yardstick against which to assess the value of the predictions published in April 2004, we include the forecast by *The Economist's* economics editor, Pam Woodall. Her global survey, published a year earlier in May 2003, spotlighted the remarkable increase in house prices in the USA, Australia, Britain, Ireland, the Netherlands and Spain. It contained an alarming forecast: '*Within the next year or so* those bubbles are likely to burst, leading to falls in average real house prices of 15-20% in America and 30% or more elsewhere over the next few years' (emphasis added). The housing bubbles did not burst. In May 2004 the mortgage lenders and government agencies that track house prices reported buoyant increases in prices across Britain. The upward trend continued in the countries surveyed by *The Economist* for the benefit of its international readership of investors and home-owners. If owners sold their properties when they read *The Economist* – to pocket their capital gains – they would have *lost* tens of thousands of dollars, pounds or euros.

Should we be worried by the inability of the experts to offer robust predictions about the housing market? The IMF analysed housing bubbles in its *World Economic Outlook* (2003). It concluded that the loss of output after house-price busts had, on average, been twice as large as the losses that followed crashes in the stock markets. Following the bursting of a house-price bubble, GDP fell by an average of 8% relative to its previous growth trend. This compared to a fall of 4% at the end of a bull run in share prices. The IMF also reported that a sharp rise in the price of houses was much more likely to be followed by a bust than as a result of a boom in share prices.

What happens in the housing sector has profound consequences for us all, whether we rent or own our homes. As employees who need to work for commercially viable firms, as savers who need a reliable return on our investments, as parents who need to plan the futures of our children with confidence ... we are all affected when the economy slips into recession. And yet, there is little consensus on how the housing sector's performance undermines the economy. At least one expert in our selection of forecasters is certain to be correct; while the majority are certain to be wrong.

§4 The Taxing Challenge

ECONOMISTS ARE curiously reluctant to learn from the past. That, at least, appears to be the case with the performance of real estate. Prof. Tim Congdon, who had attempted to alert the Thatcher government of the impending housing/debt crisis in the 1980s, looked back at what he called the puzzle that allowed 'Thatcherite monetarism' to preside over the Lawson boom bust.[24] In fact, there was no puzzle then, or during the Brown years. Money may be what the Bank of England's Governor, Mervyn King, calls 'a social or public rather than a private institution'.[25] But the combination of Brown's acts and omissions allowed private individuals to expand the money supply's credit base on the back of the collateral they accumulated in their homes.

The trouble with money is that it can be converted into a corrosive substance by the housing (more accurately, the land) market. This is not a lesson that has yet been learnt by monetarists like Congdon despite the failed experiment of the 1980s. Nearly 20 years later, he claimed that it was a mistake to equate 'the state of the housing market' with 'the state of the economy'. Investment in dwellings was not as important as oil prices, exchange rates, utility prices and other monetary phenomena.[26]

There was no consensus among the analysts, however, because they lacked a theory of the property cycle. To be meaningful, such a theory needs a timeframe, one that integrates the data into a 'narrative' that made empirical and theoretical sense. Their 2004 comparisons with the 1988/92 boom bust were untenable: they compared a point *midway* through one cycle with what happened at the *end* of the previous cycle. That was the Bank of England's mistake: it sought comfort from the claim that 'house prices and consumption did not appear to have been as close recently as during the rise and fall in house prices in the late 1980s and early 1990s'.[27] The relevant comparison is between 1988-92 and 2007-10, as I will explain in Part II.

This diagnostic failure is damaging. With current political and economic policies, we can continue to bank on failure. But once we have identified the root of our problems, the remedies can readily fall into place. That is the taxing challenge. For the solutions are to be found in fiscal, not monetary, policy.

REFERENCES

1 John Muellbauer, 'The Great British Housing Disaster', *Roof*, May-June 1990, p.16.
2 Robert Peston, 'Tony Blair has placed a huge bet on economic stability', *The Sunday Telegraph*, October 3, 2004.
3 The target rate of inflation was reduced to 2% in December 2003, when the Treasury changed the basis on which inflation was calculated to bring the UK measure into line with European conventions.
4 Stephen Nickell, 'House Prices, Household Debt and Monetary Policy', Speech, Glasgow, December 11, 2002.
5 Minutes of the Bank of England Monetary Policy Committee meeting, May 5-6, 2004, p.8. www.bankofengland.co.uk/mpc/mpc0405.pdf.
6 Kate Barker, *Securing Our Future Housing Needs*, Interim Report – Analysis, London: HMSO, 2003, p.20, Chart 1.2.
7 Gordon Brown, 'We will not rest until we have world-class public services', Labour Party Spring Conference, Manchester, March 12, 2004.
8 Mintel Survey reported by Amy Vickers, 'Credit card madness', *Daily Express*, March 17, 2004. The official indicators of consumption, saving and housing are graphically represented in the Treasury's *2004 Pre-Budget Report*, Box A4, p.180.
9 Kevin Brown, 'Savings mess that's not likely to be cleared up', *Financial Times*, March 17, 2004.
10 Richard Sykes, *Restoring Trust: Investment in the 21st Century*, London: Tomorrow's Companies, June 2000.
11 Bank of England, *Inflation Report*, August 2004, p.8, Chart 1.1.
12 Notebook, 'Dr Doom's day was the wrong call', *The Guardian*, April 14, 2004.
13 David Budworth, 'Experts warn of house price plunge', *Sunday Times*, September 5, 2004.
14 *Ibid.*
15 Martin Wolf, 'A housing market collapse draws nearer', *Financial Times*, April 16, 2004.
16 Andrew Oswald, 'Your boom is nigh: the great housing catastrophe', *The Times*, January 3, 2003.
17 Philip Thornton, 'House price boom comes to town they tried to close', *The Independent*, October 16, 2004.
18 Andrew Oswald, 'Okay, so your house price didn't crash. But just wait', *The Times*, January 12, 2004.
19 Forecast by Michael Saunders of Schroders Salomon Smith Barney Citibank, quoted in Christopher Adams, 'Glowing economic report may prompt rethink on policy', *Financial Times*, June 10, 2000.
20 Tim Congdon, 'Brown is right: the housing boom will not turn to bust', *Daily Telegraph*, April 27, 2004.
21 Henry Tricks, 'A year older – and wiser', *Financial Times*, August 7, 2004.
22 Kate Barker, Speech to CBI Yorkshire and Humber Annual Dinner, Bradford, April 28, 2004.
23 Scheherazade Daneshkhu and Ed Crooks, 'It is not all about house prices, says monetary Marian', *Financial Times*, April 28, 2004.
24 Tim Congdon, 'Money and asset prices in boom and bust', *Monthly Economic Review*, London: Lombard Street Research, May 2004, p.31.
25 Mervyn King, 'The Institutions of Monetary Policy', The Ely Lecture 2004, p.3. www.bankofengland.co.uk .
26 Tim Congdon, 'The Dollar', *Monthly Economic Review*, London: Lombard Street Research, November 2004, p.1.
27 MPC May Minutes, *op. cit.*, p.5.

2

Banking on Failure

§1 The Patterns of History

GORDON BROWN is correct; 200 years worth of evidence – the full history of the industrial economy – affords the best possible record to cross-check explanations for the repeated crises that afflict capitalism. Our investigation begins with the scientist's scepticism towards the conventional theories. There are sound reasons for our challenge. The failure to eliminate or control the business cycle, despite repeated attempts to do so, suggests that the received wisdoms do not lead governments to remedies that work. A second reason is that economics, as it is employed today, is seriously prejudiced by the dilution of some of its key concepts. Economists routinely work with economic models that treat the world as if it were composed of two factors – labour and capital – instead of the three-factor model favoured by the classical economists (see Box 2:1). This disembodies the economy from its spatial context. That, especially when we are concerned with the impact of the housing market on people's lives, creates analytical problems. For land is the key piece of the jigsaw that is the complex economy.

We begin our search for causes by considering the favourite explanation: the planning system. Imperfections in the way decisions are made about land use are held to be responsible for the shortfall of affordable homes, leading to the boom in prices. This is the explanation favoured by the construction industry. It is also favoured by the Confederation of British Industry (CBI), which needs to explain why British productivity is below the levels of its leading competitors. In December 2002 a House of Commons Select Committee published the results of its interrogation of the claim. The all-party group of MPs concluded that there was 'no evidence that planning is a significant explanatory factor for the UK's low productivity compared to its main competitors'.[1] The building industry, which ought to know where the pressure points were, appears to emit confusing signals. One of

---

Box 2:1

What's in a Name?

SCIENCE progresses by naming objects, or forms of behaviour, and then grouping them into categories. We can then discern patterns, which inspire theories that *explain* not only *what* is happening, but also *how*, and *why*. Only then can the observer hope to inject modifications that deliver the desired benefits.

The neoclassical school that originated at the beginning of the 20th century weakened this scientific process. Confusion was introduced when some of its exponents redefined key concepts. The result was a century of frustrated governance as the emerging democracies were repeatedly defeated by crises which they could otherwise have solved. Readers must form their own views on the motives for this curious history. Was it ineptness? A conspiracy of economists and their patrons? The origins of this episode in the science of political economy have been methodically traced by Mason Gaffney, a professor of economics at the University of California.*

- In *Boom Bust*, we use the concepts *rent* and *land* as defined by classical economists like Adam Smith and David Ricardo. *Land* denotes everything that is offered by nature. This includes the natural fertility of farmland, fish in the oceans, the space in which to fly aeroplanes and the minerals that we extract from Earth. Land is *not* capital, which is a man-made asset.
- The income generated by land is *economic rent*. We shall shorten this to the one word rent, the value that we attribute to urban and rural land and all resources in their natural state. This rent is not the *commercial rent* that we pay to landlords for the use of buildings and other man-made improvements on and in the land (these improvements are *capital investments*, the payment for which is interest).

*Mason Gaffney and Fred Harrison, *The Corruption of Economics*, London: Shepheard-Walwyn, 1994.

Britain's major construction firms, Taylor Woodrow, focusing on planners, claimed that output of houses was unlikely to rise further in 2005 as land became increasingly difficult to get through the planning system.[2] But on the same day, readers of *The Guardian* were informed that Taylor Woodrow's Chief Executive, Iain Napier, noted the difficulties caused by land whose price had been inflated by unrealistic expectations. 'With silly inflation prices floated, it is difficult to buy land because they have a higher perception of what it's worth,' he complained.[3]

Planning – with stereotyped pen-pushing bureaucrats attracting the animosity of hard-pressed entrepreneurs – dies hard as an explanation. Thus, against the backdrop of a decline in the construction of houses to the lowest levels for 70 years, planning was spotlighted by Kate Barker in a report commissioned by Gordon Brown.[4] Planning – zoning in the US – is an easy target, because of its association with bureaucratic procedures. We need to remove the emotive content from the discussion if clarity is to expose the real sources of friction in the housing market.

The early British town planning laws were the Housing and Town Planning Act of the 1909 Liberal government, followed by the Planning Acts of 1919, 1925 and 1932. These certainly did not hinder the construction boom of the 1930s, which delivered swathes of semi-detached family homes on estates around the major cities of England. Indeed, according to one assessment, the planning laws fostered benign institutional conditions, but there was a catch: 'In the process, landed property was transformed into a more accessible object of speculative investment'.[5]

The Town and Country Planning Act of 1947 injected a socialist edge to planning. Our assessment of its long-term impact must be made in the light of the facts. First, power resided in the hands of democratically elected government. Second, we must recall the reason why planning was felt to be necessary. Ribbon development along the nation's country roads, the urban sprawl that aroused the anxieties of rural sentimentalists, the thinly-spread investment of capital in infrastructure to provide utilities and transport which taxed the working population – these all testified to an irrational deployment of land, and therefore of labour and capital.

Planning does have an effect on construction – and property prices – through the concentration of activity in areas of containment. The net effect, however, is difficult to estimate by relying on the trends in prices. Planning restrictions that discourage construction will raise prices in those locations where the supply falls short of people's needs. On the other hand, plans issued by local authorities do assist building firms to concentrate their developments in designated areas where infrastructure is supplied by government: the economies and certainties that flow from this knowledge offset costs and they bear down on house prices.

To clarify the issues, we need to compare evidence from two areas – one with planning, the other with free-for-all construction. This is not possible for the UK, where planning laws apply uniformly across the country. The variety of zoning practises in the USA affords us some insights. We can compare, for example, the state of Texas, with its relatively relaxed approach to where people build, and Oregon, which is internationally recognised as enforcing a tight planning regime. On the face of it, the relatively low prices in Texas seem to endorse the fears of those who attribute Britain's housing problems to planning. In the 23 years up to 2003, house prices rose nearly 89% in Texas. In Oregon, they increased by 201%![6] Does this favour the need to relax planning regulations if we want affordable houses? State-wide statistics disguise the detail of what is happening on the ground. Comparing two thriving seaport cities – Houston, on the Gulf coast, and Portland, on the Pacific coast – provides important insights.

Portland's unique urban growth boundary (UGB) is acknowledged as a tight form of zoning designed to contain the sprawl that is an endemic feature of Houston's property market. Did the UGB drive house prices upwards? This proposition was tested by a policy analyst at the US Department of Justice and a professor of economics. They found that 'the UGB has had a small, and statistically weak, upward influence on house prices', with a price increase of less than $10,000 attributable to the UGB.[7] Other western cities that were not constrained by UGBs, however, had experienced comparable increases in house prices. Portland's median house price in 2000 was about the same as in other western cities.

Compared to Houston, however, Portland could claim some compensating benefits that offset the $10,000 premium. In fact, one of these benefits probably more than offsets the premium. A Rutgers University study concluded that state-wide planning ensured a more efficient use of the infrastructure while rewarding home-owners with lower property taxes. In the case of New Jersey, each new home would have cost $12,000-15,000 more without state-wide planning.[8] The UGB, which was based on land use policies integrated with public transport, probably more than paid for itself!

In addition to the cash benefits, however, there were the social and environmental attractions of a compact city and a conserved rural hinterland. Despite a sharp rise in population, Portland had contained its boundary with in-filling development on recycled ('brownfield') land. What Portland had not been able to avoid was large price increases in the 1990s due to speculation.[9] Speculation, however, is a preoccupation not altogether unknown to Houston's land owners. They doubled the price of raw land in 2003, according to the *Houston Chronicle* (March 2, 2003), and higher land costs made it harder for builders to cater for the strongest part of their market – houses priced under $150,000.

The controversy over the role of planning divides communities, with Portland's champions asking why, if sprawl and unlimited land supplies were a guarantee of affordable housing, did the average home in Los Angeles cost $30,000 more than in the Portland region? But for a clinching argument, we can return to the UK. In the 150 years before 1947, the housing and land markets featured prominently in the booms and busts of the business cycle. To what do we attribute those previous episodes? We certainly cannot blame planners! In terms of price volatility and supply falling short of demand, the patterns were consistent throughout two centuries. Land planning did not mitigate – but nor did it exacerbate – the dynamics of booms and busts.[10]

This conclusion is reinforced by trends since 1947. Total output of houses in both the private and public sectors did not deteriorate until after 1979 – the year that Margaret Thatcher came to power.[11] In the 30 previous years, under the new planning regime, output rose steadily to meet people's needs. Then, with the arrival of the pro-market Thatcher administration, the steady decline in the output of houses in both the private and public sectors began, even though the planning system was weakened and, in 1985, the Development Land Tax was abolished.

Planning, while it does not cause the periodical propensity for house prices to go sky-high, does affect the distribution of the capital gains that are made from land. These were illustrated by Kate Barker in the case of the value of a typical tract, which might be a mixture of both greenfield and brownfield land (Table 2:1). Upgrading the status of a farmer's field to residential use clearly has attractions – assuming that the market demand exists in the locality where planning permission is granted.

TABLE 2:1

Value of Land in North East England (2003)

Use	Value per hectare
Agricultural	£865-£7,534
Industrial	£80,000-£200,000
Residential	£1.15m-£1.26m

Source: Barker, *op. cit*, 2003, p.115, Table 7.1, citing data from Valuation Office Agency Property Market Report, Spring 2003.

Curiously, Barker's report did not investigate the long-run trends in land prices to arrive at an informed view on their significance to the economy as a whole. The need for the long-term perspective is crucial, for we are dealing with events that recur time and again. This suggests that we are dealing with a *systemic* phenomenon constructed on laws, institutions and conventions that were embodied in the foundations of the industrial economy. If the business cycle is characterised by a pattern that is regular in its periodicity and scale, the probability is that we are searching for a single, or a very few related, causes, and that those causes are embedded in the foundations of the system.

§2 Blame it on 'Inflation'

THE HISTORICAL perspective places in context the view that 'inflation' is the cause of recessions. Prices in general were stable throughout the 19th century. Inflation was not to blame for the instability. Between the Napoleonic War and World War I, the swings in annual percentage changes in inflation faded away like a cardiograph reading with the patient in terminal decline. With the price level at 100 in 1810, it dropped to nearly half (around 55) in the dying years of the century, and did not recover to 100 until 1918.[12]

The stability of sterling is important to note, because economists now tend to explain the property booms of the 20th century in terms of inflation: loose monetary policies were the source of the problem, according to one fashionable view of recent decades. And yet, the historical evidence shows that the booms and busts were consistent with both long-term price stability (the 19th century) and long-term price instability (the price level standing at 100 in 1940 had risen to 3,000 in 1999). In both centuries the toboggan rides in the housing market followed a uniform pattern, which suggests that there was a mechanism at work over the span of 200 years that was unrelated to inflation.

So confident were people that their savings would not be eroded by a general rise in prices, that landlords favoured 99-year leases with no provision to review their rents. They took for granted that the real value of their ground rents would not be diminished.[13] This practise continued up to the point when Britain came off the gold standard in the First World War. The Cost of Living Index in the 50 years from 1855 to the early years of the 20th century was flat, even as the price of a 3-bedroom semi-detached house rose steeply.[14] It was not until the 1970s that we can plausibly suggest that inflation disturbed people's judgments on a scale that might affect the economy. But conventional wisdoms, once embedded in the policies of politicians, are difficult to excise. Thus, in the 10 years up to 2004, Western governments employed inflation targets as their principle guiding mechanism to avoid instability, even as two of the three largest economies (Japan and Germany) experienced *de*flation, and the rest enjoyed very low price increases (in Britain's case, the government actually being concerned, at one point, that inflation was *too low!*).

Psychologically, the inflation index would have been more useful for guiding people's expectations if it registered the extraordinary increases in the price of houses. In Britain, these increased by 150% between 1997 and early 2004.

The house price virus flourished, and Gordon Brown failed to take defensive measures to protect the economy. We can predict the events of the years through to 2010 as a result of the pattern yielded by not just 200 but 400 years of land deals and business cycles. The reader needs to treat our predictions, at this point, as conjectures. But if our theory is scientifically valid, it must yield reliable predictions. So, in anticipation of the exposition in Part II, we offer forecasts of the key turning points that will deliver the first depression of the 21st century.

- After the early 1990s recession, the US housing cycle recovered in 1992 and prices rose for 14 years. This conformed to the theory elaborated on p.87 below. In 2006, the average house price fell 3%. *Identifying the correct starting point of the cycle is crucial, for accurate predictions.*[15]
- UK house prices recovered a little later, in 1994 (Graph 2:1, p.35). Prices should stall at the end of 2007 or in 2008.

This scenario is based on a periodicity whose consistency is uncanny. Basic financial arithmetic provides the mechanism that drives the timetable that may be 'read' in the pages of the history books. But for a correct reading, we need open minds. Planning and inflation were not the causes of the stop-go economy – so did this mean that Gordon Brown had succeeded in his aim to tame the business cycle? The Labour Left in Britain certainly thought so, but its ideology prevented it from recognising that an economic disaster loomed. It was misled by the economics of Gordon Brown. The main organ for left-wing opinion is *New Statesman*. Its cover story on May 24, 2004, boldly declared: 'Gordon works. Don't let Tony wreck it'. In disclosing 'the hidden agenda of the next PM', the journal took sides in the leadership contest between Brown and the Prime Minister. Brown

> prefers the dogged work of negotiating debt relief for poor countries... Labour MPs... should now summon up their courage at last, act in the interests of their natural supporters, and politely ask Mr Blair to vacate his position. They know, from his record at the Treasury, that Gordon works. They should not allow Tony to wreck it.

Because of the red herring explanations for economic instability, Gordon Brown was free to gamble with his covert Keynesian strategy: allowing people to sink deep into debt to keep the UK ship of state afloat. His last chance to elaborate an effective fiscal reform was his 2004 budget. He prevaricated. The best he could offer the House of

Commons was a 12-month consultation on what he called the 'unearned increment in land'. Too little, too late. There was now no time left to distract Britain from its historic date with the Depression of 2010. *Or had 400 years worth of economic history been dumped with the dawning of the third millennium?*

In *The Power in the Land,* I reviewed that historical evidence in detail for four countries: the USA, Japan, UK and Australia. The results were published in 1983. I was drawn to a chilling prediction: if the patterns of history were to repeat themselves, the global economy that had recovered from the slump of 1974 would survive for 18 years before 'tail-spinning into yet another deep-seated depression of even greater magnitude'.[16] The lessons of history appeared stark and inevitable to me: a global slump in 1992. I submitted warning memoranda to the UK Treasury,* and alerted the public in an economic bulletin.[17] The mandarins in Whitehall were not willing to listen. Neither was Margaret Thatcher's Tory Party. In 1996, I repeated that warning for the benefit of Tony Blair's party.[18] This warning was also ignored by shadow Chancellor of the Exchequer Gordon Brown.

Why were those warnings ignored? Was it because I had failed to offer a convincing theoretical *explanation* for the patterns of history? Those patterns may have been tediously repetitive – so that one could, reasonably, interpret them as indicators of what might happen in the future – but *why* did history unfold in this way? The gap in my knowledge was convenient for politicians who did not wish to grasp a politically difficult nettle – the remedy to booms and busts. They sought solace in the belief that there was nothing inevitable about the future.

So it appeared that I had to excavate the business cycle's underlying causes. I had to offer a convincing explanation for the patterns of history, if it existed. I followed the clues into the markets for money. Now, armed with a financial theory that provides a framework for the booms and busts, there can be no doubt that capitalism – as it is currently structured – is afflicted with a deadly virus. That virus is constantly eating away at the foundations of the market economy.

§2 The Secret of 5% Compound

PROPERTY DRIVEN booms are fuelled by the flow of credit from banks and mortgage companies. But despite the biblical censure –

---

*Policies for neutralising boom busts were also outlined for the House of Commons Treasury and Civil Service Committee, in Fred Harrison, 'The Impact of Fiscal Policy and the Land Market on the Industrial Economy', Submission, April 1983.

money is the root of all evil – money is no more than the veneer on the capitalist economy. Bankers use the laws, institutions and people's fallibilities to capture some of the extraordinary profits that are made from real estate.

We shall now begin to disentangle the elements of the business cycle, so that we can identify those features that really matter.

The *timing* of turning points in activity is all-important. To achieve an understanding of *when* events are going to go wrong, we need to identify the relationship between money and the land market. This reveals the *life* of the property cycle, which turns out to be of 14 years duration. Those 14 years set the rhythms for the house building industry which, in turn, determine the timing of the booms and busts. By mastering the arithmetical terms of the underlying financial process, we realise that forecasting the trends in the economy as a whole is not rocket science. It is more a matter of common sense.

The first fact to establish is the rate of interest at which people borrow money. The usury laws conveniently provide us with the benchmark figure: 6% for borrowers and lenders was the upper limit until 1714, when it was reduced to 5%. From that point, 5% became the key statistic that operated as a ceiling throughout the 18th and 19th centuries and deep into the 20th century. The Bank of England complied with the Usury Law (which was repealed in 1822) by maintaining its rate of discount on inland bills at 5%.[19]

Did the rate at which money could be borrowed have more to do with the struggle for political power than with religious consciences? From the late 14th century, the considerable increase in the wealth of the mercantile class occurred at a time when the landed nobility were cash-strapped – or, as Cunningham put it, 'greatly impoverished'.[20] Kings and their nobles at court needed to borrow money. Did the landowners who were working their way into the dominant role in the political structure of the kingdom use their influence to promulgate laws that put a ceiling on the rate at which they could borrow money? In a Statute of 1624 (*An Act against Usury*), usury was permitted so long as the rate of interest did not exceed 8%.[21]

The rate of interest was significant for the property cycle. This, I contend, imposed a systematic structure onto the world of business. We shall here consider the property cycle, before expanding the analysis into the general business cycle in Chapter 5.

The arithmetic was conveniently summarised a century ago by Edward Brabrook (1839-1930). He was the Chief Registrar of Friendly Societies, one of Britain's financial regulatory agencies. The societies included building societies (known as savings and loans associations in

the United States). Building societies emerged out of what were originally called terminating societies, which were financial clubs. When
every member had acquired a house, the club disbanded.

People held shares in the societies. As members they invested their
savings to build their homes. The financial trick was to make sure that

- the person who received the first house to be built (who would not
  have saved sufficient to pay for it) continued to contribute to the
  general funds of the society; while
- the last person to receive his house was willing to pay his monthly
  subscriptions for 14 years until his house was ready for occupation.

The financial juggling act was explained by Brabrook. He illustrated
the internal operations of a typical society. His reference to the 14 years
that it took to pay off a mortgage is crucial. The macroeconomic
significance of this timetable will be elaborated in the rest of this book.
But first, we need to follow how the arithmetic works to support
people's need to save and invest in the construction of their homes.

In the early building societies

> The shares are £120 each, realisable by subscription of 10s. a
> month during 14 years. Fourteen years happens to be nearly the
> time in which, at 5% compound interest, a sum of money
> becomes doubled.

Lots were drawn to decide who would get the first house to be built.
The lucky person was handed that house – but he had not saved
enough (£60) to pay for it. So he borrowed the money off the other
club members. That was deemed to be fair to everyone, for

> the present value, at the commencement of the Society, of the
> £120 to be realised at its conclusion, or (what is the same thing)
> of the subscription of 10s. a month by which that £120 is to be
> raised, is £60.

The club assembled members by advertising in local newspapers. The
money collected from the first month's subscriptions was sufficient to
stake one person with the sum that was needed to build the first
house. But what about those who would have to wait for their houses?

> [T]o protect the other members from loss, [they] would execute
> a mortgage of his dwelling-house for insuring the payment of
> the future subscriptions of 10s. per month until every member

had in like manner obtained an advance upon his shares, or
accumulated the £120 per share.[22]

In this way, the financial contributions were equalised in value and
everybody received a house. The interest rate of 5% determined the
timetable – it took 14 years to raise enough cash for everyone to secure
a home. That 5% remained the norm even when the laws on usury
were abolished (see Box 2:2). Interestingly, over the first seven years of
Tony Blair's tenure as Prime Minister (up to 2004), annual rates averaged 5.3%.[23]

Starting the money-saving and construction process in Year 1, by
Year 14 the financial club ends up with a group of contented home-
owners. Everyone has paid in the equivalent of £120 and everyone has
a house. The club disbands as the members become neighbours. This
appears to be a happy outcome. In a rational world, it would be. But
there is one problem with it. Land, unlike bricks and mortar, does not
invite rational behaviour. Land grows in value while bricks and mortar
depreciates. Land animates the propensity to speculate, while capital
favours prudent behaviour. It is the speculative activity in the land
market which distorts the economy.

Economists talk about 'houses' when they discuss the growth of
prices. In fact, the best windfall gains are not made from *buildings* on
the land.

- In the 10 years following the election of Margaret Thatcher's Tory
Party in 1979, land prices increased by 900%.[24] The building cost
index rose by 82%.
- In the five years following the recession of 1992, average residential
land prices rose by 101%, compared with 'house' prices of 25%. The
cost of rebuilding those houses rose by 20%.
- In the five years following the election of Tony Blair's New Labour
Party, land prices rose by 333%. The cost of rebuilding houses rose
by 30%.

The difference in the rates of growth in the value of land and the
cost of constructing buildings widens through time – an insight that
identifies the motive to speculate in land. Why would someone
choose to speculate in land rather than in (say) sand and cement?
Windfall gains are derived from the land market, *not* the market for
the materials that go into houses, offices and factories. Not only do
capital gains from land grow over time; but the scale of those gains is
magnified as land becomes increasingly scarce in places where people

---

Box 2:2
Terminating Societies

TO UPGRADE Britain's housing stock, people had to pool their money to buy back the land of their forefathers. Terminating societies used compound interest to equalise the benefits between members, some of whom had to wait at the end of the queue for their houses to be built.

The clubs recruited members who would provide subscriptions that were 'sufficient for a "draw", so enabling a fortunate member to buy his house at once, free of interest, but compelled to continue his subscriptions until all members were satisfied'.[1]

From the first club in Birmingham in the 18th century to the experiment in constructing garden cities in the 20th century, 5% was the cost of borrowing money from the mortgage-advancing clubs that were built on mutual self-help principles.

● Richard Ketley's club's first advertisement to recruit members appeared in 1778, and Seymour J. Price, by investigating the archival evidence, concludes that 'it would certainly be reasonable to consider 1775 as the year in which the modern building society movement originated'.[2]

● The Halifax Building Society was launched in 1853 offering £120 shares payable at 10 shillings a lunar month at 5%, "and the Tables showed that the accumulation of instalment and interest would render a share fully paid up in 13 years and seven months".[3]

● The Temperance Permanent Building Society was launched in 1854. Shares £120, and "a house was to be built for every member at a cost not exceeding £80".[4]

Halifax's records showed that 5% continued through the 1880s. That was the rate of interest which the Co-operative Permanent Building Society used when it advanced £20,000 to help build Letchworth, the first private garden city, which was built in Hertfordshire in 1904 on leasehold land.[5] Despite the ebb and flow of interest rates and the impact of taxation, 5% was the rate that northern societies were still charging in the 1930s.

1 Albert Mansbridge, *Brick Upon Brick*, London: J.M. Dent, 1934, p.30.
2 Seymour J. Price, *Building Societies: Their Origin and History*, London: Franey, 1958, p.24.
3 Oscar R. Hobson, *A Hundred Years of the Halifax*, London: Batsford, 1953, p.25.
4 Seymour J. Price, *From Queen to Queen: The Centenary Story of the Temperance Permanent Building Society 1854-1954*, London: Franey, nd, p.8.
5 Mansbridge, *op. cit.*, p.19.

---

need to live and work. In Britain's residential sector, for example, 50 years ago, the land's value as a proportion of the market price of a typical house was around 15%. This proportion has almost trebled, and represents over 40% of the price that people pay for a newly built house in South East England.[25]

This contrast in prices is repeated throughout Europe (Table 2:2). In the relatively stable economies, such as Denmark's and Germany's, the rise in the cost of building materials is almost zero. Contrast this with the rate of increase in the price of land, which in Germany was double the rate for house prices over the 20 years to 2001. Apart from tiny land-starved Luxembourg, the UK experienced the widest contrast between building costs and land prices.

TABLE 2:2

**House and Land Prices and Building Costs,
Selected European Countries:
annual growth rates, 1980-2001 (%)**

	House prices	Building costs	Land prices
Belgium	1.2	-0.5	1.8
Denmark	1.0	0.0	1.2
Germany	0.5	0.1	1.1
Luxembourg	2.6	0.3	6.3
Netherlands	2.3	0.0	1.9
Austria	3.5	1.2	3.1
Portugal	0.4	0.7	2.8
Sweden	-0.2	-0.4	1.3
UK	3.0	1.4	5.2

Source: *Structural factors in the EU Housing Markets*, Frankfurt: European Central Bank, March 2003, Table 21, p.16. All prices are real, deflated with the private consumption deflator. Germany refers to West Germany. Data for Austria was from 1987-99, and for Portugal from 1988-2001. Land prices refer to the following periods: 1990-9 (Netherlands and Austria); 1980-98 (Sweden); 1981-2000 (UK).

With advances in productivity, competition tends to even out the relative costs of labour and capital, so the *increasing gains* from innovations surface as increases in land values. Land price increases outpace the rate of growth of the economy.[26] The macroeconomic significance of this was implied by Alan Greenspan to bankers in America.

In evaluating the possible prevalence of housing price bubbles, it is important to keep in mind that home prices tend to consistently rise relative to the general price level in this country. In fact, over the past half century, the annual pace of home price increases has been approximately 1% faster on average than the rise in the GDP deflator.[27]

Compounding those annual increases leads to enormous wealth gains for those who own land. There is one reason only why the price of land will outpace the prices we pay for bricks and mortar, combustion engines fitted into Ford automobiles, PCs, biros, the labour services of mechanics and chefs, digital cameras and domestic services: the monopoly power that compromises the market economy. The land market – where the supply of the raw material is in fixed supply – has the characteristics of a natural monopoly. Contrast this with the markets for labour, capital and consumer goods, where – if prices and profits rise – the supply is increased and prices and profits return to their competitive levels. The outcome, as competition bears down on wages and profits, is increasing returns to a growing, productive economy. These have to find a home somewhere. *They are captured in the land market.* Periodically, people realise that the best returns for their money are to be found in real estate: they begin to speculate in the capital gains from land. They talk about bricks and mortar, and of 'trading up in the housing market'. They are, in fact, relying on trends in the land market. And as they pour money into property, so this leads to the violent swings in land prices that ultimately crush the enterprise economy.

The scale of the exploitation of the land market is awesome. In the US, for example, in 2002, as the stock market crumbled around the ears of the dot.com millionaires, people 'cashed out' – withdrew as equity – a staggering $700bn from residential real estate alone.[28]

The cyclical character of the land market, which is the basis of the volatility of 'house' prices, may be seen in Graph 2:1. This is based on data compiled by FPDSavills, the real estate company that methodically tracks trends in the UK land market.[29] It relates land prices to house prices. The swings in land prices are more violent than those for 'house' prices. In the Lawson boom (1988-9), land prices rose by nearly 80% compared to the 25% increase in house prices.

House prices lag behind the ups and downs in the land market. For the purpose of analysing the economy, house prices ought to be treated as no more than a proxy for land prices. This means that we must 'read' house prices to account for the reality on the ground. The timing of turning points are misleading by about 18 months, if we want to use information on housing as a leading indicator of what to expect from the economy. If we are looking for signs of a downturn, it would not be shrewd to monitor prices in the windows of the local estate agencies. Rather, you need to know whether the deals in the land market between owners and prospective buyers have stalled. If they have, you know that the game is up.

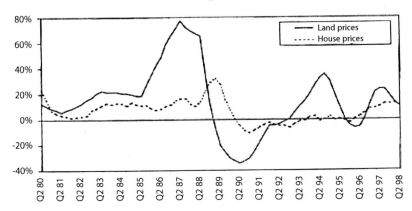

GRAPH 2:1

Land Prices Anticipate House Prices

In the land market, prices take off into the stratosphere at the point when speculation is at its most intense. They come down with an almighty crash, heralding what then happens in the High Street and the jobs market. After the Lawson boom, land prices fell by 60% to June 1992. They then rebounded with a rise of 60% by 1995, as builders regained their confidence and started to construct new homes.

These stark statistics conceal the human consequences of the violent amplitudes. Rising land prices, for example, cause builders to economise on the space they devote to each house. As values rise, so the density of development is intensified. As houses become un-affordable, the incentive to crush more houses onto smaller plots is increased. For most people the occupation of smaller spaces is not a lifestyle choice; it is a survival response to the prospect of becoming homeless.

The insights that we have now begun to offer into the dynamics of the capitalist economy – anchored in the land market – do not appear in the curricula in the universities. Students are encouraged by their professors to study the labour and capital markets. The outcome, for public policy, has been fatal. It was this legacy that New Labour inherited when it entered the 1997 general election. The prospects for Gordon Brown's British economy were bleak, but he had the time after the election contest to restructure the economy.

Brown's policies did not seem to convince some parliamentarians, who were worried that something was missing from the government's mix of policies. The House of Commons Treasury Committee decided that an enquiry was needed to determine whether asset prices should be part of the remit of the MPC. And there was a further problem that needed to be interrogated. David Ruffley, a Conservative member of the Treasury Committee, voiced their concerns:

> We want an immediate review into the operation of inflation-targeting as it relates to the unsustainable boom in housing. We also want the National Audit Office to go into the Treasury to check the economic cycle assumptions aren't being fudged.[30]

Nothing was to come of these anxieties – nothing that would motivate a paradigm shift in the Treasury's model of how the economy worked, and the government's priorities for public policies. Nothing that could forestall the crisis years that would follow events in the land market in 2007/8. If a government knows what it is doing, it needs just three years to put in place the reforms that would automatically generate a restructuring of the economy. Gordon Brown's last chance was his budget of 2004. He did not grasp that opportunity, so time was up for Britain. But the depth of the Depression of 2010 would also depend on the scale of the misjudgement by policy-makers in the largest economy in the world: the USA. If they, too, ignored the lessons of history, their escape into a state of virtual reality would cost the rest of the world dearly.

REFERENCES

1   Jean Eaglesham, 'Business attacks Commons inquiry on planning', *Financial Times*, December 13, 2002.
2   Maija Pesola, 'Woodrow sees benefits from Connolly buy', *Financial Times*, August 4, 2004.
3   Heather Tomlinson, 'Mortgage lenders' house price figures are flawed, says builder', *The Guardian*, August 4, 2004.
4   Kate Barker, *op. cit.*, pp.11-12, Chs. 8-9.
5   Michael McMahon, 'The Law of the Land: Property Rights and Town Planning in Modern Britain', in M. Ball, V. Bentivegna, M. Edwards and M. Folin, *Land Rent, Housing and Urban Planning: A European Perspective*, London: Croom Helm, 1985, p.103.
6   'OFHEO House Price Index Shows Dramatic Increases in Fourth Quarter 2003', Washington, DC: Office of Federal Housing Enterprise Oversight, March 1, 2004, Table, p.8. Because of the breadth of its sample, the OFHEO House Price Index is the most comprehensive index of single-family house prices.
7   Justin Phillips and Eban Goodstein, 'Growth Management and Housing Prices: The Case of Portland, Oregon', *Contemporary Economic Policy*, July 2000, p.341.
8   Rutgers University, *Impact Assessment of New Jersey Interim State Development and Redevelopment Plan*, 1992.
9   Phillips and Goodstein, *op. cit.*, p.342.

10 Related to the planning thesis is the claim that the green belts around urban
    conurbations are a cause of the shortage in the supply of affordable houses. This
    is no more than a special case of the planning explanation. The green belt became
    sacrosanct environmental space in the 1950s. Throughout the 19th century, the
    green fields were policed by private owners, mainly the aristocrats who had carved
    up the nation into their grand estates. They were never averse to construction of
    houses when the rewards attracted them. Still, boom busts in the housing sector
    inflicted their disturbances on communities.

11 Barker, *Securing our Future Housing Needs*, *op. cit.*, p.177, Chart A.1.

12 OECD, *United Kingdom*, Paris: OECD, 2000, p.46.

13 I owe this observation to Ronald Banks. In the 1950s, property owners were still
    selling buildings with long ground leases that did not include rent review clauses.

14 *The Emerging Residential Investment Sector*, London: FPDSavills, Summer 1988, p.2.

15 The Office of Federal Housing Enterprise Oversight (*op. cit.*, p.6) claimed that the
    housing market took off in 1994. If investors and home-buyers accepted this date,
    they would conclude that the rise in prices would end in 2008. But data from
    financial institutions and trade associations that track real estate prices showed
    the recovery beginning in 1992. This implied that the long-run growth, if it lasted
    14 years, would end in 2006. Getting the starting point right is imperative if
    economists are to use real estate, and especially the land market, as a leading indi-
    cator of the future course of the economy. In 2006, more than 25 US mortgage
    lenders were bankrupted because home-owners were unable to service their loans.
    In March 2007 the UK's biggest lender in the US market (the HSBC) reported
    losses of $10.6bn when its sub-prime mortgages turned sour.

16 Fred Harrison, *The Power in the Land*, London: Shepheard-Walwyn, 1983, p.302.

17 'Boom on Course for the Crash of 1992', *Economic Intelligence*, No. 1, 1988, London:
    Centre for Incentive Taxation.

18 'Land-price threat to Blair's party', *INSITE*, London: Land Policy Council,
    December 1996, p.1.

19 H.A. Shannon, 'Bricks – A Trade Index, 1785-1849', *Economica*, August 1934, p.313.

20 W. Cunningham, *The Growth of English Industry and Commerce during the Early and
    Middle Ages*, Cambridge: University Press, 1922, 5th edn., p.384.

21 W. Cunningham, *The Growth of English Industry and Commerce: The Mercantile
    System*, Cambridge: University Press, 1907, p.154.

22 E.W. Brabrook, *Provident Societies and Industrial Welfare*, London: Blackie, 1898,
    p.120.

23 According to Paul Tucker, the Bank of England's Deputy Director responsible for
    financial stability, the 'neutral' interest rate in Britain was probably 5% to 5.5%.
    This was the rate at which monetary policy neither stimulates nor constrains the
    economy. David Smith, 'Bank's market man is ready for rate rises', *Sunday Times*,
    April 25, 2004.

24 Land Price data derived from bulletins published by FPDSavills.

25 FPDSavills, *Residential Research Bulletin* No. 25, Spring 1998, p.4.

26 Harrison, *The Power in the Land*, *op. cit.*, pp.85-8.

27 Alan Greenspan, 'Home Mortgage Market', Remarks to the annual convention of
    the Independent Community Bankers of America, Orlando, Florida, March 4,
    2003 (via satellite); transcript, Washington DC: Federal Reserve Board, p.4.

28 *Ibid.*, p.2

29 Savills *Quarterly Residential Research Bulletin*, Summer 1996 and Summer 1997;
    FPDSavills *Residential Research Bulletin*, No 26, Summer 1998.

30 Scheherazade Daneshkhu, 'MPs warn Brown over risk to growth and prosperity',
    Financial Times, January 17, 2003.

3

The American
State of Virtual Reality

§1 New Economy, Old Alchemy

DOT.COM FEVER was incubated in the fertile reaches of California's Silicon Valley. A new – virtual – reality was born.

A tract of 284 acres owned by Russian Orthodox nuns above Half Moon Bay, 30 miles south of San Francisco, would have sold for $1m in 1996. When the nuns put the land on the market in June 2000, the asking price was $2.84m. As the bids came in, the price rose to $3.5m.[1] Making millions of dollars out of thin air was manna from heaven for the nuns and for those who already owned a slice of the land of the free.

For others, however, the New Economy had a surreal quality which took them for a ride. Literally. You could see them every night, hard-working employees of Silicon Valley. They bought tickets for the No. 22 bus that runs through the valley. It was dubbed Motel 22 because it was home for the homeless. After a day's work, they paid $3 and rode up and down the 26-mile route during the dark hours until it was time to report for work the next morning. With the emergency shelters crammed, there was nowhere to go for people who held respectable jobs. Their incomes ought to have been sufficient to support a family. They were not: those incomes fell short of the cost of renting in an area where the median price of houses was $270,000.

The reasons for the divide between those with homes, and gainfully-employed people who slept in automobiles, were not difficult to unravel for builders in the San Fernando Valley. The construction industry identified three explanations for its reluctance to erect low-cost apartment blocks:

- high land prices;
- not-in-my-back-yard (NIMBY) opposition from those already housed; and

38

● taxes that raise the cost of housing above what many people could afford.[2]

If the Wall Street and City of London analysts had concentrated on how the convergence of those three factors would bear down on the emerging electronic age, they would have saved their clients a great deal of financial grief. They did not do so. Consequently, as the dot.com prosperity took hold, the building industry shifted away from the provision of homes that were within the budgets of most families, to the luxury properties that would attract rents above $1,000 per month for a one-bedroom apartment. California was the First State of Virtual Prosperity. A state where the number of mega-rich folk increased exponentially, at a rate exceeded only by the very poor – two groups that squeezed the middle class. Was this really the age of a New Economy, or a new twist on the old theme?

The electronic revolution allowed the new gurus to interpret facts to suit their money-spinning myths. Crucial to the promotion of the State of Virtual Reality was a doctrine that distorted people's under-standing of the power that perverts the way we create wealth. Fine-tuning the doctrine is an exercise that is undertaken at the beginning of each of the boom busts that has dislocated the economy of the past two centuries. For the dot.com age, the sanitised version of history was articulated by Andreas Schmidt, Chairman of AOL Europe, the joint venture between America On-Line (the world's biggest internet service provider) and Bertelsmann, the German media group. AOL, through its merger with Time Warner (owner of CNN and Warner Bros.), became one of the leading corporations shaping the character of the electronic economy. According to Schmidt, the internet would have a comprehensive impact on our lives:

> There isn't just a change going on in one industry – it's a whole new economy. Those that don't realise it will be history. Two hundred years ago in Britain all the land was owned by lords and that was where the money was. Then these guys started putting up factories and they became the ones who were running the economy. The shift occurring today is every bit as seismic as the industrial revolution.[3]

This spin on history was riddled with twists of the facts that would not matter if they did not deflect people's minds from a realistic appreciation of sound economic principles and rational public policy. It was understandable that the gurus of virtual reality should want to promote the notion of a post-industrial age. The myths, however, like the fatal viruses that invade PCs, contaminate our knowledge of the way in which people earn their living and support their communities through the delivery of resources to pay for shared services.

For people like Schmidt, it was important to claim that there were discrete breaks between the agricultural era that was based on land, the industrial era that was based on capital-intensive factories, and the Information Age based on microchip technology. Such disjunctions legitimised a future in which computers were hardwired to a New Economy. The damage caused by this caricature of history stems from the way that it fragments awareness of the structure of political power. The nature of that power has existed since the feudal era (which was overtly financed by land rents) up to the present (which is covertly manipulated by those who seek to maximise their accumulation of land rents).

Curiously, the most powerful testimony against the Schmidt doctrine was the analysis by Karl Marx. His insights affirm the seminal role of capitalists in the wealth-producing process. Marx was the most enthusiastic exponent of the unique qualities of capital; that was why he called his book *Das Kapital*. He was also capitalism's most potent enemy. And yet, in what must be one of history's exquisite ironies, Marx noted in one of the most neglected insights that he had to offer that

> The capitalist still performs an active function in the development of this surplus-value and surplus-product. But the landowner need only appropriate *the growing share* in the surplus-product and the surplus-value, without having contributed anything to its growth.[4]

In his voluminous portrait of economic history, Marx endorsed the conclusion that flowed from classical economic principles: rent (which was privatised in the late feudal era) continued to manifest itself in the buccaneering era of the 19th century industrial entrepreneur. Throughout the 20th century, although challenged by the Tax State, at no time was the powerful role of the land market over the destiny of the capitalist economy weakened. Armed with such insights into how income is distributed, the revolutionary traumas of the 20th century might have been avoided. It did not work out like that, because Marx was one of the myth-makers. He did, however, correctly distinguish land from capital, and he emphasised the influence that landowners exercised over the Captains of Industry. He noted in *Critique of the Gotha Programme*: '[T]he monopoly of landed property is even the basis of the monopoly of capital'.[5] That appreciation of the reality of the power structure in the 19th century remained valid in the 20th. But by his emphasis on capital as the site of conflict, Marx added his doctrinal prejudices to the conceptual ambiguities that were to undermine attempts to formulate sound public policies.

One of our objectives, then, is to decode the language used to defeat our best private and social interests. Central to the new analysis is the appreciation of the role that land plays in our lives.

One level of analysis relates to land as a physical entity. More significant, however, for the commercial and industrial economy, is the treatment of land and nature's resources as a flow of rental income. Both of these dimensions are central to the correct analysis of the digital age. To trace the evolution of the importance of 'land', we begin with illustrations of the first dimension in the course of commerce in its pre-electronic form.

Real estate is the backbone of many corporations that appear to rely on the sale of the products that they manufacture. McDonald's, for example, famous for beefburgers, relies more on real estate for its profits than on mangled meat. Location is critical. In June 2001, as the Internal Revenue Service (IRS), the US tax authority, was considering granting yet more favours to the real estate sector, the value of McDonald's portfolio became the subject of Wall Street analysis. McDonald's property and equipment was valued at $8bn. It was one of the largest real estate owners in corporate America, with 12,800 US restaurants and over $1.4bn in rental income from 10,100 franchised outlets in 2000.[6]

Acquiring land is not just a matter of locating the store close to customers. Possession is part of corporate strategy for controlling markets. It is a means of depriving others of the opportunity to sell to consumers. This was understood by Aşda, the British supermarket chain that was bought in 1999 by Wal-Mart, the giant US retailer. In the mid-'90s, Asda offered hundreds of thousands of pounds to Manchester City Council for a piece of land. According to evidence given to the House of Commons Environment Select Committee, the money was not so much for the purpose of acquiring another outlet for Asda; it had more to do with denying a rival, Quick Save, the opportunity to construct a store on the site. Present at the meeting where the money was offered was council leader Graham Stringer, who was to become a Cabinet Office minister in the Blair government. He testified that Asda's bid was motivated by the fact that 'they did not want the extra competition'.[7]

The defensive acquisition of strategically located sites is a traditional strategy for cornering a market. The power to exclude competitors stems from the fact that land is in finite supply in the locations where it matters, near to customers and the business infrastructure. The dot.com companies were shrewd enough to know that their success depended, in part, on their ability to hoard land. According to Steven Comfort, Vice President for sales at eGroup, a San Francisco company: 'If you're confident in your business model, you don't rent the space you need now, you rent three times as much space as you need now'. This strategy has the effect of pushing up demand for space and consequently rents, making it more expensive for everybody else. The electrifying impact of internet companies on real estate was dramatic in New York, where in the dying years of the 20th century these companies were responsible for nearly doubling rents in the scramble for scarce office space. In doing so, they drove out traditional tenants in the printing and garment industries.[8]

So where did the dot.coms get the money to outbid the product-making/selling industries? We now embark on uncharted waters. For the dot.coms did not churn out profits from services delivered to customers. The money to pay the rent was from speculators who believed they could become rich by buying the shares of start-up companies that had not yet delivered a product to market.

§2 Sky-High Rents

MEDIA PUNDITS represented internet share deals as built on nothing except a name. The dot.com suffix was supposed to be all that was required to extract the cash from investors' pockets. In fact, this contention was another layer of confusion over people's minds. Silicon Valley's whiz kids had found the electronic pathway into one of nature's untapped niches. The internet was a new way of connecting the earth's surface with one of the invisible natural resources above earth. The transmission of electronic messages is via the electromagnetic spectrum. To access the airwaves it is necessary to erect antennae in prominent locations from which to beam signals to mobile telephones and a web of cables below the ground which link to computer terminals. This was the physical infrastructure that supported the World Wide Web, which is the body of knowledge hovering above the cables and computers. The 250,000 millionaires who worked in Silicon Valley had found a new way to speculate in land.

Land is defined by economists to include all of the resources provided by nature. The fantasy world of virtual reality was anchored in the tangible resources of nature, which are treated as free for the taking by those who stake their claims before others realise the economic potential that nature is yielding to us all. It was the Wild West land rush all over again. The covered wagons were swapped for four-wheel drives, but the risks and rewards were much the same: many of the path-breakers would lose their shirts, but a few would end up mega-rich, because they held on to the biggest 'ranches'.

First, however, the pioneers of the heavens had to solve one little problem: how could they tap the rental value of the new frontier when the customers were not tooled up in sufficient numbers to cross into the Promised Land? The solution was a new variant on an old theme, one that had been tried and tested in the 19th century railroad-building programme. At the cusp of the 21st century, the answer was to be found in one word: *securitisation*. This was the impatient speculator's method of making people pay today for the revenue of a product that would not be made and sold until tomorrow or even next year. The stream of rental income that would *one day* be generated by the radio spectrum was capitalised and sold to investors. The investors assumed that, by buying this stream of income at today's prices, they would secure a capital gain. The catch that made the deal speculative (and which would guarantee that most investors would end up as losers) was that little rental income was being generated that could be capitalised.

For one group of operators, however, the securitisation formula was not speculative; in fact, it was a certain money-spinner. They were directors who received shares when their company – or someone else's dot.com – was offered for sale to the public. That was when the value of the shares was untested in the market. For those with knowledge of the quicksand foundations on which the companies were floating, the shrewd decision was to off-load the shares immediately. According to an investigation by the financial services committee of the US House of Representatives, in the case of Goldman Sachs, shares in stock market flotations were allocated to executives of 21 companies with which Goldman had (or would like to have) a banking association. The recipients included former Enron chief executive Kenneth Lay. Some of them had no intention of being long-term investors. They 'flipped' the shares immediately, to ensure that they capitalised – and pocketed – the future income well before anyone else could see what the future held. That was just as well – for them. According to the congressional committee, of the 22 firms brought to market by Goldman Sachs, which they studied, two-thirds had since lost at least 96% of their value.[9]

Box 3:1

Enron: A Case of Bad Apples?

ENRON was the first company of the dot.com collapse to surface as having employed accountancy techniques to conceal its debts, and to camouflage the filtering of money into foreign tax havens. Enron's former chief financial officer, Andrew Fastow, was charged in October 2002 with fraud, money laundering and conspiracy at the energy firm which had gone bankrupt in 2001, costing investors billions of dollars.

President Bush was familiar with the corporate sweetheart deals that were behind rip-offs such as those at Enron. He was a beneficiary when Harken Energy bought his company at an astonishingly high price. It fared badly, but concealed its failure. The stock price was sustained long enough for Bush to sell most of his stake at a large profit – with an accounting device identical to one of the techniques employed by Enron. Professor of economics Paul Krugman described the ploy: 'Corporate insiders create a front organisation that seems independent but is really under their control. This front buys some of the firm's assets at unrealistically high prices, creating a phantom profit that inflates the stock price, allowing the executives to cash in their stock.'*

In the Bush case, Harken lent the money that was used to pay for Aloha Petroleum; this created a $10m phantom profit, which was sufficient to conceal three-quarters of the company's losses in 1989. Bush was on the company's audit committee. Later, as the incumbent in the White House, he characterised his failure to follow the rules as no more serious than a motoring offence.

*Paul Krugman, 'How Bush firm used accounting scam', *The Guardian*, July 9, 2002

When the creative accounting procedures behind the securitisation scams were finally exposed, the politicians were anxious to claim that the crooks were deviants; that the problem was not attributable to weaknesses in the rules of the economic game. It was of little comfort for people who saw their savings and pensions wiped out to be told by the President, George W. Bush, that they should place the blame on individual bad apples (see Box 3:1).

The losers in securitisation gambles were not only the people who staked their savings on glossy brochures that packaged dreams. Taxpayers who underwrite the decisions of governments were also penalised when the deals turned sour. That was what happened with the great boom in the shares of American railway companies. The federal government granted free land to companies that would lay the tracks to connect coast to coast. The capital cost of clearing the ground, drilling tunnels through mountains and building the metal tracks was enormous. The revenue from the sales of tickets would hardly cover the costs of the rolling stock. The land that was bequeathed to the railway companies was initially of little economic value. This was because much of the investment was pushed into marginal lands where people could barely make a living. The railway construction boom was, in other words, a classic example of land speculation. The fortune hunters persuaded governments to cover the losses incurred in building the railways by offering subsidies (tax-payers' money) which could be invested in the infrastructure that would attract migrants to the new locations and raise the value of their land.

The rail operators were not interested in ensuring that taxpayers who had to foot the bill received value for their buck. They were concerned with the alchemy of land speculation. Their job was to convince governments that one day the economies of the outlying townships would generate rents and profits. In the meantime, however, many speculators did not want to wait for their rewards. So they sold the shares in the railway companies at a value which presumed that a stream of rental income was actually being generated from the land which they held.[10] The trade in US internet shares that began in 1995 had all the hallmarks of the 19th century mania for railway shares.

The dot.com mania infected the shores of Britain. The boom in sky-high rents began in 1999, but it did not take long for gullible people to form themselves into investment clubs. They pooled their savings and met in pubs to decide which of the dot.com shares they would buy. The bubble at the end of 1999 was followed by three days of share trading in the new millennium which saw a fall in value of £100bn in the City of London. The small-time gamblers were in good company. George Soros, the financier known as the man who once broke the Bank of England, also suffered big losses from the plunge in hi-tech stocks. His Quantum Fund was reported to have suffered a drop in value of $600m (£365m) in the first week of January 2000. In 1999 the IT hardware sector had risen 700%: in 2000 its shares dropped 15% in one week.

This did not deter the 'day traders' in America. They used the new technology on desks in the corners of their bedrooms and living rooms to buy and sell the shares of colourfully named companies. The US equity market was now like a low-life junkie. It was hooked on the fate of IT stocks which made up about a quarter of the value of the US market.

In London, the daily deals on the stock exchange doubled to 120,000 during 1999 thanks to people's fervent belief that they were the pioneering winners in the fortune hunt on the new frontier. The best deals were easy to spot.

- ARM Holdings designed chips for semiconductors. It began trading on the London stock market in the middle of 1998. Eighteen months later it was valued at £6bn – which was £2bn more than the blue-chip ICI.
- Yahoo! the internet portal, rapidly acquired a market value greater than General Motors.
- Amazon.com started as an online book retailer before branching out into groceries and pharmaceuticals. By the end of 1999 it was valued at $20bn *even though it traded at a loss.*
- Sage, the accountancy software group, saw its value grow by 28,000%.
- Freeserve, the internet access company, had not made a penny in profit when it was floated. Its shares were priced at £1.4bn.

The US telecommunications and IT sector became bigger than any other share market in the world. Even though companies in the real world were ill-equipped to deal with the predicted increase in global e-commerce, the share speculators were not deterred. Stock brokers reported that some clients did not even know the name of the company in which they wanted to invest their money – they identified the enterprise from descriptions picked up from internet bulletin boards. The motto, according to dealers, was 'buying tomorrow's stocks today'.

Sceptics began to recall the lessons of history. Previous fast-growth industries such as railways had not produced substantial profits for investors, because competition cut returns to levels that were comparable to other sectors. But when people are gripped by the fever of speculation, bad news is swamped by the hype. The tales of personal good fortune ignited the imaginations of people who had spent their lives earning wages and just covering their costs of living. Tales like the one about Dave Stanworth, who believed he was Britain's first internet millionaire. He was the 33-year-old Birmingham man whose family had had so little money that cash in the house was hidden behind the sofa when the rent man called. He left school with no qualifications and worked as a bricklayer, a bookie, and by mailing Christmas cards from Santa Claus before he took a computer course by correspondence. His big idea was to establish an internet site which reviewed computer games. He started in a room above a barber's shop. Games Domain achieved a global following in 1995, receiving 11,000 'hits' a day from 70 countries. He sold the site for $3m worth of shares in Attitude Network in February 1997. This was the news that hit the headlines and lured people into dreams about making similar fortunes. They were not interested in knowing that the value of Stanworth's shares went into freefall when Attitude Network sold out to theglobe.com, which then hit a bad patch."

Shares in dot.com companies were the new currency. Employees agreed to take part of their wages in the form of stock options. Hiring university whiz kids without paying them cash became an attractive business proposition in the US. Akamai Technologies offered stock options to students at the prestigious Massachusetts Institute of Technology in exchange for work during vacations. The value of those stocks soared to eight times their initial value when the company went public in October 1999. Students became millionaires (on paper). Their idol was Bill Gates, the Harvard drop-out who created Microsoft and became the richest man in the world.

The internet bubble was assisted by the manipulation of accounting rules to inflate earnings and artificially reduce costs, so that the dot.coms could report profits.

- *Labour costs* were disguised by not paying salaries. Stock options inflated earnings but concealed costs.
- *Advertising costs* are a major outlay for companies with no goodwill or brand recognition (and precious few products to sell to the customers they had not yet acquired). These were written off immediately so that they would not appear as a debit on future profits.
- *Barter trades*, as with the exchange of advertising deals, were treated as revenue to inflate the income of companies that were short on sales.
- *Equipment* was acquired based on deferred payments. The transaction would be entered in the books of hardware manufacturers as revenue. The favourable rebates and credit deals appeared to cut start-up expenses.

Such artful devices were substituted for the hard-headed assessments that are supposed to feature in business plans. Young entrepreneurs weaned on interactive video games were not interested in 'old economy' constraints such as the need to identify a market for prospective products. They were more concerned with the 'story' that would attract investors. The pace was fast, the penetration superficial, the commitments non-existent so far as the infrastructure of commerce was concerned. Caution was history. Investors wanted to believe that the 'new economy' was 'wired' in a new way, making it easier to launch a new operation rather than having to work through the painful process of re-engineering an old enterprise to increase productivity and profits. In the 'new economy' the risk was in ignoring the opportunities that came and went with the speed of light, offering no mercy for those who felt the need to pause and think. Reflexes were honed on the joysticks, where the inversion of reality was consolidated. Bricks and mortar had no place on the screens in this world of software. Outputs were not products on a conveyor belt, but zeros on electronic ledgers.

Extrovert Dan Wagner knew how to sell such dreams. He relished appearing at a City presentation dressed in a Donald Duck waistcoat. The grey suits may not have appreciated his taste in attire but they liked his commercial style. In October 1997 his loss-making high tech Maid took over Knight Ridder Information for what was described in the financial press as an audacious £261m. The deal was sold as the world's largest online data and information supplier. The financiers helped Wagner to raise $190m (£120m) from a share placing, and debt of $270m. With the right story, it seemed that anything could be achieved in high finance. Three years later the man whom tabloid newspapers dubbed 'the new Bill Gates' was obliged to abandon his dreams. In March 2000 he entered talks to sell the core of his business for a price that fell short of what he had paid for the business in 1997.[12]

Professional people quit their jobs to trade shares from their homes. But there was one big difference between the classic case of the landowner selling his location for a fortune, and the pursuit of easy rent-capitalised profits. In the first case, if the owner is willing to wait, he or his heir was guaranteed to make a killing: land was the tangible asset *par excellence*. But speculators who do not hold title deeds, and whose time horizons are short, can lose everything in the gamble. That's what happened when day trader Mark Barton ran up losses of more than $120,000 (£75,000). As his despair deepened, he went into a rage. He relieved his tensions with murder. In the two days leading to July 29, 1999, he bludgeoned to death his wife and two children. He then went on a shooting spree, killing nine people at two day trading firms in Atlanta, Georgia, and wounding 13 others. Then he committed suicide.

§3 The Economic Law of Absorption

THE INTERNET was dubbed the information superhighway. That accurately portrays the way in which we can now transcend time and space to transform many aspects of our everyday lives. But understanding the commercial prospects is crucial for two reasons. I will discuss the good news first.

People working a distance from mainstream markets found the internet a life-saver. Their commercial universe was expanded from the local to the global at the press of a few buttons on the keyboard. That was the way in which a secondhand book store in the rural county of Shropshire, England, found that it could literally open its door to the world.

Shropshire's entry into history was an accident, stemming from a decision over where to locate a road. The development of towns like Shrewsbury, the birthplace of Charles Darwin, was the result of a deviation in the Roman rule of constructing roads by the formula of 'minimum effort'. The direct route from London to the north-west was through Chester, which was the garrison town from which the Lancashire plain could be controlled and the western end of Hadrian's Wall patrolled. But when the Romans built Watling Street, they turned left towards a hill called the Wrekin. On the north side of the Wrekin they built Uriconium, which was headquarters of the 14th Legion from about 50 AD. The strategic reason for this road-building deviation was that the Romans had failed to pacify the Welsh tribes. Watling Street was made to loop westwards to enable them to consolidate their western flank.

On the basis of this military necessity, the hamlets that would become strategically important were brought into history. To reach the unruly mountain tribes in Wales, the Roman legionnaires would march through a gap in the foothills now occupied by the town of Church Stretton. Here, retailers still depend on the number of people who trudge past their shops every day. Or at least they did until the arrival of e.commerce. For the bookshop run by Roger Toon in the High Street, the screen on the word processor became his window onto the world. In one instant, the catchment area for customers leapt from a backwater lane to the farthest corners of the globe. Financial analysts confidently predicted that electronic commerce on a global scale would increase in value from $2.6bn in 1996 to hundreds of billions of dollars in the next century.

But Roger Toon did not allow the 'New Economy' to distract him from the economics of the old economy. Location continued to matter, even in geographically remote places like Church Stretton. Mr. Toon bought his property in 1993, at the bottom of the previous recession. He paid £93,000 and spent £25,000 on improvements. Ten years later he decided that the top of the cycle had been reached for his property, a mixture of residential and commercial use on the High

Street. He sold it for £272,000, delivering a profit of £150,000. While reaching into the ether with his book business, Toon kept his feet firmly planted on the ground. He re-located to a rural home outside the town, and was still plugged into the global marketplace through his desktop PC.

Now the bad news: the electronic age will emboss a new layer of deprivation on society. This is an *unavoidable* outcome of the economic impact of digital technology under our present combination of property laws and tax policies. The reason is summarised in two words: cost cutting. Computers cut the costs of commerce and industry, but the consequences of this in the electronic age is no different from the previous revolutions in science and technology. The railways of America did cut the costs of transporting beef from the mid-west to the restaurants of New York. The refrigeration of cargo ships did cut the cost of New Zealand lamb and butter for the housewives of Britain. Likewise, computers cut the costs of secretarial work in offices and the inventory stocks held in factory warehouses. The new method of collating and processing information transforms many traditional practices, reshaping much of the landscape of our lives. In banking the cost of an internet transaction is estimated to be about 7p. This compares with the 37p cost at a call centre and the 70p cost at a conventional bank branch.[3]

Corroboration that computers improved productivity for the 'old economy' came from three Nobel Prize-winning economists. They employed a historical perspective to explain that there had been 'one innovation after another,' as it was put by Kenneth Arrow, professor emeritus of economics at Stanford University. 'The telegraph marked the first time we could eliminate distance ... Electricity's most important impact was its use in the factory'. For James Buchanan, professor emeritus at George Mason University in Fairfax, Virginia: 'The closest analogy for the Internet today is the automobile in the 1920s'. Car production gave an immense boost to the manufacturing sector, but that did not stop the stock market from crashing in 1929. Lawrence Klein, professor emeritus of economics at the University of Pennsylvania, forecast that the productivity gains would continue right up to 2010.[4]

Who benefits from the reduction in production costs? The answer is found in what I call the Economic Law of Absorption. The land market is a giant sponge. It soaks up the value that is not taken by people in the labour and capital markets. The speed and the scope by which revenue is transformed into net income (that is, after paying for the use of labour and capital) and paid as rent to the owners of land

and natural resources depends on particular circumstances. Here are some examples.

● *Costs are cut when science and technology enable entrepreneurs to produce the same output with fewer inputs of labour and capital.*

Whether employees pocket part of the savings depends on the demand for their skills. In the late 1990s, computer programmers were in short supply. They were a mobile workforce in an industry that was expanding. Their wages were bid up: they captured some of the gains that resulted from the new technology. But that flow into wages would only last for as long as firms needed to upgrade their technologies. When the work was completed and new firms had moved into the sector to bid down the super-profits, the net gains from new technology would be soaked up as rent. The diffusion of computer skills would adjust downwards the wages of programmers. Ultimately, the net economic benefits of the Information Age would be absorbed as rent.

Occasionally, however, part of the net gains can be intercepted by entrepreneurs who can limit the competition they face. That was the allegation against Marsh & McLennan, a major New York insurance broker. New York State Attorney General Eliot Spitzer claimed that the brokers had derived super-profits from the New Economy's cost-cutting productivity gains. Under the headline 'Finger Points at the Broker Barons in their Rent-Collectors' Castles', a *Financial Times* journalist reported that, assuming Spitzer's suspicions were at least partly correct,

> Marsh & McLennan – and perhaps others – have moved beyond acting as entrepreneurs seeking profit in a competitive market by providing a useful service, to becoming rent-seekers.[15]

The journalist, John Dizard, traced the source of the rents that had become available. They were due to 'the dispersion of computing power, communications bandwidth, and internet transparency [which] have reduced transaction costs. The increased access profits going to major insurance brokerages are an anomaly'. In time, through competition – which the Attorney General, in this case, was able to impose on the insurance sector with the mere threat of legal action – those profits would cascade down as windfall gains for landowners.

● *Governments reduce production costs when they cut taxes.*

The 'enterprise zone' is an example of how prices are affected by taxation. The experiment in trying to boost economic activity by overriding the constraints imposed by taxes was popular in Britain and the US in the 1980s. The logic was that entrepreneurs would invest in deprived areas if they were granted tax 'holidays'. Who benefited from the tax relief? The net benefits were instantly transformed into rent and an increase in the selling price of land within the zones. The rapidity with which this was accomplished was made possible by the fact that the land was generally vacant (originally marginalised, in the main, by the disincentives of taxation). Investors realised that the easiest way to maximise the collection of trouble-free rent was to minimise their investment in value-adding activities. The result was a bias in favour of warehouse activities that employed few workers. The local economy did not derive significant benefits. The ingenuity was in creating economic vehicles that could most efficiently recycle the tax benefits into land rents.

When the history of the new Information Age is fully documented, economic historians will demonstrate that the major gains of the post-industrial era went into the pockets of landowners. Marx was correct on this one point at least: rent would constitute 'the growing share' of the nation's income. But this particular road to riches is beset with risks waiting to engulf the unwary. This lesson was learnt the hard way in California.

Silicon Valley had benefited from the greatest concentration of venture capital in the world. At its peak, in 1999, $26bn was invested in the region. When the computer age dawned in the arid reaches beyond the Californian coastline, a prime site for a macho HQ became one of the must-have trophies. Palm, the iconic maker of hand held computers, paid $220m (£141m) for 39 acres in San Jose to proclaim its mighty status. It had a $1.2bn cash pile to burn, and everything seemed possible. When the crash came, the value dissolved like snowflakes in the sun. In March 2003 the company announced that it would write down the value of its property to $60m.[16]

With the bursting of the bubble, it was symbolically appropriate that the seven modern glass buildings that housed Excite@home, the bankrupted internet access provider, stood empty along Highway 101. Landlords found themselves holding properties they could not rent. By the summer of 2001 landlords were offering bonuses to prospective tenants. Vacancy rates were pushed to their highest level since the beginning of the business cycle in 1992. The vacancy rate for commercial property along Highway 101 was 1.3% at the beginning of the new century. Two years later it stood at 15%.

The legacy of the Great Spectrum Rent Robbery was transmitted by Wall Street to every part of the US economy. Meanwhile the homeless who could not even afford the reduced rents continued to spend their nights sleeping in their cars or cruising the highway on board Motel 22.

REFERENCES

1 Michael McCabe and Marshall Wislon, 'Priced Out of Land', *San Francisco Chronicle*, July 22, 2000.
2 Something similar happened in London where nurses, firemen, policemen etc. could not fill job vacancies because they could not afford accommodation.
3 Dominic Rush, 'Internet Giant prepares for shake-out of dinosaurs', *The Sunday Times*, February 6, 2000.
4 Karl Marx, *Capital*, London: Lawrence and Wishart, 1962, Vol. III, p.623. Emphasis added.
5 *Critique of the Gotha Programme*, in Karl Marx, *The First International and After*, London: Penguin, 1974, p.343.
6 Norma Cohen and Andrew Edgecliffe-Johnson, 'IRS to allow real estate spin-offs', *Financial Times*, June 7, 2001.
7 Anthony Barnett, 'Tory's environment chief is "green belt destroyer"', *The Observer*, February 6, 2000.
8 'Silicon Alley changes New York market', *The New York Times*, from a feature in the *South China Morning Post*, January 19, 2000.
9 Vincent Boland, 'Congress names Goldman's 'new economy' friends', *Financial Times*, October 4, 2002.
10 Fred Harrison, *Wheels of Fortune: Self-financing Transport Systems & the Tax Reform Dividend*, forthcoming.
11 Juliet Jowit, 'Playing a game of fortune on the web', *Financial Times*, London, January 5, 2000.
12 Caroline Daniel, 'The deal that marks the death of Dial-a-Dog', *Financial Times*, March 21, 2000.
13 OECD, *EMU One Year On*, Paris, 2000, p.68, Box 6.
14 Alan Goldstein, 'Milken panel evaluates impact of technology', *Dallas Morning News*, March 10, 2000.
15 John Dizard, 'Finger points at the broker barons in their rent-collectors' castles', *Financial Times*, October 18, 2004.
16 Scott Morrison, 'Property crash sends chill wind through Silicon Valley', *Financial Times*, March 3, 2003.

4

The Incredible Alan Greenspan

§1 The Troubles with Bubbles

THE GLOBAL ECONOMY felt the impact of the terrorist attack on September 11. Once again, a random event came to the rescue of economists who could not offer scientifically valid predictions. Few of them had an inkling of the downturn that would begin in 2001. The hijacking of passenger jets, two of which were crashed into the twin towers of the World Trade Centre in New York, became the convenient explanation for the recession that gripped the world in 2002.

As the economic news ,unfolded during the winter of 2001/2, people were told that output in the US and UK had fallen at the fastest rate for *nine* years. The number of Americans out of work and claiming benefit rose to an *eighteen* year high, according to the US Department of Labor. These periods – nine and 18 years – were not the result of crazed terrorists plotting in their training camps in Afghanistan. As we shall see, they are derived from a timetable that is built into the DNA of the capitalist economy.

Bankers who failed to anticipate the looming crisis paid a heavy price. In 2002 alone, investment banks in Europe and the US were expected to write off more than $130bn in loan losses.[1] They had taken their cue from the central bankers and, above all, they felt entitled to interpret the boom of the late 1990s as secure in the hands of Alan Greenspan, the Chairman of the US Federal Reserve Board – America's central bank. The speculators chose to ignore the fiasco during the previous turning point in the US economy. In September 1990 Greenspan denied that the US was in recession. In fact, the recession had begun three months earlier, in July. The hapless Greenspan was not helped by the National Bureau of Economic Research (NBER), which is widely accepted as the arbiter of business cycles in the US. It registered the onset of the July 1990 recession in April 1991 – a month after the recession ended.

Is it any wonder that people believe that the workings of the economy are beyond comprehension? That they are victims of dark forces which are even beyond the influence of sovereign governments? That the rational way to operate is to treat the economy as a casino – which, in Britain, is what investors took the opportunity of doing in the housing market (Box 4:1)?

This outcome is the result of one solitary fact: economic theory, as it is applied by its practitioners, fails to treat rental income as the economy's *pressure gauge*. As a consequence, the mightiest economies periodically collapse into a mess because the experts at the steering wheel turn Nelsonian blind eyes to the vital information that is registered on that gauge.

Box 4:1

Gambling with Your Home

IN BRITAIN, investors bet on whether people's homes will go up or down in value. Using the latest techniques in calculating risks, gamblers may get rich by anticipating a drop in house prices that would be ruinous for the families who live in them.

The spread betting firm, City Index, enables punters to play the housing market like others bet on dogs at a greyhound stadium, by taking positions on its Property Futures Book.

Banks that fuel the bubbles seek to avoid the risks to their financial viability. They have devised ways to offload risks onto others – the people who rely on a stable stock market for the returns that will pay their pensions. They employ instruments like credit derivatives. These shift the risks of losses, ultimately, on to the people who are trying to save money.

When the International Monetary Fund (IMF) rang alarm bells over the unsustainable level of house prices in Britain, which it said could undermine the economy, it reassured the bankers that they were in "strong enough shape" to withstand a price slump. This contrasted with prospects for "highly indebted households [which] could be vulnerable to increases in interest rates or unemployment".*

* Ashley Seager, 'House crash would derail economy, warns IMF', *The Guardian*, April 22, 2004.

And so, people are invited to draw comfort from small mercies. For example, Alan Greenspan's claim to a congressional committee on 16 July, 2002, that financial rip-offs of the dot.com kind occur but once a generation was supposed to be reassuring. Within the previous few weeks, millions of hard-working Americans learnt that their savings and pensions had disappeared into secret accounts in tax havens. Alas, we all have but one life to live. If, during that lifetime, our carefully-husbanded pensions are stolen from us, leaving us destitute in old age, it is of little comfort to learn that the plunder of our wealth is not likely to occur again until our children are the victims.

But the assessment offered by the venerated Chairman Greenspan was suspect. For he also declared that the opportunities for stealing other people's money, through financial transactions on the bourses, were increasing. If that prognosis is correct, the rip-offs will be more frequent than once a generation.

Metaphysical skills are needed to translate the economic prognoses of the Chairman of the Federal Reserve. When he communicated with the nation – most often through his statements to congressional committees – he sought to reassure with optimistic news. He perfected the strategy during the dot.com crisis. This led people to believe that a crash could be avoided by fine-tuning the nation's interest rates. The economy crashed, with a recession stretching from 2000 into 2001. Was this predictable? Was it avoidable?

In Chapter 2 (§2) we saw how the financial arithmetic in the house building industry dictated a 14-year construction cycle. In Part II, we shall test the logic of the arithmetic against the facts of history. Here, for present purposes, we need to introduce a refinement of the 14-year cycle. From the historical evidence, we discover that the cycle is divided into two distinct phases by a mid-cycle mini-boom. The two 7-year phases match the average period that owners live in their homes before selling and moving. In the UK, they also match the average time it takes to deliver new commercial property to market – from the time that a project is conceived and financed through to construction and delivery to tenants or purchasers.[2] How does this assist us in anticipating events after the global recession of 1992?

In the US, the housing market began to recover in the final three months of 1994. If our thesis has merit, house prices would take seven years to reach boiling point in 2001. That is what happened. Prices peaked in the first three months of 2001.[3] *The timing was perfectly aligned with what we would have expected, if we had correctly read the texts of economic history.* The peak prices were unsustainable. Something had to give. The economy buckled. So according to our theory of history, *the US economy would have slipped into recession even without the frenzied share dealing in dot.com start-ups.*

Alan Greenspan, if he had paid attention to the land market, would have had that historical insight at his disposal; he would have known that the US had a date with recession in 2001, and he would have had the opportunity to recommend pre-emptive strikes by Congress. He failed that test.

A second opportunity to redeem himself arose when the economy recovered. With house prices surging, was the US locked into a housing bubble? Was this a bubble that would terminate in the depression of 2010? Incredibly, Greenspan disparaged the idea of a housing bubble. It was true that America's home-owners had enjoyed substantial increases in the price of their properties. But, emphatically: 'A sharp decline, the consequences of a bursting bubble, however, seems most unlikely'.[4]

Economists concurred. Shelly Dreiman, senior economist at the OFHEO, who oversees the construction of that organisation's authoritative House Price Index, concluded: 'The price increases of recent years diminish significantly when prices are divided by income. This would suggest that prices are not currently near the peak of a bubble'.[5] Not at the peak – but *when* would those prices hit the peak? What would inflate that bubble? What were the key signals that would alert the families who needed to make decisions on how much to save, which assets to include in their portfolios, whether to reduce their debts and sell their homes to live somewhere affordable?

The evidence that would lead to sensible answers to such questions was not beyond the reach of economists. Greenspan might have looked closer at the research published by the OFHEO. In carrying out its duty to stress test the two government-backed mortgage finance organisations (known as Freddie Mac and Fannie Mae), the OFHEO had published a study on the forces that might disrupt the economy. That report was submitted to Congress in February 2003. Attention was drawn to the real estate bubbles of the previous two decades, including those that developed in US farmland, Swedish and Japanese commercial real estate and Thailand's residential and commercial property sectors. But what drove those bubbles to unsustainably high peaks – so high that they had to terminate in full-blown collapses of the property markets? And why did a real estate crash have to drag down the rest of the economy with it? The literature on real estate cycles was hesitatingly coming to terms with the reality. This is how a senior economist at one of the US Government's financial agencies analysed the processes that feature in a bubble:

> Recent studies explain the emergence of those bubbles in terms of the unique characteristics of land and moral hazard behaviour by banks. Those studies observe that land is different from some financial assets (such as stock) in that it is in fixed supply, and that it is generally not possible to sell short individual tracts of land. The studies suggest that those conditions imply that optimists will set the price of land, since only people who already own land or who are interested in buying land will influence land's market value. If a group of agents controlling sufficient wealth becomes sufficiently over-optimistic about

land values, a bubble may emerge. Whether a bubble in land prices emerges depends largely on the behaviour of lenders, who can refuse to lend to optimists. Moreover, as rising land prices increase the value of the collateral backing loans, the value of lender assets and capital also increase, which encourages additional lending, in a self-reinforcing process.[6]

Where banks and mortgage-lending institutions were protected by government guarantees – creating the risk of reckless lending – 'the bursting of the bubble may cause widespread insolvencies that may require a government to consider a bailout. That outcome has occurred in commercial and agricultural real estate and, occasionally, in local or regional real estate in the US and other countries'.[7]

Failures in market discipline of banks contributed to many of the banking crises that occurred around the world in the 1980s and 1990s.[8]

The OFHEO study also warned that worse bank-fuelled bouts of land speculation might emerge in the future, for 'recent changes in the banking system and the financial sector are making safety and soundness regulation increasingly difficult'?[9] The computer and the internet contributed to this climate of heightened fragility in the financial system. They made it possible for banks to remove the personal link between themselves and the people who borrow their money. The friendly neighbourhood bank manager with his pulse on the local economy was a personality consigned to the past, replaced by call centres that were created to cut costs and speed up the creation of credit. This is 'out-sourcing', or 'disintermediation'.[10] As the first global business cycle gathered its pace in the 1990s, the financiers no longer had their personal fingers on the creditworthiness of their clients. The crash, when it came, would once again catch the bankers by surprise.

Bankers would not be solely responsible. Politicians create and preserve the rules and institutions within which people operate. The US, recovering from the dot.com crash, was stimulated by the adrenaline of President George W. Bush's massive tax cuts of $1.35 trillion over the years to 2011. With the stock market out of favour, where better to invest this money than in the rock-solid ground beneath our feet? President Bush knew the reality, as we heard in his self-acclamatory State of the Union Address to Congress in January 2004:

Americans took those dollars and put them to work, driving this economy forward. The pace of economic growth in the third quarter of 2003 was the fastest in nearly 20 years; new home construction, the highest in almost 20 years; home ownership rates, the highest ever.

Money continued to pour into property in 2004, consolidating the trend that made real estate the most rewarding asset over the previous 20 years. Since 1980, house prices had risen by 355% in Rhode Island, 306% in California, 294% in Washington, DC. Twenty states enjoyed price appreciation of more than 200% in that period. But housing was also the epicentre of the chaos in the capitalist economy, causing the booms and busts that repressed people's incomes, encouraged urban sprawl and raised the taxes that had to be spent to fund infrastructure.

Did people – especially the home-owners who had managed to pay off their mortgages – want to hear this bad news? Could this be the reason why politicians avoid an honest interrogation of the housing market? After all, it was plausible to offer less disturbing explanations for house prices. Demographic trends were one such escape route into the collective denial of the national pastime – speculating in the capital gains from land. The age profile of the American population was changing rapidly. The Baby Boomers of post-World War II had bought their homes in the 1970s, and the number of young first-time buyers declined thereafter.[11] As an explanation for house prices – and the propensity to speculate in land, and the macroeconomic impact of those prices on people's daily lives – the demographic thesis was flawed. It did not take account of rising incomes. In the final decades of the 20th century, as incomes rose, people demanded larger homes in more desirable locations. This drove up the price of those locations – land. That, in turn, forced builders to economise by constructing houses on smaller plots in places like Portland, Oregon. It also led to the sprawl of Houston and the other Texas towns, as developers reached further into the hinterland for cheaper agricultural acres on which to build houses that people could afford. This was represented in the media as good news. 'Housing appreciation is still above inflation and that's very good,' pronounced Shelly Dreiman of the OFHEO.[12] Prices were running at more than twice the rate of inflation – well above the rate of increase in people's wages. This meant that homes were becoming less affordable. Alan Greenspan presided over these events, as people accumulated consumer debts that exceeded $1.5 trillion in 2004 – an all-time high. The US, like Britain, was dead on-course for the Depression of 2010.

§2 The Colour of Money

ALAN GREENSPAN acquired the status of a colossus. The financial
commentators lionised him for keeping the US on an even keel during
the financial crises in Asia and Russia in 1997 and 1998.

Greenspan was central to confidence in the global markets. While
he smiled and reassured, giving small touches to the tiller whenever a
modest act of intervention was perceived by investors to be necessary
to protect the value of their assets, the sun shone. But beneath the
veneer of calm, something was going wrong.

The most sensitive short-term tool for government engagement in
the economy is monetary policy. The Federal Reserve is charged with
maintaining the money supply at a level that ensures the containment
of 'inflation', which was deemed to be the leading indicator of the
health of the economy. But to vary the rate of interest, the Federal
Reserve must be able to track the money supply – M3, as it is called,
which is the broad definition.[13] Unfortunately, economics had degener-
ated to the level of a subjective art form for most of its practitioners.
One result, as two distinguished professors pronounced on the money
supply, is that 'the exact definition of 'the' money supply is as much a
matter of taste as of scientific necessity'. Economists have been able
to define more than a dozen different money supply concepts.[14]

As the US inflated its indebtedness to astronomical heights, the
fragility of the financial pyramid depended on the absolute trust that
people were willing to vest in Greenspan. So long as *he* knew what was
going on, *and* was happy; *and* he was alert to the need for marginal
trimmings to the financial sails, all would be well. But what if the
Chairman of the Fed lost his compass? That was an inconceivable
proposition! But the Chairman of the Board did not know what was
going on. He said so, publicly, under cross-examination in Congress.

On February 17, 2000, the House Banking Committee convened to
receive a report from Greenspan. Dr Ron Paul, a Republican from
Texas who is an exponent of 'sound money' policies, grilled the
Chairman. He pointed out that M3, over the previous three years, had
been far above target growth rates. He added that if he, a physician,
practiced medicine as inaccurately as that, his patients would die.

Greenspan replied by acknowledging that it had become *increasingly difficult to define what money was*. That was a startling confession.
For if the Chairman did not know what money was, how could the
Federal Reserve be guiding the US economy away from the dangers
that awaited unwary investors?

Congressman Paul pounced. He asked: 'So it's hard to manage something you can't define?'

Greenspan admitted: 'It is not possible to manage something you cannot define'.

The economist charged with managing the US money supply, who exercised fateful influence over the value of the dollars that were swishing around the world, admitted that he was not able to fulfil his obligations. The US economy was in uncharted waters, but the public was kept ignorant. None of the major wire services put out the news that the Chairman of the Federal Reserve was no longer managing the nation's money supply ... the credit pyramid had expanded to frightening proportions, but the only way to prevent panic was to maintain in blissful ignorance the people who saved and invested their earnings.

Congressman Paul, by profession an obstetrician who represents the 14th District of Texas, was sceptical about the economic information available from official sources. In an interview with Jay Taylor, the author of a financial newsletter, he spelt out the realities that confront people on the street:

> From a free market viewpoint, we have a lot of inflation if you look at the money supply, at the inflated prices for financial instruments, if you look at the cost of certain things like housing and medical care and education. As an interesting aside on this, one of my kids three or four years ago bought a house. Recently he chose to upgrade into a larger home. So in just three years, with this very modest house he made $30,000. So, I said, this is fantastic. But then the government continues to say there is no inflation. Of course they fudge the Consumer Price Index numbers and they don't even look at the cost of buying a house. They use another calculation that brings the increase in cost of housing down to something like 3% per year. But when I ask people in my district if they think there is no inflation, they think that's a joke. They simply don't believe what the Alan Greenspans of the world are telling us.[15]

The notable feature of the mounting housing crisis was the way in which government and its agencies failed to shout the truth from the rooftops. They prejudiced an informed public debate by obscuring as a 'paradox' the association of a crisis with prosperity. This word was repeatedly used by the US Department of Housing and Urban Development (HUD). In particular it noted that because the 'cost of housing' was increasing faster than the rate of inflation, 'economic good times are paradoxically creating a housing crisis for many Americans'.[16]

What HUD called the 'Megaforces Shaping the Future of the Nation's cities' had enabled 8.7 million households to become owners between 1992 and 1999. The national home ownership rate reached 66.8% by the end of the century – and then broke the record barrier in the first quarter of 2000 to reach an all-time high of 67.1%.

> Paradoxically, the economic growth that is increasing employment and home ownership in most of the Nation's cities is driving up rents and housing prices for many Americans.[7]

The dictionary defines a paradox as 'that which is apparently absurd but really true'. Why should the housing experts at HUD, armed with the best information and computer power in the nation, classify the housing crisis as flowing from something that was 'apparently absurd'? This characterisation fosters a sense of unreality about the relationship, one that discourages remedial action. Subliminally, people are invited to believe that this situation is not the logical outcome of a mechanism internal to the laws that drive the economy.

Language can be manipulated to place a full stop on further thought. The word 'paradox' was calculated to deter the penetrating questions that might cast light on the tragedy of house price trends that were eclipsing people's ability to afford shelter for their families; of progress with poverty. While the US government ended the century with surplus cash in its coffers – and able to pay down the national debt – millions of its citizens sank deeper into personal debt because of the cost of housing.

In 2003, outstanding residential mortgages totalled more than $6.6 trillion. The equity that people had in their homes, as a percentage of the value of household real estate, was at a record low. People were burdening themselves with so much debt that family finances would contribute towards the termination of growth around 2007-8.

The social consequences were embedded in what HUD called 'The Strong Economy Paradox'.

- The supply of affordable housing was not keeping pace with demand.
- Higher incomes and more people in work 'has the negative effect of pricing some families out of affordable housing'.[8]
- Many low-income earners had to work at two or three jobs just to pay the rent.
- Escalating prices deprived people of homes near the available jobs, so that teachers and firefighters could not live in the communities they served.

- The expansion of businesses was compromised by the inability to hire employees.
- Officials in 28% of the cities that were surveyed said a serious or very serious shortage of homes existed for upper-income households.[19]

'This housing paradox is especially affecting the hot high-tech markets around the country,' recorded HUD.[20]

In 1997, an all-time record was breached – 5.4m very low-income families paid more than half their income for housing or lived in severely inadequate housing. This represented a 12% growth in 'worst case needs' households since 1991, a pace of deterioration that was nearly twice as fast as the 7% growth of all households over the 1990s. As the number of low-income families increased, the number of affordable housing units decreased, a decline of 5% (more than 370,000 units) in the six years up to 1997. For every 100 extremely-low-income households, there were only 36 units both affordable and available for them to rent.[21]

For Wall Street financiers, the bubble would continue to inflate for as long as Alan Greenspan was able to keep the show on the road. *Their* streets were lined with gold. For people who had to work for wages to pay for the roofs over their heads, however, the trust that was needed to stabilise the economy was absent. For them, the statistics were a magical mystery brew that delivered a soothing message, but they meant very little in the real world. How could people develop independent ways of making sense of what was happening in the world if the experts were messing with their minds?

§3 Oil on Troubled Waters

IF MONEY *is* the root of all evil, we would expect central bankers to provide us with all the information we need to combat the demons that use the lust for loot to attack our lives. Could it be that money animates wars? The question is relevant, here, because some people believe that wars cause recessions. They wonder whether those wars are sometimes induced by the pursuit of rents from petroleum. That connection was promoted by opponents of the Bush administration's decision to attack Saddam Hussein's Iraq in 2003.

There is a second, and possibly associated, reason why a scientific understanding of money would be helpful in the global age. The US trade deficit, which escalated to $2,700bn, might be the cause of political panic in Washington. Could that amount of dollars slushing around the global economy render the US vulnerable to foreign manipulation? That was one fear in relation to Saddam Hussein, who controlled a large slice of the world's oil reserves. The geopolitics of this situation go back to the decision by the OPEC countries to denominate oil deals in dollars. Iraq decided to ditch dollars in favour of the euro. Might that have aroused anxiety among the Texas advisers to President Bush?[22]

These are questions which, if they are to be forensically evaluated, need to be supported by a theory of land and rent, as well as an understanding of money. For, historically, wars have been related to rent-generating natural resources. And oil-rents do affect the industrial economy. But this does not mean that they *necessarily* result in mass unemployment, or that they inspire democratic governments to launch armies against countries that have not threatened them with weapons of mass destruction. Here, then, are issues that ought to exercise the central bankers who advise governments.

The evidence is ambiguous.

- A *drop* in oil-rents may occur at the same time as a violent territorial conflict. That is what happened during the anti-Taliban war in Afghanistan at the end of 2001, when oil-rents dropped but US unemployment escalated from 4% to 6%.
- The OPEC cartel flexed its monopoly power and drove up the price of petroleum in 1974. But that was the year in which, according to our theory, a recession would strike the USA anyway. The recession and rise in US unemployment cannot be attributed to the Yom Kippur war in the Middle East.
- The Iran-Iraq conflict doubled the real price of oil in 1979, but this was too early for the mid-cycle recession that our theory predicted for 1983. As it happens, the US downturn occurred 12 months earlier, when oil prices were on a downward trend.
- The first Gulf war, in which Allied forces ejected Iraq from Kuwait, saw a spike in oil prices in 1990. The US went into recession – but this was within 12 months of the end-of-cycle recession that our theory predicted for 1991/2.

Al-Qaeda's attack on the Twin Towers in September 2001 occurred well after the onset of the mid-cycle downturn which our theory predicted for 2001. The subsequent onslaught on the Taliban regime in Afghanistan had no implications for oil prices or unemployment in the US, and the onslaught on Baghdad in the Spring of 2003 was a distraction from the dynamics of the mid-cycle recession. But because of the absence of agreement over the roots of capitalist instability, economic analysts were disposed to clutch on to President Bush's adventure in Iraq in March 1993 as an explanation for global travails. The global economy hit the bottom in 2001, nine years after the end of the previous 18-year cycle – an outcome that could have been predicted with a high degree of confidence in 1992!

One would have expected that economists who advise government would have resolved the question of whether the 'shocks' of sudden and high increases in petrol prices have the power to disturb the productive economy. There has been a curious silence on this matter. It was an issue that Alan Greenspan preferred to avoid, but he was trapped into addressing the issue during a question and answer session via satellite between London and Washington. He was asked whether there was a causal link between oil prices and economic growth. Sitting in the London conference hall was Ashley Seager, a business reporter from *The Guardian*. He noted Greenspan's reluctant answer.

> I was going to duck that question. It's a very difficult one. The impact of oil prices on an economy is difficult to infer and there's no automatic policy response. We found that despite the fact that most of the recessions of the last 40 years have been preceded by an oil price spike, the problem is that we create these elaborate models for policy responses and we put in oil prices [but] they don't create a recession in the models. This means either the connection is false or that there is a non-linearity in the response of economies to oil prices.[23]

There was a chasm of incomprehension between theory and reality. Why? Sceptics have a saying about models: if you put garbage in, you get garbage out. But in this case, was the problem less one of scientific reasoning and more a desire to avoid the implications for public policies?

§4 Guardians of Our Minds

A KIND OF insanity is embedded in our civilisation. We continuously disrupt the lives of people who are guilty of no crime, by condoning the cyclical booms and busts that constrain capitalism from achieving its full potential prosperity. We foster profligacy in the use of natural resources, which underlies the tensions between nations. To preserve these anomalies, it is necessary for the guardians of our minds to contain our thoughts. We must not be allowed to recognise the truth even when we are walking all over it.

Is this an unfair characterisation of the way in which knowledge is ritually processed by politicians and their advisers? Does perverse socialisation coerce us into accepting irrational behaviour that we would otherwise reject? Consider the case of Her Majesty Queen Elizabeth and the Chairman of the US Federal Reserve.

By 2002, Alan Greenspan had chaired the central bank for 15 years. He took up his post months before the stock market crash in 1987. The US and world economy crashed into a deep recession in 1992. From then on, it was helter-skelter in the world markets. Russia, over which the US government exercised considerable influence, saw its economy crash in 1997. Contagion swept Asia a year later, felling some mighty tigers. Brazil and Argentina continued Latin America's remorseless commitment to crises. And to cap it all, in 2000 the US economy stalled before its slide into three quarters of declining output that spilled into 2001. This was more than enough to qualify as an official recession. And what did Her Majesty do in 2002? Prevailed upon by the mandarins of conventional economic wisdom, she announced that Alan Greenspan would be honoured with a knighthood. His qualifying achievement? His 'contribution to global economic stability'.

One man appreciated the irony behind this testimony: Alan Greenspan! In a speech in Jackson Hole, Wyoming, which he delivered a few days earlier in August 2002, Greenspan put the nail into the myth of his reliability as the guardian of stability. He said 'it was very difficult to definitively identify a bubble until after the fact'. How do you stabilise the economy if you cannot even spot a looming bubble?

Greenspan's confession was incongruous. In December 1996, he warned of 'irrational exuberance' on the economic horizon. He failed to take preventative action. Why? Not through vacillation, he assured the world. Rather, 'it was far from obvious that bubbles, even if identified early, could be pre-empted'. Corrective action, apparently, was a contradiction in terms: it might induce an even bigger recession.

When the facts no longer make common sense, it becomes necessary to retreat to metaphysics. This was how Greenspan convinced people into believing that he knew what he was doing. The mental gymnastics are difficult to unravel. Thus, when he changed his mind, he claimed that 'it was very difficult to definitively identify a bubble until after the fact – that is, when its bursting confirms its existence'. In the world of unreality, what you see is not necessarily what you get.

The Greenspan model of the economy was fatally flawed because it excluded the one variable that featured in every boom bust over the past 200 years in the United States: the land market. In every significant economic collapse, the central operating mechanism was the land market. People experienced the helter-skelter prices through the value of their homes. But according to Greenspan, in congressional testimony to a House of Representatives Committee: 'The type of underlying conditions that create bubbles are very difficult to initiate in the housing market'.[24] In fact, far from fearing the inflation of residential assets, he was confident that robust gains in this sector would offset the weakening effect of a declining stock market on the nation's consumption habits. In that testimony on Capitol Hill, the one man on whom a nation relied for economic wisdom betrayed a cavalier attitude that would guarantee the destruction of people's hard-earned wealth.

Greenspan may have been worthy of a knighthood, but not for his capacity to stabilise the economy. He allowed himself to fixate on monetary policy as the antidote for unstable trends, and the stock market as the primary site of that instability. But out of 24 boom episodes in *equity* prices in the OECD countries since 1970, only three were followed by busts: Finland in 1988, Japan in 1989 and Spain in 1998. In 19 booms in property prices, 10 were followed by busts. The study which yielded these results understated the facts in relation to real estate. The Finnish and Japanese equity bubbles were intimately associated with ferocious episodes of land speculation. In Japan, that process was shrouded by trading in the stocks of companies that were land-rich. Even so, the relative importance of the property sector compared with stock markets is abundantly clear.[25] It ought to have featured in Greenspan's calculations. Instead, he denied that the housing market could contribute to the bubble that disrupted the US economy in 2001. Like NASA, which could not believe the high readings that revealed the ozone layer crisis, Greenspan could not comprehend the significance of extraordinary rates of increases in the prices of residential real estate – and especially the price of land.

What, then, was the purpose of the ritual presentation of the knight's badge of honour to Alan Greenspan? Of one thing we can be sure: the ceremony would distract the pensioners whose savings were wiped out by the billion dollars on the stock exchanges during the summer of 2002.

We cannot hold Greenspan exclusively responsible for the booms and busts during his stewardship of the US central bank. Nonetheless, his privileged role is one that influences policy throughout the world. His contribution to the mid-cycle recession at the turn into the 21st century was particularly damaging. The problem was not just with his failure to advocate remedial action against the dot.com conflagration. He legitimised the *debacle* by lending credence to the notion that the

US had entered the Age of the New Economy, when, in fact, it remained hostage to the fortunes of the Old Alchemy – speculation in the rents that can be extracted from land and nature's resources.

We need to hold civil servants like Greenspan accountable for failing to diagnose the propensity for instability that is built into the capitalist economy. This instability was alluded to by Greenspan as 'creative destruction'. His use of colourful language disguises ignorance and powerlessness by suggesting that we should be grateful for the turmoil on the bourses. Should we not be thankful for an economics of chaos that resurrects creativity out of the acts that destroy people's hard-earned wealth? That is the logic behind the Greenspan camouflage. That turmoil spells financial disaster for millions of small-time savers who cannot afford the luxury of creative destruction.

The periodical destruction of wealth is *not* driven by a law of nature. It is based on man-made laws. They can be rewritten. But before we examine them, we need to demythologise the powers of individuals whom we lionise. Greenspan is one of those individuals, an archetypal figure who is feted by presidents. He had access to the information and theories that could have led him to issue public warnings that might have encouraged governments to adopt enlightened policies. Instead, in 2000, as the bubble was about to burst, Greenspan reassured people that 'I see nothing to suggest these opportunities [of high rate of return productivity enhancing investments] will peter out any time soon'. Within two years, US stock market indices would collapse by more than 25%. If we have to exonerate Greenspan from *causing* the booms, he can be indicted in the court of public opinion for doing nothing that would mitigate the busts. Was he worthy of a KBE, a Knight Commander of the Order of the British Empire?

In the asylum, we can understand why the inmates need mind games. They fill their haunted lives with fantasies that appear to give substance to the dreamlike quality of their everyday existence. Thus it was that one group of corporate directors persuaded themselves that they ought to honour Alan Greenspan for his stewardship of the dot.com era. In November 2001 he was awarded the Enron Prize for Distinguished Public Service – six weeks before Enron declared itself bankrupt, leaving thousands of employees without their pensions. Investors who thought their money was safe in the shares of that energy trading company were impoverished.

Likewise with the pronouncements of governments. Their actions appear purposeful, but they tend to maroon us ever deeper in The Land of Virtual Reality. A contribution to the theatre of mysticism was played out on September 26, 2002, when the Chairman of the

Federal Reserve presented himself at a private audience in Balmoral, the Queen's Scottish retreat. There, he was honoured with the trappings of his chivalric status. As Her Gracious Majesty's wine flowed at the lunch given for America's central banker, the other financial technocrats who claimed to know what they were doing presided over the continuing collapse in what was the worst stock market bubble in 100 years.

One analyst noted on the jacket of his book *The Boom and the Bubble: the US in the World Economy*: 'The pundits are no nearer an understanding of what drove the boom, why the boom turned into a bubble, or why the bubble burst'.[26] Because of the holes in knowledge, economists are free to play fast and loose with information about the housing market. Thus, the central bank of central bankers, the Basle-based Bank for International Settlements, claims that 'Unexpected stock market gains are the most important surprises explaining unanticipated house price growth'.[27] For those who know where to look for the clues, booms in house prices are *not* unexpected, and the driving motivation behind those prices is capital gains from land – not from stocks and shares.

Our investigation will seek to fill the void in our knowledge of what drives market euphoria, and why the housing sector inflates into a bubble that always bursts. We need answers to questions such as these:

- How do boom busts emerge in free markets where people are supposed to be rational investors and consumers? Few people gain from the stop-go cycle.
- Why can we predict – many years in advance, and with remarkable precision – turning points in the economy? Economists deny the validity of such foresight.
- What can be done about economic instability? Humiliated finance ministers retreat to the claim that the business cycle is rooted in natural law – there is no remedy for it.

To address these questions we need to return to the beginnings of the Industrial Revolution. To understand the logic that drives the housing markets, we need to reconstruct an episode in a public house in Birmingham, England. It was here that a group of drinkers quaffed their ale and ruminated over how they could afford to buy back land that had been taken from their ancestors by the feudal aristocracy...

70 *Boom Bust*

REFERENCES

1 Lina Saigol, 'Investment banks to write off record losses', *Financial Times*, October 7, 2002.
2 Liz Peace, Chief Executive, British Property Federation: personal communication.
3 Office of Federal Housing Enterprise Oversight (OFHEO), *House Price Index History for USA 1990Q1 to 2003Q4, op. cit.*, p.6.
4 Alan Greenspan, 'Home Mortgage Market', Remarks to the annual convention of the Independent Community Bankers of America, Orlando, Florida, March 4, 2003 (via satellite); transcript, Washington DC: Federal Reserve Board, p.4.
5 Shelly Dreiman, 'Using the Price to Income Ratio to Determine the Presence of Housing Price Bubbles', Washington, DC: OFHEO, *House Price Index Fourth Quarter 2000*, March 1, 2001, p.8.
6 OFHEO, *Systemic Risk: Fannie Mae, Freddie Mac and the Role of OFHEO*, Washington, DC, 2003, p.19.
7 *Ibid.*, p.20.
8 *Ibid.*, p.21.
9 *Ibid.*, p.22.
10 Forrest Pafenberg, *The Single-Family Mortgage Industry in the Internet Era: Technology Developments and Market Structure*, Washington, DC: OFHEO, January 2004, p.28.
11 N. Gregory Mankiw and David Weil, 'The Baby Boom, the Baby Bust, and the Housing Market', *Regional Science and Urban Economics*, 1989.
12 Michele Derus, '7-year Housing Upswing Going Strong in Year 9', *Milwaukee Journal Sentinel*, September 7, 2003.
13 M3 was defined in the *Federal Reserve Bulletin* (April 1991, pp.A13, A14) as including coins and paper bills, savings in deposit accounts and travellers' cheques, overnight repurchase agreements and overnight Eurodollars, general-purpose and broker-dealer money market mutual fund balances, large-denomination time deposits (with balances of £100,000 or more), term repurchase agreements and term Eurodollars, and institution-only mutual funds balances.
14 Paul A. Samuelson & William D. Nordhaus, *Economics* 12th ed., New York: McGraw-Hill, 1985, p.271.
15 Jay Taylor, 'In Defense of our "Unalienable Rights"', *Gold & Technology Stocks*, Woodside, NY, May 11, 2000, p.6.
16 HUD, *The State of the Cities 2000*, Washington, DC: US Department of Housing and Urban Development, 2000, p.iii.
17 *Ibid.*, p.viii.
18 *Ibid.*, p.51.
19 *Ibid.*
20 *Ibid.*, p.52.
21 *Ibid.*, p.57.
22 John Chapman, 'The real reasons Bush went to war', *The Guardian*, July 28, 2004.
23 Comment by Alan Greenspan, via satellite, to International Monetary Conference, London, June 8, 2004. The transcript was provided to the author by Ashley Seager, who summarised Greenspan's comments in *The Guardian* Notebook ('Greenspan at a loss'), June 9, 2004.
24 Alan Beattie, 'Top advisor shares Greenspan optimism on economy', *Financial Times*, July 18, 2002.
25 Michael D. Bordo and Olivier Jeanne, *Boom-Busts in Asset Prices, Economic Instability and Monetary Policy*, NBER Working Paper, May, 2002.
26 Robert Brenner, *The Boom and the Bubble*, London, Verso, 2001.
27 Scheherazade Daneshkhu, 'Stock market "may hit UK homes boom"', *Financial Times*, September 9, 2002.

PART II

Genesis of the Boom-Bust Cycle

5

Rent and the 18-Year Cycle

§1 The Repetitive Syndrome

CONSTRUCTION is a leading sector of the economy. Its performance in Britain has been traced back to 1700 by J. Parry Lewis, who documented that history in *Building Cycles and Britain's Growth*. From his reading of the evidence, he was led to ask 'whether qualitative evidence confirms the suggestion that building moved in long swings with troughs approximately 18 years apart throughout the 18th century, and on into the beginning of the 19th, where statistics of brick production enable us to be more confident about the course of activity'. He concluded: '[W]e may assert quite briefly that qualitative evidence does, on the whole, support the inference drawn from the statistics'.[1]

Instability was the characteristic feature of the construction trade. Booms and busts occurred with alarming regularity, but there was something uncanny about that instability. The repetitiveness became predictable. What drove those cycles? If we knew, we could formulate policies to thwart the proclivity to collapse into bankruptcy every 18 years. Lewis suggested that this periodicity was 'more probably associated with the impact of war'.[2]

Wars appeal to historians as explanations for recessions.[3] One of them argues that wars grow out of the economy: 'Growth creates the economic surplus required to sustain major wars among core powers. But these large-scale wars drain surplus and disrupt long-term economic growth'.[4] That wars damage the economy is incontrovertible, but that does not mean that they constitute the mechanism that drives repetitive cycles.

H.A. Shannon, in his famous index of 18th century brick production, inferred a causal connection between wars and construction. He cited contemporary evidence of life in London in the 18th century, quoting one author as stating: 'Each war is said to have checked building operations in London; builders' labourers joined the army or navy and materials became dearer, while peace brought a renewed outburst of building activity'.[5]

But does the propensity to declare war recur with the precision that is necessary to make sense of the economic patterns? Table 5:1 provides the dates for the peaks and troughs in the 18th century. This is based on data for timber imports. Brick production, Lewis found, confirmed the trends drawn from the timber trade.

If there is substance to the conjecture that wars animated the cycles in construction, we need a theory that *explains* why the British government engaged in military conflicts with such predictable regularity as to bequeath a regular pattern to the house building industry. That theory would also have to account for the provocative actions of other governments, over which the British had no control – but which conveniently conspired to deliver 18-year cycles in economic activity. Without a theoretical explanation, advocates of the case for war are left to defend the astonishing proposition that random events accidentally occur with almost clockwork precision over the course of a full 100 years – and, as we shall see, for a further 200 years, all the way to 2001!

TABLE 5:1

The Economic Cycle: Britain in the 18th century

Peak	Trough	Duration between peaks	Duration between troughs
1705?	1711?		
1724	1727?	19	16
1736	1744	12	17
1753	1762	17	18
1776	1781	23	19
1792	1798	16	17

Sources: J. Parry Lewis, *Building Cycles and Britain's Growth*, London: Macmillan, 1965, p.14.

The average duration from trough to trough, and from peak to peak, was 17.4 years. There were six booms in construction in the 18th century, with the final peak in 1792. All of them, with the exception of the weakest of these expansions, which peaked in 1736, are held by the advocates of the war thesis to be the result of the depressing effect of the wars and the way that these affect the availability of funds during periods of peace. Is it plausible to claim that there was an internal logic to the war-making process that resulted in the staggering of economic activity in such a regular pattern?

The 18th century was militarily turbulent. Kings jousted for territorial dominance. They had to borrow to pay for mercenary armies, which raised the cost of borrowing money. This would have had a negative impact on industries that relied on credit. Beginning with troughs of the cycle described by Lewis, we find the following.

- The 1711 trough was preceded by English victories at Almenara and Saragosa in 1710. The war with Spain seemed to be going well at this point.
- In February 1727 England engaged in war with Spain. England had captured Gibraltar in 1704, and the Spaniards laid siege in a bid to recover the rock.
- In 1744, France declared war on England.
- On January 4, 1762, England declared war on Spain and Naples.
- 1780: near year's end, England declared war on Holland, and in February 1782 England lost Minorca.
- Revenge for England. Spain having declared war on Britain in 1798, the British recapture Minorca in that year.

To rely on these military adventures to account for the periodicity of economic activity, we have to develop some improbable hypotheses. One might be a conspiracy between the kings who ruled England, Spain, France and Naples to time the pursuit of their territorial ambitions on the basis of aspirations that fitted into a neat timetable averaging almost 18 years. Might the whims of land-hungry kings deliver this pattern, one which (with hindsight) could be predicted with great accuracy? But whims are likely to be random in their character: we cannot plausibly rely on them to provide a scientific explanation for such a remarkable sequence in history.

There might have been something peculiar about the British monarchy's penchant for wars that clocked on and off in time to create 18-year economic rhythms, but how would Lewis and the other historians explain a similar periodicity in economic activity in the United States in the 19th century? The US was not prone to military conflicts of a kind that would account for people's investment decisions in the American real estate market.[6]

It would be more satisfactory if we could identify an operational logic that periodically punctuated the economy with a full stop. Can we suggest a mechanism to compete with the war thesis?

The evidence from within the building industry itself may provide the clues. We need to identify seemingly discordant trends which sow the seeds of destruction. To begin our interrogation of the evidence,

we suggest that the finite supply of land constitutes an explanation
that we could test. The way that people are affected by the land
market, of course, is contingent on the legal and institutional framework within which that market operates. These, therefore, also have
to be scrutinised to determine whether they support the notion that
land somehow segments the modern economy.

Timber imports in the 18th century appear to be linked to the
mediating effects of the land market. That is a conjecture which
analysts who lived in that century would have regarded as reasonable.
One of them, writing in 1805, traced the links:

> Since the beginning of the 18th century, the reintroduction of
> furnaces and forges for making and working iron, has enhanced
> the value of wood considerably, and the tenants have found the
> means of improving part of their lands into meadows, and
> preserving their woods for the use of the furnaces; *which has
> raised the value of the land*, within these 50 years, to many times
> the value it was of before [emphasis added].[7]

Something unique happened as the economy accumulated capital
and developed new technologies. As the supply of marketable goods
increased (reducing their price by satisfying demand), in the land
market the impact on prices was in the reverse direction – upwards.

Lewis, in championing the war thesis, would not be impressed by
the claim that the problem lay with the dynamics of the land market.
We could address his scepticism by offering two observations.

First, the performance of the building industry in the 18th century
was similar to what unfolded in the 19th and 20th centuries. That fact
was recorded by historian J.H. Clapham. In reviewing the terms on
which 'the numerous small speculative builders, whom some call jerry-
builders' operated, he concluded:

> Their methods have remained the same until our own time –
> the land rented in hope, materials secured on credit, a mortgage
> raised on the half-built house before it is sold or leased, and not
> infrequent bankruptcy.[8]

Thus, whatever the causes in the 18th century, it appears that they
continued to make their presence felt in the 19th century and into the
20th century – all the way through to the beginning of the 21st century.
Wars did not cause the large-scale bankruptcy of building firms in
Britain in the early 1970s and early 1990s. We need to look deeper.

Secondly, we might ask: how would Lewis rebut our thesis about
the land market? Unfortunately, he admitted that he was not qualified

to offer an informed view about the way land affects the urban economy. At the end of his methodical review of all the available evidence on the housing industry going back to 1700, he reported, on the penultimate page of his study, in a footnote:

> *Since writing this book*, the importance of a thorough study of urban land economics has become apparent to me. It is a subject which is peculiarly neglected in England.[9]

Given the importance of land as an input to the building industry, one would have thought it important to assess the economics of urban location before writing a book called *Building Cycles and Britain's Growth*. At any rate, we are obliged to consider the legal, fiscal and institutional features which, taken together, constitute the land market, if we are to claim with credibility that land is the basis of business cycles. This means we have to explore the origins of commercial property rights in land and the social framework within which these were marketed.

§2 Origins of the Land Market

A MARKET in land could not exist at the beginning of the 16th century, because there was no supply of land to trade. Land was held by the feudal classes for the power and social status that it accorded as well as for the rents from tenants. This changed with Henry VIII's dissolution of the monasteries in the 1530s. Vast amounts of land were claimed by the Crown, which then chose to sell it. Historians have chronicled the sales from 1540 onwards. 'Here at last was the supply which the market had been waiting for,' wrote Joyce Youings, who studied the dissolution for her doctoral thesis. The properties of 800 religious communities were put into circulation. The Crown dictated the terms of the sales. There were over 300 purchases in 1589-90 alone.[10]

> Men expected to pay a fair but not excessive price and most were content with an immediate return of 5% on their capital outlay. Few were likely to improve on that in their own lifetimes.[11]

It took time for the real estate market to mature. The full trading conditions were in place by 1600, with scriveners acting as conveyancers, cartographers as land surveyors and solicitors doubling up as real estate agents and mortgage advisors.

Out of a sample of over 3,000 transactions involving yeomen as purchasers between 1570 and 1640, in well over half the purchase price was under £100, implying an annual value of under £5.[12]

During the last half of the 16th century, the commissions that were instructed to sell the land on behalf of the Crown were told to require 20 years' purchase of the net current annual value, which is the gross rent less any fixed outgoings such as bailiffs' fees.[13] That translates into a rate of interest of 5%. This was 'the normal formula'.[14] Youings, from her reading of the parchments that track the break-up of the monastic estates, stresses that 'most purchasers were prepared to pay a fair price: they could neither afford inflated prices nor did they really hope for bargains unless they were leading politicians or civil servants'.[15]

What was the logic behind this formula? This was the question that a professor of epidemiology, Dr George Miller, asked himself. He wanted to know why a multiplier of 15 to 20 years for rent recurred time and again through the ages.[16] Why was 5% the favoured rate of interest? He concluded that the answer lay with the average length of the adult working life. During the Middle Ages and through to about 1870, life expectancy in England averaged 35 to 40 years.[17] A young adult who acquired land could not expect to enjoy it for more than 15 to 20 years. Paying a price that exceeded the rental income did not make commercial sense. The Crown prescribed terms that were consistent with people's life expectancy. The 20 years/5% formula made biological and economic sense.

The cost of borrowing money was higher than 5%, because the money markets were not yet efficient. Efforts were made to curb the rate of interest through the Usury Laws, which reduced the permissible rate from 8% in the 17th century to 6% in the 18th century. A 6% capitalisation rate implies a purchase price for land at 16.6 years' worth of rents, which was close to the average adult lifespan of 17.5 years. The legal interest rate appeared to converge with the duration of the working life of a tiller. That interest rate also related to the surplus income of the land that a farmer could afford to yield as rent and still make a living.

Does this financial history fit with the onset of the business cycle and its average duration of 18 years? Our analysis starts with a consideration of the evidence for assuming that volume trading in land on a commercial basis originated in or around 1600.

Youings is cautious.

> A great deal of the monastic land was resold by the original grantees, some of it changing hands many times, but the market

was not so brisk, nor the speculation so rife, as many writers have suggested.[18]

Nonetheless, Youings describes activity in the decade up to the turn of the century in which a large amount of Crown land was sold at enormously increased prices. What she called 'the land flow' included parcels that were turned over several times. Here was a bunching of sales in which prices were driven up to 40 years' worth of rents. 'Even so the sale price probably never quite caught up with the real value of land in terms of economic rent,' reports Youings.[19] This was the first land boom in which, on a socially significant scale, people made money not by producing wealth but by transferring title deeds. Prices peaked above affordable levels and finally had to be reduced to attract buyers. The Crown was forced to offer purchase by instalments to maintain sales. The land revenue of Elizabeth 1st between the years 1598 and 1603 totalled (after deductions) £150,827.[20]

Was this the beginning of a pattern? Was the 17th century divided by sharply defined periods of heightened activity in the land market?

Working on the basis of an average adult life of about 17 or 18 years during the century, as owners died their land would have been relinquished to the next generation. Some of that land was retained within the family, with farms passing from father to son for two generations before it was put back on the market.

TABLE 5:2

Hypothetical Dates for Intensified Sales of Land

1600
1617.5
1635
1652.5
1670
1687.5
1705

The theoretical framework for our analysis is provided in Table 5:2. Revealingly, by working our way through the century in multiples of 17.5 years, the century's sequence ends in 1705. Lewis put a question mark against 1705 (Table 5:1) as the peak of an economic cycle, with 1711 (also with a question mark) as the trough. He records that there had been a house building boom during the previous 10 years, but there had been a 'set-back'.[21] Can we remove the doubt? Was 1705 the link year between the agricultural economy of the 17th century and the heightened tempo of capital formation in the 18th century which laid the foundations for the Industrial Revolution? Christopher Clay reports that, between 1704 and 1713, freehold land sold for 17-19 years' purchase – an average of 18 years (Table 5:3). Was this coincidence?

TABLE 5:3

Movement of Land Prices

Period	Normal spread of prices	Remarks
1646-50	14-16 years' purchase	Abnormally low
1650-64	18-20 years' purchase	Recovering
1665-89	16-18 years' purchase	Falling
1690-1703	20-22 years' purchase	Rising
1704-13	17-19 years' purchase	Falling

Source: C. Clay, 'The Price of Freehold Land in the Later Seventeenth and Eighteenth Centuries', EcHR, 2nd ser, XXVII, 1974; cited in Christopher Clay, 'Landlords and Estate Management in England', in Joan Thirsk (ed.), *The Agrarian History of England and Wales*, Vol. V: 1640-1750, Cambridge: Cambridge University Press, Table 14:1, p.173.

Over the final 50 years of the 17th century, what Clay classified as the 'normal spread of prices' between 1650 and 1703 averaged 18 years, the expected working life of the people of England. It is beginning to appear that the terms of these transactions in the land market laid the foundations for the 18-year economic cycle. The average life of the business cycle in the 18th century (Table 5:1) was 17.4 years, which is as close to the adult life expectancy as one could expect. But how would this timetable generate instability of the kind that we associate with cycles? By itself, it would not do so. There is no logical reason why one 18-year period should not be succeeded smoothly by another 18-year period, in line with the growth of the population. For ruptures within this process we need to identify rules or institutions that impede sustainable growth.

Monarchs and the aristocracy evolved the rules and routines that incubated the speculation in land which featured in the emerging enterprise economy. Scholars tend to underestimate the role of speculation at the inception of the new market.[22] The way that land dealers operated is well understood. Landowners

> managed, by judiciously-timed sales, to raise the money necessary to buy carefully chosen portions of the monastic lands.

They did, on occasion, borrow money and even speculate in land which had not yet been paid for.[23]

Historians need to scrutinise the conditions that made the timing judicious for land speculation,[24] to evaluate the activity that unfolded into a systematic pattern. What made it worth some people's while to borrow on the open market at what were deemed to be usurious rates of interest (6% or 8% or more) to buy an asset that would yield 5%? Could it be that they were not interested in the stream of income? That they were pursuing a capital gain?

The evidence that is accumulating identifies a confluence of influences in the 17th century that shaped the economic life of the 18th century; influences that are more plausibly related to the modern business cycle than the proposition that warfare was responsible for repetitive booms and busts. People exploited Crown land, the rents for which were below their market value. Dealers realised that they could achieve capital gains by trading land. This enabled them to accumulate cash from speculation rather than from the labours of entrepreneurship. The nobility facilitated the commercial market. The number of manors they owned dropped from about 3,400 in 1558 to about 2,200 in 1600.

Land did continue to provide elevated social status and access to political power, qualities that were defused through the increasing number of transactions. The emerging market was founded on insider dealing – well-placed courtiers made the largest short-term profits 'especially by buying, and later selling, under-valued Crown land'.[25] Youings, in noting that speculation was a minority activity, believed that the impact could safely be ignored. As lawyers, merchants or government officials, speculators were 'mere birds of passage, who, without having more than a marginal effect on the price of land, served a useful purpose, especially in the dispersal of the smaller units'.[26] Should we accept her view that it was safe to ignore 'those who bought land only to re-sell within a very short time'? These people initiated a new social process. *Previously people captured the benefits of land by conquest or theft. Now, that outcome was legally enshrined in the land market,* in which payments were a pure transfer of income that involved no reciprocal obligation to add to the wealth of the nation.

The 16th century monarchs were derelict in their duty as stewards of the common wealth. In alienating Crown lands, kings and queens diminished the long-term flow of rents into the coffers of the exchequer. Their actions contributed to the transformation of the social status of rent. Hitherto, rent was the social revenue that paid for what we would today call public 'expenditure. By selling land in the new market, monarchs aided and abetted the courtiers in turning rents into private revenue. In doing so, they institutionalised the process of redistributing income from those who earned it to those who wished to live without working. There was to be nothing to match that redistribution until the second half of the 20th century, when the working population hit back with its variant of 'welfare' economics. Monarchs and aristocrats privatised the social income (rent), while the socialists socialised the private income (wages).

We will attempt to quantify the impact of this pathological inversion of incomes in Part IV. First, however, we must elucidate the way in which the economics of an agrarian society metamorphosed into the dynamics of the industrial economy. Our starting point is the Industrial Revolution, when urban centres came under pressure from migrating workers who had been displaced from the farms by enclosures. They needed jobs, and they needed homes. Those homes had to be affordable, and they had to be financed. Could a mechanism be invented that would raise the output of houses to meet the increase in demand? It could. Would that mechanism synchronise with the propensity to speculate in land? It would. It was called the terminating society.

§3 Terminating Societies

OUR QUEST for the origins of the modern economy's booms and busts leads us to a pub in Birmingham.

What happened under the watchful eye of the publican, Richard Ketley, as he poured the jars of ale one evening in 1775, needs to be considered in the context of two challenges facing Britain. One was the onset of the Industrial Revolution. This historic development was chronicled by Adam Smith (*The Wealth of Nations* was published in 1776). As a displaced population converged on towns like Birmingham, the demand for dwellings grew in leaps and bounds. The second consideration was that property prices at that time were racing towards a peak (Table 5:1 suggests the peak was in 1776). People without capital found great difficulty in acquiring property. But if a way could be found for them to band together to pool their savings and buy their way into the property market, the housing problem might be solved. The terminating society was the solution, and the credit for inventing it goes to the ale-drinkers in Richard Ketley's pub.

Birmingham was a modest market town located on the side of a hill

by the River Rea. It had an undistinguished history, although a settle-
ment occupied this location going back to the time of the Norman
conquest. It began to expand from about 1700, so that by 1821 the
number of houses had increased from 2,504 to a little more than
17,300. The town was clustered around streets that formed two
crosses. The ingenuity of the townsfolk emerged in the reign of
Charles II. The toy trade began to flourish, an early indication of the
creativity of the people of this part of the Midlands. By the 1830s the
town was aflame with the enterprises that were clustered around
forges and furnaces, and 'The vicinity abounds with many pleasant
villas and retreats of its opulent manufacturers'.[27]

Here was the epicentre of a red-hot revolution. Ores were liquefied
and turned into wondrous objects that could be sold throughout the
world. But the Industrial Revolution needed a financial revolution. It
started with the group of men who clubbed together to pool their
savings to buy a piece of land. This agreement was the model for the
first financial institution dedicated to the mass construction of family
dwellings. But the patrons of the Golden Cross in Snow Hill,
Birmingham, also contributed something new to the business cycle.
Without knowing it, the artisans and professionals who built and paid
for the houses – some to live in, others as investments to rent out –
created the institutional framework for the modern boom bust. They
agreed that the landlord, Richard Ketley, would serve as their banker.
They celebrated the 5% interest deal by quaffing ale. They could not
have known it, but their financial ingenuity would send shock waves
throughout the emerging world of conveyor belt production. Over the
following 25 years, more than 20 societies were founded in the
Birmingham area alone. They made possible an explosive growth in
construction. In doing so, they intensified the demand for scarce land
within commuting distances of the factories.

In the agricultural age up to the 17th century, construction in rural
areas was based on a timetable of one to two years to build each
dwelling. Finance came from the average profits from farming over
the course of five years.[28] At the beginning of the 18th century, however, the structures that passed for dwellings could not serve the needs
of people living in towns. The technological possibilities were transformed by the economics of mass production. The West Midlands,
from Ironbridge in Shropshire to the Black Country around
Birmingham, set the rhythm for capital formation and entrepreneur-
ial activity. This region was the cradle of industrialised output,
symbolised by the iron bridge that spanned the gorge cut by the River
Severn in the hills near Wellington, in Shropshire.

For the financial innovators who met at the Golden Cross, the
terminating society was the way to redeem the injustices of the past.
Their ancestors had been dispossessed of land by the enclosures,
but they could buy back some of that land with the support of the
shareholders' meeting.

The members of the first terminating society could not have anticipated that the efficiency with which they raised the money to buy land
would also nourish the virus that periodically brought the economy to
its knees. Even today, scholars have difficulty in identifying the causes
of the 19th century building cycles.[29] The most distinguished investi-
gator, Simon Kuznets, who exhaustively documented the data for the
upswings and downswings, admitted that there was a problem in
explaining them.[30]

The sequence of events was not a mystery. Lewis provides one of
the clearest *descriptions* of booms and busts in the housing market.

> As the building boom develops so it assumes a character and
> impetus of its own. As each house is built and occupied, so the
> attractions of solid investment become apparent; and the prof-
> its to be made out of building operations, out of speculative
> building and selling, and *out of appreciation of land values* attract
> still further. Craftsmen set up as master-builders, and in the
> larger towns a vast number of people in one way or another
> become responsible for launching a flood of projects, large and
> small ... The first in the field succeed, and their profits encour-
> age others to follow suit, until, with a startling suddenness, it is
> overdone. Houses remain empty for longer, rents stop rising,
> and may even begin slowly to fall, and further building ceases to
> be an attractive proposition. Many of the houses will have been
> built with borrowed money, and the inability of the builder to
> rent or to sell them leads to his bankruptcy.[31]

The failure to formulate corrective strategies for the booms and
busts in the building sector is remarkable, for there is no doubt that
the housing market did not operate efficiently at the beginning of the
19th century. To start with, there was a critical shortage of dwellings.
The shortfall in England was identified in the Census of 1811, which
recorded the presence of 2m families occupying 1.67m houses. The
problem of adequate shelter was not a purely construction problem,
however, for streets of overcrowded houses went side-by-side with a
vast number of vacant dwellings. In England and Wales in 1801, about
57,000 houses were unoccupied; this, when the number of families
exceeded the number of houses by well over 300,000.[32]

The market for housing was not working efficiently; and yet, the market was supposed to place a premium on the efficient allocation of resources. The rules were supposed to guide people into using the resources they gathered from nature, or which they made with brain and brawn, to the best possible effect. This, evidently, was not the case at the end of the 18th century; and it is not the case today, in the 21st century.

Prices are supposed to alert us to the potential waste of productive inputs, so that we can shift resources between alternative uses. Prices signal the existence of bottlenecks (which cause prices to rise) or unwanted surpluses (which we recognise when prices drop). When it comes to property, however, the evidence of 400 years tells us that there is something peculiarly exceptional about real estate which defies the rules of the market. Unfortunately, governments are reluctant to monitor too closely the trends in the property market.

This is not the case in the labour market, where the hoarding of employees, for whatever reason, is actively condemned as inefficient. Hoarding affects the performance of other enterprises, which are denied the labour they need. To monitor this inefficiency, governments employ a statistical measure which indicates the scale of the problem. A comparison of OECD countries shows that Japan, Italy and France were among the worst offenders as revealed by the labour hoarding indicator index.[33] Similar measures compare and quantify the under-use of capital equipment, which helps statisticians to measure the 'output gap' in the economy.

Armed with this information, you would think that economists would have pinpointed the root cause of booms and slumps. Had they done so, governments would have been able to adopt remedial measures that consigned economic instability to history. Could our failure to do so be the result of a fatal absence of vital information? Is the absence of that data the result of imperfect theory, which distorts our assumptions about what is important and what is trivial? Significantly, there is one curious exception to government enthusiasm for collating statistics – land.

The account of the business cycle that we shall elaborate suggests that when a wealth-creating machine harbours predators, its productive successes also nourish the seeds of its own destruction.

● Capital accumulation causes the rate of interest to decline over time. This ought to be glad tidings for working people. It means they can acquire labour-saving devices that produce the goods they want by using fewer resources (including their own labour). But there is a downside to this trend: when the rate of interest declines, the price of land is raised. Under the present rules, this makes it increasingly difficult to establish new enterprises as land becomes increasingly unaffordable.

● According to the philosophy of the free market, competition equalises everyone, and everything, to produce the best of all practical worlds. But while Capital needs Land to function, Land is not so dependent on Capital. This unequal relationship stems from the fact that land is in finite supply, and whoever monopolises it has the whip hand.

To understand why capitalist markets do not produce the outcomes that one would expect, we have to understand the economics of the land market. Our analytical starting point is the building cycle. Because the pattern that emerges is so predictable, it yields its own clues. To follow those clues, we have to shift our focus from Birmingham, England, in the late 18th century, to Chicago in the United States in the 19th century.

§4 The Chicago Plot

HOMER HOYT was a real estate researcher who carefully collated data on land values in the Windy City. He discovered that the price variations conformed to a pattern that averaged 18 years.[34] This pattern was common to other towns and even continents.[35] I interviewed Hoyt in his Washington apartment in 1978. He believed that the 18-year periodicity of the 19th century had disappeared in the 20th century.

I was not satisfied with the way he diminished the significance of his remarkable findings. Hoyt had gone on to enrich himself as a land speculator on a major scale, but there is no reason to believe that this coloured his attitude to his famous statistical discovery. In any event, while I was confident that the 18-year pattern had been maintained during the 20th century – disturbed only by the implosive power of two world wars – I was not able to offer a theoretical explanation for the *duration* of that trend. A convincing explanation was needed, one that took into account the dynamics of house building. Such an explanation can now be offered. A stylised representation of the theory is presented in Figure 5:1. The trend line of economic activity is divided into the component parts that constitute the 18-year period.

If we take the trough of a recession as the starting point, we find that it takes about two years to recover from the state of deepest

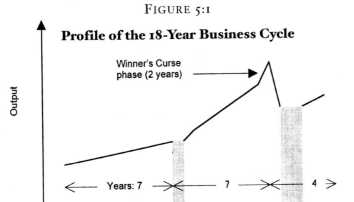

FIGURE 5:1

Profile of the 18-Year Business Cycle

inactivity. At the other end of the growth phase, the downturn from the peak of growth to the trough takes about two years. But before examining these turning points, we shall describe the middle 14 years of the cycle. The period of growth is divided into three segments. The purpose of this exercise is to find some satisfactory answers to questions like: why is the growth phase unsustainable? Why does it last for just 14 years?

In the building industry of the 18th and 19th centuries, production would last for as long as it took for people to buy the land and pay for their homes to be built. The duration of this process was 14 years. This period was determined by the cost of borrowing money (the real rate of interest averaged 5%). In principle, there was no reason why one terminating society should not have been smoothly succeeded by another terminating society. Growth could be sustained. The potential of the building industry would be set by the rate at which the population grew. Unfortunately, the constraint on the supply of houses was not related to demographic trends.

Three factors appear to account for the cyclical termination of building activity. The first is associated with the finite nature of land. Because, *inter alia*, tax policies and property rights permit the hoarding of land, prices escalate faster than the growth of people's incomes. Those already inside the property market are generally secure, so long as they do not get greedy. Those outside the property market are left to sink, as prices rise beyond what can be afforded on average (let alone below average) wages. Result: the housing market implodes, and it has the weight to drag down other industries with it.

The second explanation is emphasised by Dr. Michael Hudson,[36] who has combined the teaching of economics at US universities with analysis for Wall Street financial institutions. He stresses the role of credit. Banks insist on using land as collateral. As land values multiply, so the capital base of financial institutions expands. This enables them to accelerate the increase in loans to the owners of property. In the early phase of the construction cycle, debt appears to facilitate the expansion of economic activity. Eventually, however, the point is reached where increases in interest rates turn the loans into an intolerable burden. Debtors are horrified to discover that interest payments absorb all the net rental income. Indeed, many operators in the real estate sector realise that they are paying back more than the inflow of rents. The motivation to build ceases, mortgage credit dries up and the construction sector contracts.

The third explanation was suggested by John Maynard Keynes and has been more recently elaborated by Mason Gaffney, a professor of economics who devoted a lifetime to dissecting the role of the land market in the capitalist economy. He stresses the wasteful investment of capital and the diminishing returns to people's savings, which consequently leads to a contraction of economic activity. This aspect will be explored later in this chapter.

Because of the convergence of such influences the economy was not geared to smoothly launch successive phases of construction without interruption. Our narrative begins with the first phase of the upswing.

The Recovery Phase   Following an end-of-cycle recession, new growth starts which lasts for about seven years. It ends with a revision in people's business expectations. This is an empirically derived feature of the cycle. The association representing mortgage lenders in Britain has documented the average duration of house-buying loans for long enough to be able to conclude that the average life of a mortgage in the housing market is just over eight and a half years.[37] This breaks up the 18-year cycles into two parts of approximately equal duration linked intimately to the financing of homes.

The convergence of deals in the housing sector towards the middle of the 18-year cycle produces an intensity of economic activity that manifests itself in a boom in the price of land, followed by a recession.

The Explosive Phase   Recovery from the mid-cycle recession launches activity in the housing market for seven years. This activity takes place at a higher level of growth, and the dealing in houses assumes special characteristics. The phase has to be divided into two distinct periods.

The first lasts for about five years. The price of land accelerates markedly, as the economy grows, but the public pronouncements of alarm are restricted by governments to 'house' prices. With increasing frequency, politicians warn of the need for disciplined behaviour. This message is aimed, in particular, at wage-earning employees. They are admonished for wanting to increase their wages at rates that exceed the rate of growth of the economy. Wage settlements at 4% are met with outrage by analysts who overlook the fact that the average price of land is accelerating in double-digit numbers.

Investors become incautious. People treat their homes as investments rather than as safe havens for their families. The media fuels the mass psychology that encourages the belief that they ought to 'trade up' as a way of increasing their wealth. A few doomsayers realise that a bubble is in the making that will end in tears. But the peals of the warning bells are drowned by greed and the fear of missing out on super-profits.

The Winner's Curse The third phase of the 14-year growth period lasts for about two years. The trades in housing are now almost exclusively driven by the motive to speculate in the prospect of reaping huge windfall gains. The price of land takes off in an almost vertical trend under the influence of what is known as the Winner's Curse.[38] This is the period of frenetic trading in which prices can no longer guide people towards rational decisions based on what something is worth. This is most evident in the real estate market. Investors become reckless to the point where the winning bids for property are made by people who make the greatest upward errors in their assessment of what a site is worth. The psychology is primitive: the property must be acquired at any cost. So convinced is the purchaser that a windfall fortune is there for the taking that he will outbid all-comers, whatever it takes. As prices escalate, the gap between reality and fantasy widens to breaking point.

In the market for houses in Britain, the Winner's Curse is signalled by the advent of 'gazumping'. Vendors double-cross people to whom they have already agreed to sell, in favour of a latecomer who trumps the price that the previous bidder last thought of. This is the process of random errors in action on the doorstep. The winner's success is a curse to him and everyone else: the price is unbelievably high.

The market is left with owners who think they have won – they own the deeds – but something odd happens. They discover that others are hesitating, unwilling to take the land off their hands. The market goes into the economic doldrums. That is when the horror dawns: the properties cannot possibly yield the returns that would make sense of the prices that were paid for them. The housing market crashes; and, suddenly, the gale sweeps in ...

When competition pushes land prices above the levels that working people can afford, the social consequences are unique. The reckless bidding for works of art at auction, for example, does not damage the interests of other people, not even when those prices were forced to record levels by Japanese corporate purchasers in the 1980s. Even if the prices subsequently dropped (as they did, following the recession of the 1990s), other people did not suffer from the imprudent treatment of paintings as investments. This is not the case when people overprice land. The speculator dries up the supply of sites, because he is obliged to hoard the property until he can find someone willing to fulfil his unreasonable expectations. Meanwhile, his successful bid has helped to raise the prices of comparable sites, so the consequences of his unrealistic expectations are transmitted to other people.

When the Winner's Curse forces land prices into a skyward trajectory, we know that the economy is in the grip of a complete loss of reality. Land dealers (including families who 'trade' their homes) base their prices on expectations about future increases. In the United States, this premium has been calculated at over 70% of the price of land during boom times.[39]

By creating an artificial scarcity of land, the prospects for creating new jobs and sustaining output are terminated. The shortage of affordable sites is matched by the shortage of affordable money. Liquid capital becomes scarce.

- Banks expand their credit on the back of the spiralling price of land. People are tempted to dig themselves deeper into debt. There comes a point where they can no longer finance their mortgages. For some of them it is cheaper to walk away from their property. A rise in the number of non-performing loans signals a crisis in the financial sector. Panic sets in.

- Over-investment in capital intensive projects adds further upward pressure on interest rates. Speculative building in the commercial sector is one reason why the payback period of investment is dragged out at the expense of jobs. Imprudent government investment in public infrastructure (to cater for sprawling towns, for example) is the second major reason why the flow of capital stock begins to seize up.

The land speculator is in the vanguard of this process. As the price of his asset reaches the highest peak, those elected as the guardians of the economy appear to be in a state of deep sleep. So entranced are they with what appears to be a healthy state of growth that they invite accolades for themselves rather than alerting people to looming dangers. A typical example was the display by Nigel Lawson when he presented the Chancellor's Autumn Statement to the House of Commons on November 1, 1988.

Britain was halfway up the slope of the Winner's Curse. Lawson was euphoric. He claimed credit for what he regarded as an incomparable achievement – 'no other major economy has such sound public finances'. Britain was on the financial precipice, peering into a deep chasm, and the chancellor was inviting Parliament to cheer him on for his wise management of the economy. He uttered the details of the timetable which we have stylised in Figure 5:1, but he did not have the theoretical insights to interpret the trends.

> The continuing vigour of the British economy is testimony to the transformation that has taken place in the supply side of the economy, a transformation which has enabled the seven years to 1988 to record a combination of strong and steady growth unmatched since the war.

Seven years of growth ... but the chancellor did not realise that he was presiding over the onset of the final phase, the Winner's Curse. He lulled the House of Commons into a state of somnolence with this assurance.

> In short, after two years of *unexpectedly* rapid expansion, growth next year is forecast to return to a sustainable level ... The prospect that lies before us is yet further testimony to the success of the policies we have been pursuing these past nine and a half years.[40]

Gordon Brown glared at the chancellor from the Opposition benches, but he was equally unable to comprehend the significance of what Parliament had just heard. The seven years of growth were up; people were recklessly bidding fantasy prices for land, and in the following few months the housing market would go into the doldrums as the market seized up. Britain was about to collapse into a severe recession, and the stewards of the economy were misreading the dials on the economic compass.

TABLE 5:4

Prices of Bulk Residential Land

	Price, 1987: £ per ha.	Change in Price 1986/7: %
Inner London	4,100,000	51.2
Outer London	1,687,000	44.5
South East	818,000	28.1
East Anglia	625,000	39.1
South West	440,000	24.6
East Midlands	233,000	26.2
West Midlands	245,000	24.4
North West	192,000	15.4
North	185,000	12.3
Yorks & Humber	181,000	13.1
Wales	137,000	12.7

Source: Graham Hallett (ed.), *Land and Housing Policies in Europe and the USA: A Comparative analysis*, London: Routledge, 1988, p.139, Table 7:1, derived from Inland Revenue Valuation Office data in *Property Market Report*, London: RICS Publications, 1987.

Table 5:4 highlights what was happening in the land market as Lawson lauded his performance. The data emphasises the variable levels of speculation: the most ruthless, reckless activity takes place in South-East England, where the illusion of a fortune from capital gains leads land dealers into bidding prices that are 40% or 50% higher than those paid in the previous year. No economy can make sense of such increases, least of all the residential market when wages are rising by 4% or 5% a year. The only way to restore sanity, under those conditions, is through a collapse. But it is not just the speculators who suffer; innocent people are also dragged down.

Another dramatic example of the Winner's Curse in action is worth recalling. It emphasises that the treasure which the speculators are hunting is not land in its physical state, but the rent which can be milked from the natural resource. The British government, this time with Gordon Brown as chancellor, was the steward of the nation's electro-magnetic spectrum. The Treasury offered to lease five licenses to telecommunications companies. The spectrum was needed for the use of third-generation mobile telephones. What was this finite natural resource worth? The government was persuaded by economists commissioned by the Economic and Social Research Council to find out by offering the licenses at auction. The Treasury expected to raise £1-2bn. On March 6, 2000, when the first bids were delivered, telecommunication experts raised their expectations to £5bn. This would be a fine windfall for Britain's taxpayers! As the bids escalated in leaps and bounds, soon passing the £10bn mark, the alarm bells began to ring. Wasn't this a price too high? The *Financial Times* (April 3) reassuringly editorialised:

> Governments are much less likely than phone companies to find the right economic price for scarce wireless spectrum. An auction is therefore the most efficient way to allocate the resource, as well as to capture a proper rent for taxpayers.

Fears mounted that one of the five winners out of the 13 contenders – after overpaying for the right to monopolise the natural resource – might default. But once people are in the grip of speculative fever, common sense flies out of the window. As with every phase of intense speculation, the sums offered were bid in a blind way. The telecommunication companies had no way of knowing the value of the services that would be delivered by the next generation of mobile telephones. Analysts warned that the bids might jeopardise the commercial viability of the companies. As bids breached the £20bn mark, investors became alarmed that they would not see a fair return on their money. In the end, the winning bids added up to more than £22bn. This saddled the winners with debts that did jeopardise their commercial viability. British Telecom paid the price – it bid £10bn more than it had expected to secure its licenses – when, in March 2001, it had to go cap-in-hand to the financiers in the City of London to try and cover its £30bn debt mountain. The outcome was a classic case of land speculation, which was no more acceptable because the seller was the government representing taxpayers' interests.

The bidding errors of the telecom giants were transmitted to the rest of the economy via the impact on the stock exchange. When a speculator has outsmarted himself, the debt burden can affect the owners of shares. That was the case with Vodaphone, one of the firms that outbid others to claim a G3 license. Vodaphone proved to be a consistent underperformer over the four years to 2004. Because of its size on the FTSE 100 of quoted companies on the London stock exchange, it contributed to the overall poor performance of the index compared with share performances in New York, Australia and Japan.

The Recession Phase John Maynard Keynes, the economist who devised a strategy to help governments to avoid recessions, examined the historical evidence and concluded that recessions lasted from three to five years. This empirical evidence provides us with an average duration of four years.

Keynes, in *The General Theory of Employment Interest and Money*, identified the important starting point for an account of what happens
during the upswing. The illusions of the boom cause an excessive supply of particular types of assets. There is a waste of resources, or what
Keynes called 'misdirected investment'.[41] Why should rational people
invest resources in a wasteful way? Keynes pointed out that an essential feature of the boom was spurious expectations about the yield on
investments. Investments that might yield 2% during full employment
are made 'in the expectation of a yield of, say, 6 per cent, and are valued accordingly'. The error of optimism is followed by the 'error of
pessimism' in which investments that would yield 2% are expected to
yield less than nothing, which is the prelude to the collapse of new
investment. That leads to unemployment. 'We reach a condition
where there is a shortage of houses, but where nevertheless no one can
afford to live in the houses that there are.'[42]

The terminal segment of the business cycle is the V-shaped crash
into the trough of the recession, and the upward climb back to the
start of the recovery phase. But how do we account for an average
period of four years? The answer was provided by Keynes.

In the previous period of optimism, the future yield that people
expected from their savings, which are invested in capital equipment,
is assumed to be sufficient to offset opposing tendencies. The contrary trends include the growing accumulation of capital goods, their
rising costs of production, and the rise in the rate of interest.
Eventually, however, investors discover that the returns from what is
technically called the marginal efficiency of capital are not what they
expected. The market falls 'with sudden and even catastrophic force'.[43]
Insofar as they can, people switch their savings into cash. There is a
reaction against productive investment, which accelerates the decline
in the formation of new fixed capital.

How does this help us to understand the recession timetable? For
Keynes, the timetable was dictated by such considerations as the
length of the life of durable assets and the costs of carrying the surplus
stocks that consumers were unwilling to buy. These would produce a
timetable which would have

> an order of magnitude which is not fortuitous, which does not
> fluctuate between, say, one year this time and ten years next
> time, but which shows some regularity of habit between, let us
> say, three and five years.[44]

In Keynes' view, then, based on empirically observed behaviour,
it takes an average of four years to elapse before the economy

experiences a sufficient shortage of capital to raise investors' expectations that they will receive a satisfactory return on their money. The time element has to allow for the use, decay and obsolescence of the capital that has been rendered redundant in the post-boom phase. For Keynes this timescale was a stable function of the durability of capital.

The second influence was the cost of carrying the surplus stocks. This had to be absorbed in the face of the indifference of consumers who, rather than spend money, struggle to keep their jobs and pay their bills during the hard times.

> The carrying-costs of the stocks will seldom be less than ten per cent per annum. Thus, the fall in their price needs to be sufficient to bring about a restriction which provides for their absorption within a period of, say, three to five years at the outside. Now the process of absorbing the stocks represents negative investment, which is a further deterrent to employment ...[45]

Again, the second component in the recession phase takes an average of four years to work its way through the system. So both components – adjusting the return on capital to levels acceptable to investors, and getting rid of old stock – deliver a period that rounds off our 18-year timetable. Keynes' analysis links the reasons for, and periodicity of, the recession, to the pattern and timing of the growth phase.

What does our description of the business cycle reveal?

- The evidence from the housing sector supports the 18-year cyclical timetable.
- The cycle is present irrespective of the distinctive characteristics of the economy: one with the benefit of a resource-rich land mass (USA); or where people occupy a country that is bereft of natural resources (Japan); or where the population is deemed to be large relative to its territory (Britain); or where the population is very small in relation to the land mass (Australia).

The evidence points to two overlapping and contradictory layers of activity.

- The 14-year duration of activity in the housing market generates investment and consumer satisfaction. This is associated with the expansion of valuable goods and services for sale in the marketplace.
- Land hoarding and speculation leads to waste and unearned riches as a section of society cashes in on the rocket-powered rises in land prices, before many of them fall into their own traps.

The common denominator over the last 300 years is the ability of people to pay for the construction or purchase of houses: affordability. The *production* cycle in the market for residential property lasts for as long as it takes for people to pay to build or purchase the house. This period turns out to be 14 years, and is tailored to the cost of mortgages. Does this abstract account actually reflect the way people behave?

§5 The Unpublished Evidence

THE EMPIRICAL data to support the 14-year growth phase is sparse in the literature, because economic historians have not been directed by their theories to look for it. Lewis drew on the unpublished material of one scholar, Bernard Weber, to chronicle aspects of the industrial economy that had escaped attention. Weber's papers report what he called 'scraps of information on the average number of year's purchase offered for house-property' covering 1872 to 1907. The data was from houses sold by auction in Glasgow. 'The striking feature of the series is its resemblance to the long waves of house-building.'[46]

TABLE 5:5

Average Number of Year's Purchase of House-Property Sold in Glasgow (1872-1907)

1872	14.3	1886	12.8	1901	14.9
1876	17.0	1891	13.0	1906	13.0
1881	13.5	1896	14.1	1907	12.1

Source: Lewis, 1965, p.159.

Table 5:5 lists the prices paid. These constitute more than a *resemblance*. They are the core of the waves of house building, as construction interacted with supply and demand. In the 35 years up to 1907, rational people bid prices for houses in Glasgow that represented an average of 13.85 years worth of rents. As corroboration of our 14-year growth phase, that is as close as one can get to empirical corroboration of a scientific hypothesis.

Weber knew that activity had to be examined from the point of view of building costs and the rate of interest as well as the level of rents and property prices. His notebooks include calculations that integrated these variables. Two findings are relevant for our analysis. The first concerns the total cost of inputs. These fluctuated around a very narrow band during the second half of the cycle, if anything, actually declining. Labour costs rose fractionally, but these were more than offset by the decline in the cost of building materials.[47] So price pressures from 1870 into the beginning of the 20th century were not generated by the costs of labour or materials. Prices did soar in 1876, which happened to be the take-off point for the second half of the 18-year cycle that terminated in 1884 (the trough year was 1886).

The second issue concerns the cost of land. This has to be inferred. The index measuring the profitability of house ownership soared away from the early 1870s up to the early 1880s, increasing by more than a third over the second half of the 18-year cycle. Who pocketed the difference? Not the carpenters and plumbers who built houses, or the entrepreneurs who supplied bricks and mortar. The boom in prices could only have been to the benefit of the owners of land.

But why can't people simply keep on paying higher prices? Why does the construction and purchase of homes come to a grinding halt with the certainty of the arrival of blossom in spring? People's wages do not rise as fast as the price of land. There comes a time where houses are unaffordable. Bearing in mind the 5% interest payable on mortgages, the average price that people can afford tends to be the annual rent multiplied by 14 years. When people are driven to offer more than 14 years' worth of rents, the affordability index explodes. The building industry grinds to a halt.

So with the regularity with which summer is followed by winter, the cycle that begins when houses are affordable (Year 1) terminates in Year 14. That is the year in which houses are priced at levels that are prohibitively expensive for prospective buyers. As a leading sector of the economy its travails are multiplied many times over as the effects course through the financial sector.

In an economy built on rational principles, the first terminating societies would have been smoothly succeeded by new terminating societies. Growth would have been on a gentle upward incline based on demographic trends and technological progress. In reality, as building projects began to terminate, people discovered that the capitalist system was not able to launch a new phase of construction without first going through the trauma of recession, in which prices could be forced down to affordable levels.

And so the financial clubs whose members met in pubs metamorphosed into building societies in Britain and savings and loans institutions in the United States. Working people deposited their savings with them, for safe-keeping, but – unwittingly – these institutions were drawn into an economic routine that undermined their mission.

People aspired to homes that afforded the security of the rock-solid castles of their dreams. But as house prices soared, for many of them mortgages turned into a working lifetime of debt and grief.

REFERENCES

1 J. Parry Lewis, *Building Cycles and Britain's Growth*, London: Macmillan, 1965, p.15.
2 *Ibid.*
3 W.W. Rostow, *British Economy of the 19th Century*, Oxford: Clarendon Press, 1948, pp.16-17.
4 Joshua S. Goldstein, *Long Cycles: Prosperity and War in the Modern Age*, New Haven: Yale University Press, 1988, pp.15-16.
5 Rostow, *op. cit.*, p.16, n.1, citing H.A. Shannon, 'Bricks – A Trade Index', *Economica*, 1934.
6 Nor could this explanation account for the 18-year land-value cycles in countries as culturally diverse as Japan and Australia, which I have documented in *The Power in the Land*. See also Ch. 13 below.
7 Thomas West, *The Antiquities of Furness*, Ulverston: George Ashburne, 1805, p.33.
8 J.H. Clapham, *An Economic History of Modern Britain: The Early Railway Age 1820-1850*, Cambridge: University Press, 1967, p.164.
9 Lewis, *op. cit.*, p.372, n.1. Emphasis added.
10 Joyce Youings, *Sixteenth-Century England*, London: Allen Lane, 1984, p.159.
11 *Ibid.*, p.162.
12 *Ibid.*, p.170.
13 *Ibid.*, p.161.
14 Joyce Youings, *The Dissolution of the Monasteries*, London: George Allen and Unwin, 1971, pp.121, 125.
15 *Ibid*, p.126.
16 George Miller, *On Fairness and Efficiency*, Bristol: Policy Press, 2000, p.184.
17 E.A. Wrigley, R.S. Davies, J.E. Oeppen and R.S. Schofield, *English Population History From Family Reconstitution 1580-1837*, Cambridge: Cambridge University Press, 1997, p.541, Fig. 8.3.
18 Joyce Youings, 'The Church', in Joan Thirsk (ed.), *The Agrarian History of England and Wales*, Vol. IV: 1500-1640, Cambridge: Cambridge University Press, 1967, p.349.
19 Youings, *Sixteenth-Century England*, p.161.
20 Sidney J. Madge, *The Domesday of Crown Lands*, London: Frank Cass, 1968, p.43, Table XI.
21 Lewis, *op. cit.*, p.15.
22 Youings, *Dissolution*, pp.127-8.
23 *Ibid.*, p.131.
24 A pioneering study in this field is by J.E. Kew, 'The Disposal of Crown Lands and the Devon land market, 1536-58', *Agricultural History Review*, XVII, ii, 1970.
25 Youings, *Sixteenth-Century England*, p.166.
26 *Ibid*, p.176.
27 Ashley Boynton-Williams, *Town & City Maps of the British Isles 1800-1855*, London: Studio Editions, 1992.
28 R. Machin, 'The great rebuilding: a reassessment', *Past & Present*, No. 77, November 1977, p.48.
29 C.W. Chalklin, *The Provincial Towns of Georgian England: A Study of the Building Process, 1740-1820*, London: Edward Arnold, 1974, pp.251-5.

30 Simon Kuznets, *Capital in the American Economy*, Princeton University Press, 1961, p.424.
31 Lewis, *op. cit.*, p.56. Emphasis added.
32 *Ibid.*, p.26.
33 OECD, *EMU One Year On*, Paris: OECD, February 2000, p.176, Fig. A4.
34 Homer Hoyt, *One Hundred Years of Land Values in Chicago*, Chicago: University of Chicago Press, 1933. For the remarkable association between booms and busts in land values between 1855 and 1930, and the 5% interest rate, see Fig. 80, p.352.
35 Harrison, *Power in the Land, op. cit.*
36 Interview with author.
37 BMRB Survey 1993, p.33, Table 8.5.
38 Paul R. Milgrom and Robert J. Weber, 'A Theory of Auctions and Competitive Bidding', *Econometrica*, Vol. 50, 1982, p.1094.
39 Karl L. Guntermann, 'Residental Land Prices Prior to Development', *Journal of Real Estate Research*, Vol. 14 (1/2), 1997.
40 *Hansard*, November 1, 1988, Cols. 826, 827. Emphasis added.
41 J.M. Keynes, *The General Theory of Employment Interest and Money*, London: Macmillan, (1967), p.321.
42 *Ibid.*, p.322.
43 *Ibid.*, p.316.
44 *Ibid.*, p.317.
45 *Ibid.*, p.318
46 Lewis, *op. cit.*, pp.158-9.
47 Christopher Powell, *The British Building Industry Since 1800*, London: E. & F.N. Spon, 2nd edn., 1996, p.92.

6

The Patterns of History

§1 The Get-Rich-Quick Schemes

ECONOMIC HISTORY spanning four centuries, it appears, can be divided into 18-year segments going from bust to bust. Does the historical record support the thesis that the building industry was central to the mechanism that drives those cycles? In Chapter 5 we reviewed the evidence for the existence of those cycles in the 17th and 18th centuries, but how did the influence of the life-cycle of farmers transcend the Industrial Revolution and perpetuate itself, in adapted form, in the 19th and 20th centuries?

The Usury Law reduced the rate of interest to 5% in 1714. We have seen that this delivers a building cycle of 14 years. Was it coincidence that 1714 was divided from the next recession (1727) by a period of between 13 and 14 years? Why did construction fail to proceed smoothly after 1727? Was a financial logic set in motion that gave a precise shape to business activity? What is beyond dispute is that, if we date the modern building cycle from the year that 5% became operative, the duration between cyclical troughs averaged 17.4 years (Table 5:1). This delivers four cycles in the 18th century which, we suggest, were plugged into the financial logic of the 5% rate of interest on borrowed money. To determine whether there was continuity after this period, we must scrutinise the evidence for the 19th and 20th centuries.

We need a starting point. We may choose one of two dates. One could be the meeting in the pub in Birmingham, from which we could move forward in 18-year jumps to compare our hypothetically-derived dates with the outcome of historical events. Alternatively, we could take a recession that is within living memory – say, the 1992 trough – and move backwards in 18-year steps and extrapolate into the future. If our theory is consistent with the historical evidence, this second approach ought to return us to the year in which the ale-drinkers convened their first meeting in the Golden Cross pub (1775).

The recession of 1992 reduced GDP *per capita* in most of the advanced capitalist countries.[1] We will take this date as our starting point. This yields the timetable set out in Table 6:1.

For a snapshot guide to the history of booms and busts, we may take as our primary text a book that was written by Thomas Johnston. He was born in the small Scottish town of Kirkintilloch in 1882. He was appointed Lord Privy Seal and a Privy Councillor in 1931, and as a Labour Member of Parliament he served as Secretary of State for Scotland during the Second World War. In 1953 he was made a Companion of Honour, and appointed a Governor of the BBC in 1955. His public service concluded as Chancellor of Aberdeen University. He died in 1965. His credentials, as an astute observer of the British political and economic scene, are impeccable.

TABLE 6:1

The 18-Year Business Cycle:
Britain from the Industrial Revolution to the IT bubble

Primary recessions	Mid-cycle recessions
1776	1785?
1794	1803
1812	1821
1830	1839
1848	1857
1866	1875
1884	1893
1902	1911
1920	1929
1938	1947
1956	1965
1974	1983
1992	2001
2010*	–

*Prediction

In 1934 Johnston published *The Financiers and the Nation*, a history of financial shenanigans from 1824 to 1931.[2] His brush-strokes are bold; he captures the vitality and futility of the 19th century with pithy descriptions that reveal a keen analytical mind and a passionate anger against the waste that stemmed from human folly.

And so boom and slump, slump and boom has gone on, decade
after decade, the severance of fools from their money. As every
fresh crop of small accumulators saved sufficient to invest, and
looked around hopefully for some 'certain security' with an adequate interest yield, lo! always there opportunely appeared some
plausible leader of finance with a get-rich-quick scheme, casting
it before his victims as an angler casts his flies for trout.[3]

The smooth talkers may have wrapped their schemes in financial
wizardry, but it was the land speculator who parted people from their
money; and then many others from their jobs, creating the anxieties
that lead to suicide, depression, shattered dreams ... but let us
approach the historical evidence as it unfolded, to discover whether
the dates in Table 6:1 were turning points. Recall that one of our
landmarks in the history of the building industry was the formation in
1775 of the first club to finance the construction of houses. We can
assume that their collaborative house-building activities began within
12 months (1776), which we have postulated as the beginning of an
18-year cycle. If it was, the end-of-cycle crash would have been in or
close to 1794. Thus, as we see from Table 6:1, in retracing British
history we identified

- 1776 as the beginning of an 18-year cycle. This theoretically derived
  date coincides with the empirically derived peak in the economic
  cycle which is listed in Table 5:1 (page 74). And
- 1794 as the end of a cycle up-tempered by the new financing
  arrangements for building houses. Was 1794 the turning point
  between two 18-year periods? What was significant about that year,
  on the ground?

1794   For Lewis, the peak of the construction cycle was 1792.[4]
Johnston calls 1793 'the black year'. The City Council of Liverpool
faced a complete collapse in the local banking system. On March 20,
the Mayor reported that 58 merchants urged the council to secure a
loan from the Bank of England to enable the City to survive 'the dis-
tress which had engulfed the people'. Parliament issued a special Act
which entitled Liverpool to issue negotiable notes for a limited period,
to be lent at a rate of interest slightly below 4.5%. The citizens weathered the storm, thanks to what the Webbs described as 'the boldest
financial step recorded in the annals of English local government'.[5]

What caused this trauma? Speculation focused on the rent-yielding
opportunities presented by canals. These carried the raw materials to
the great factories that were sprouting in the north, and the products

back to the new consumer markets. So intense was the speculation in canal construction and reckless the expansion of credit, that the price of urban land rose beyond what people could afford. In Liverpool, the Vicar of Walton on the Hill put his finger on the human costs of land speculation:

> The increase of the commercial Town' of Liverpool by covering the neighbouring townships with villas, pleasure grounds and cow pastures has occasioned for many years a material decrease in Corn land.[6]

To acquire space, the cotton weavers had to pay 'enormous rents'. In doing so, they displaced agricultural workers who were reduced to a state which provoked food riots.

An 18-year cycle which began in 1776 did terminate in 1794. Was a new cycle of 18-year duration launched?

1812 What was described as the 'phrenzy of speculation' gripped the nation, followed by 'depression and heavy unemployment as the out-come, especially in Lancashire and around Birmingham. Bad trade led to lower wages and unemployment, and effectively reduced the demand for housing'. A single issue of *The Manchester Mercury* in 1812 reported riots in Bristol, Truro, Leeds, Macclesfield, Stockport and Birmingham 'as high potato prices added to the misery of depression'.[7]

Writing in 1817, Samuel Taylor Coleridge, in his *Lay Sermon*, iden-tified the internal mechanism of a repetitive trend. Booms and busts occurred 'at intervals of about 12 or 13 years each [as a result of] certain periodical Revolutions of Credit'. Towards the end of this period, which strikingly echoes our 14-year period based on house-building mortgages, people throw caution to the wind. They embark on a 'tempting and encouraging headlong Adventure, Want of prin-ciple, and Confederacies of false credit ... the movements of Trade become yearly gayer and giddier, and end at length in a vortex of hopes and hazards, of blinding passions and blind practices'.[8]

1830 Speculation in shares and commodities was noted as a social phenomenon in 1825, and the heat was on within a year. People threw money at ludicrous ventures. The significant impact, from the view-point of investment and employment, was in land. In 1826, 60 banking firms stopped payment and the nation went through 'one of the most tremendous and searching convulsions ever experienced in any country', according to Charles Canning, a Conservative MP before his elevation to the House of Lords.[9]

In this great crash of 1825-26, hundreds of thousands of humble folk were stripped of all they possessed, not because of specu-lation or gambling in which they themselves had participated, but because the bank directors to whom they had for safety entrusted their slender savings had rashly and madly adventured them in crazy and wild-cat hazards and follies in the search for profits.[10]

Investment in railways slacked (1828-31), and the building industry hit its trough in 1832.

1848   The crash reminds us that governments create the legal and institutional context that makes it possible to seduce people into reck-less speculation. In the three years leading to 1847, Parliament autho-rised the investment of £250m to construct 9,500 miles of railway. The public investment in the communications infrastructure raised the price of land, but there was no compensating fiscal stabiliser to prevent the economy from imploding.

George Hudson, the Railway King, owned 1,000 miles of track. He was one of the most spectacular victims of the bust. '[P]rojects worth absolutely nothing were sold and resold at swollen prices during the next decade until 1847, when the whole edifice toppled over again, and in ten railway corporations alone the unfortunate shareholders lost no less than £78m sterling'.[11] Six banks failed. Johnston rounds off his account of this period by identifying the chain of guilt:

First the promoters, the landlords, and the Parliamentary lawyers had plundered and robbed the railway concerns; then the financiers had arrived, and the result of their manipulations with railway stock had been such that it had become absolutely unsaleable; hundreds of thousands of families were ruined, and there ensued such widespread devastation and panic as the country had not seen before nor – even including the depression in the years 1921-33 – since.[12]

Parliament was dominated by landowners and their lackeys. An example of their power to rig politics in their favour is offered by the Land Clauses Consolidation Act 1845. Far from enabling government to redistribute income in favour of the people working in factories, and those who invested their savings in capital equipment, this Act ensured that compensation was paid to landowners. But compensation was not sufficient. They were also granted a 10% *solatium* – defined in *Chambers Concise Dictionary* as 'compensation for disappointment, inconvenience or wounded feelings'. This extra payment was to offset the loss of option due to compulsory purchase by the railway companies, which disregarded the fact that the owners did not create the value for which they were being compensated.

The British economy was also being affected by what was happening in the colonies. There was a surge in construction in Australia, with an associated land boom. The Colonial Banking Regulations that were introduced in 1846 came too late. Although they sought to ban loans that rested on property as collateral, or to hold land except for the conduct of banking business, the legislation was sidestepped: building societies borrowed from banks and lent on to speculators.

1866 Esau Hanson does not feature as a personality worthy of note in the history books, but he was symbolically important in the annals of the business cycle. At a meeting at the Old Cock Inn on December 23, 1852, a group of Halifax citizens met to form the Halifax Permanent Benefit Building and Investment Society. Esau Hanson, a manufacturer, was among them. In the following May he became the first to borrow from the Halifax. He was granted a mortgage for £160 (two full shares at £80 each) with repayments set at £13 a year for 13 years.[13]

Hanson was a man of means, for in those days the most expensive planned homes cost £155 to build.[14] It was possible to build a house for as little as £80 in the 1850s with the aid of a 5% mortgage. In Hanson's case, his repayments continued through to the termination of the business cycle in 1866. Testimony that this was the end of the cycle was offered by no less an authority than that most famous student of the British economy, Karl Marx. In 1864 he confided that he was cashing-in on the frenzied activity. He wrote in a letter to a friend:

> I have, which will surprise you not a little, been speculating –
> partly in American funds, but more especially in English stocks,
> which are springing up like mushrooms this year (in furtherance
> of every imaginable and unimaginable joint stock enterprise),
> are forced up to a quite unreasonable level and then, for the
> most part, collapse. In this way I have made over £400 and,
> now that the complexity of the political situation affords
> greater scope, I shall begin all over again. It's a type of operation
> that makes small demands on one's time and it's worthwhile
> running some risk in order to relieve the enemy of his money.[15]

Within 12 months (1865), Britain was back in recession. Some players found that the risk to which Marx referred carried a heavy price. George Hudson got his comeuppance. He was sentenced to nine months' imprisonment for not paying a large debt. But for his gigantic railway frauds, perpetrated during the previous cycle, he escaped scot-free.

The misery of 1866-7 was due to 'extravagant speculation and gambling'.[16] The story of the last 40 years of the century was 'Alternating booms and slumps; crooks and prospectuses of glittering gains to be had from investments at home and abroad; the savings of thousands of families periodically swept away by cheats and frauds operating as company promoters and investment bankers'.[17]

1884 Something happened in the housing market in 1884, concluded Lewis, but his index of rents, while 'useful as a guide to changes in the housing market ... cannot tell us what'.[18] In the five years to 1875, 477,000 housing units were built. In the five years to 1880, 531,000 houses were completed. This was the peak, with the number falling to 402,000 up to 1885.[19]

Another index of activity was the construction of ships from the great yards on the Tyne, in the north-east. In Jarrow, seven years of growth in the output of shipping tonnage peaked in 1883, collapsing in 1884. The shipyard workers once again experienced 'bad times'. Ellen Wilkinson, who was Jarrow's Labour MP in the 1930s, recorded the way people were forced to respond to the events of 1884.

> With little or no resources to fall back on the first move was to effect an economy in rent. Two, three or more families would move together into one house. Rent was halved or even further reduced, but the overcrowding was appalling. Large families were herded into one room. At the same time some streets of houses would almost be empty.[20]

These indices do not *explain* why 1884 was such a bad year for working people. Lewis, who favoured the theory of war as the cause of the 18th century cycles, could not account for what was driving the 19th century cycles. He noted of the construction industry: 'Clearly, something happened to this market around 1875. Clearly, too, something happened around 1884. But the index cannot tell us what'.[21]

The mystery needed elucidating, but the message from the markets could not be deciphered from the number and the price of transactions. Could this be because the author had neglected to take into account the role of the land market (as we noted in Chapter 5, §1)? Lewis trained in mathematics, and he was recognised as an authority on the economics of the building industry. His book was a major work of reference. And yet, his explorations were into an industry which, for the purpose of understanding the dynamics of the market, was for practical purposes a spatially disembodied entity. If educated people like Lewis did not know what was driving building cycles and Britain's growth, what chance did politicians have of implementing laws to smooth the booms and busts?

1902 Financial scams reached such an outrageous scale by 1898 that the Lord Chief Justice (Lord Russell of Killowen) informed the City of London that 'rampant fraud' was 'touching all classes, involving great pecuniary loss to the community, loss largely borne by those who are least able to bear it'.[22] He singled out a property deal in West Africa that was sold for £48,000, which did not exist. After the 'property' had been sold, an agent was sent out to buy some land for £140 from a tribal chief which was supposed to fit the description on the deeds of the property! Between 1890 and 1897, the Official Receiver reported that £28.1m was lost,[23] a sum that disappeared through companies that were wound up.

1920 The boom bust that would have preceded the 1920 recession did not take place. The First World War was like dynamite thrown into an oil-well that was aflame: the blast destroys the fire. The war deflected the cycle in land speculation. In 1914 the Treasury pumped out an enormous sum of money to finance military operations against Germany, which smothered the looming recession in the UK.

1938 Following the housing boom of the mid-'30s, Britain, like the other European economies, was heading for a recession in 1938.[24] But by the middle of the decade the European powers began to stoke up their munitions industries in anticipation of another territorial conflict. As the land boom weakened the furnishings industry, the manufacturers of tanks and explosives compensated with the aid of government funds. This countervailing economic weight offset the crash that was in the making. The price for heading off the recession was a volcanic eruption that claimed the lives of millions of people.

1956 The hypothetical end of the cycle that straddled the Second World War would be 1956. Land speculation was absent in the '50s. Families still relied on rations cards for their groceries. There was no scope for a building boom and land speculation. Recession did not occur. The devastation of Europe's cities and industrial base was so extensive that it required a massive rebuilding programme spread over a decade before the economies were back to some semblance of pre-war 'normality'. The capital creation programme had to be sufficient to generate income at levels people had come to expect before the war. This investment was sustained right up to 1955. The recession that would otherwise have occurred was stillborn. The price paid for avoiding that recession was measured in the mutilated lives of people who struggled to rebuild their families after the amputations of the world war.

1974   Historians agree that the European economies were back to their normal economic rhythm in the mid-'50s. That coincides with our expectation that 1956 would have been the beginning of a new cycle. But something new had now entered economic life. Because of the world war and the investment programmes that followed, the building cycles of the leading industrial economies were synchronised. The first post-war 18-year cycle would be on a European scale and would terminate, according to our prediction, in a depression in 1974.

   In popular mythology, the recession of the early 1970s is attributed to the maliciousness of the oil sheikhs who used OPEC, the petroleum cartel, to push prices to record heights. The extraction of oil-rents from the industrialised countries did aggravate the productive economy. OPEC's actions fit our general analysis concerning the negative impact of monopolists who manipulate resource rents to their private advantage. Still, the OPEC intervention was not the sole explanation for the recession of 1974. An examination of the property markets during the late 1960s reveals in technicolour detail the predictable outcome of the cycle in the land market.[25]

1992   I had predicted the 1992 recession in *The Power in the Land,* which was published in 1983.[26] The peak in the land and housing markets was in 1989, followed by the crash into the recession that was officially dated as occurring in the first quarter of 1992.

   There was some agreement among economists as to the cause of the recession. According to the IMF:

> Recent research suggests that high housing prices have affected the United Kingdom's overall macro-economic performance. Household savings declined dramatically during the financial liberalisation of the 1980s, apparently because households, believing they had more money, were willing to take advantage of the new rules that allowed them to withdraw part of their home equities as refinanced mortgages. After providing an initial boom in consumption, this drop in personal savings resulted in less financing for the business community.
> As in most countries, the business sector in the UK is a net

borrower and the household sector is a net saver, so when household savings declined, upward pressure was put on interest rates. These pressures eventually led to increased inflows of foreign capital and a deterioration in the balance of payments capital account.

At the same time, the soaring house prices in the greater London area tended to prevent unemployed workers – primarily from the north of England and Scotland – from moving to an urban environment where they might find jobs. Estimates put the overall unemployment rate at some 2% more than it would have been had workers been able to move freely to look for work.[27]

Analysts in the property industry were shocked by the collapse in house prices in 1992. Lacking a theory, they offered instant judgments of this kind: 'Many people do not believe that the housing market can ever be as it was in the 1970s and 1980s again. Mind you, that is exactly what they thought in 1977 and 1983 following the mid-70s and early '80s slumps. Is 1994 really that different?'[28] Even in the depths of the recession in 1993, while people were losing their jobs and house prices were declining, the price of land grew by 18.2% for the whole country and 28.2% in the South East. Savills, the London-based estate agency, reported: 'Land price rises would appear to be based on speculation by developers'.

The good times in the housing market could never repeat themselves ... until mid-way through the next cycle, in 2001!

2010   The first mass-unemployment recession of the 21st century would grip the global economy in 2010. The events that laid the foundations for this cycle are analysed in Part 3.

This review of the historical evidence confirms the theory that economic activity is most fruitfully analysed in terms of 18 year segments. The periodicity is linked to the construction cycle, which is shaped by the financial mechanisms and the pursuit of windfall gains from the rents of land and nature's resources.

§2   The Mid-Cycle Crises

THE 14-YEAR construction cycle, I explained in Chapter 5, was divided by a mid-cycle boom bust. The hypothetical dates are listed in Table 6:1. (p.101). The crises of the early 1980s and the crash of 2001 were the midway points of two 18-year cycles. So was 1929, the mid-way point in the interwar cycle. But how far back does the historical record go for written confirmation?

We would not expect the first 18-year cycle to be disrupted halfway through it (1785), because the first batch of mass-produced houses were not yet complete. The commercialisation of the residential sector on a mass scale would take time to emerge. Nevertheless, the heightened tempo of the new economic mode of production was registered in the expansion of investment in the emerging industrial centres. So was there a mid-cycle recession in 1803?

1803   Lewis records that there was increased availability of credit at the turn into the 19th century; war with France increased investment in blast furnaces, and a score of factories were constructed in Manchester in 1802. The cumulative effect was to increase the demand for houses. But the economic progress could not be sustained, and 1803 was marked by a 'general depression'.[29]

Was this a coincidence, or the start of a historical pattern? Referring back to the dates in Table 6:1, we have to review the evidence for my claim that the economy was disrupted in or around 1821, 1839, 1857 and 1875 and the mid-point in cycles at the turn into the 20th century. The record does suggest that the pursuit of rental income from land and natural resources was leaving its deadly mark on the economy at these points in time.

1821   From 1818 the price of wheat dropped and the marriage rate rose, a trend that came to a halt in 1821. Poor Relief rose steadily to 1822. Meanwhile, the construction of houses proceeded to a peak in 1819, and 'in 1821 came a minor trough, before an even mightier surge continued the long upswing'.[30] Despite the inaccuracies of the statistics, Lewis concludes that 'building must have paused in the early twenties'.[31] And this time, there was no war to blame. What about our competing thesis? Was speculation present on a socially significant scale? Lewis acknowledges that the trends up to 1822 were affected by

> speculation which was a principal cause of the minor crisis that temporarily reversed the direction of the economy. It is tempting to examine the matter more fully, and to attempt to determine more precisely the mechanism involved, but to do so would take us too far from our main purpose which is to examine the major cycle on whose upswing this was but a ripple ...[32]

Here was a missed opportunity. If Lewis had excavated the causal mechanism that explained why '1821 marked a trough', he might have convincingly explained the major cycle that attracted his attention (the explanation for which could not be a war).

1839   The tempo was fully established, and the people with money were out to exploit the opportunities. Forty-two new Joint Stock Banks were floated in 1838 to cope with new commercial ventures. Total currency in circulation increased in one year by over 50%. 'Soon there was a run upon these mushroom banks and another commercial crash, and thousands of families were ruined.'[33] Scarcely had the ruin befallen people, than the money-lenders were again pouring depositors' money into new land speculation – this time, heavily linked to railway schemes.

1857   Britain's burgeoning industrial centres needed investment in infrastructure, to make life tolerable for urban dwellers. An improvement in the quality of life, for which people were willing to work, would have increased their ability to generate even greater income. But that would also have raised the rents of land. This was a two-edged sword. If rental income was public revenue, it would have provided the resources to make communities more habitable. But because rent was privatised, its owners could extract wealth out of the working population and diminish the quality of their lives – for, instead, they had to bear the cost of public services out of taxes on their earned incomes. Thus, in Dudley, not far down the road from Ironbridge in the West Midlands, in 1852 the average age of death was 17 years, which was attributed to the absence of piped water in the town and the dumping of human excrement in all 'back streets, courts and other eligible places'.[34] If the high rents of land in the town had been invested in piped water and sewage systems, the residents of Dudley would have raised the output of their industries and also enjoyed a longer life expectancy. Instead, the rents were leeched away; thereby diminishing the welfare of the folk of Dudley even further.

The panic of '57 went global. Speculation in land in the United States attracted British banks and commercial houses, which speculated on their own accounts. When the bubble burst, the British financial edifice crashed. Wednesday, November 11, 1857, was called Black Wednesday. The City of Glasgow Bank closed its doors. Financial houses in the City of London were insolvent, and between September 7 and November 12, according to Disraeli in the House of Commons, 85 firms terminated their operations with liabilities of at least £42m. Once again, the Bank of England stepped in to issue notes in excess of its legal limits to try and boost trade and stem the financial crisis.

The Banker's Magazine, noting what was going on in Australia, editorialized: 'The evil to be feared ... is Land Jobbing, which shows an extent of speculation highly imprudent and even dangerous ... the new banks, in seeking business, will do wisely in lending no encouragement to the extravagant prices land and house property have now reached'.[35]

1875 No sooner had the country been swept by indebtedness and unemployment following the crash of 1866, than, towards the end of the decade, it all began again, particularly with railway companies. 'Ruin and devastation swept the land, and for the third time in 23 years the Bank Charter Act of 1844 had to be broken and the Bank of England ordered to issue notes in excess of its legal powers.'[36] But this time, there was a new spin on what had become a recurring refrain. In 1875, Parliament appointed a Select Committee to investigate speculation in foreign lands. 'In the three previous years it was estimated that some £60m of British money had been lost in foreign speculation ...'[37]

The bankers, in venturing abroad in search of profits, were also revealing their aristocratic aspirations. For them, economic success was marked by the purchase of country estates on which they could assume the airs of the lord of the manor. Their business decisions were skewed towards land speculation, even if that meant prejudicing commercial enterprise on their home territory. Francis Fukuyama noted how class attitudes intruded to distract financiers.

> This reflected a deeper social cleavage ... between the financiers, working out of the City of London, and the manufacturers in northern cities like Liverpool, Leeds, and Manchester. The former were more easily assimilated into Britain's upperclass culture and tended to look down upon the less refined, more pragmatically educated industrialists from the grimy towns of the North. They often opted for safety and stability, in preference to the long-term risks inherent in funding new industries, and as a result the British electrical and automobile industries never received the level of financing they needed to make them competitive. As was typical throughout British economic history, development was hobbled by class and status barriers that undercut the sense of community and erected unnecessary obstacles to economic cooperation.[38]

The commercial timidity of the financiers did not deliver greater stability for the British economy: it fostered land speculation that wrecked the creative enterprises of the despised towns of the North. When they realised they had been reckless in advancing credit to townsfolk who were buying up farmland, they pulled the plug on the credit. Prices collapsed. Over the course of 20 years the price of farmland had soared, but

> At last, as we all know, the crisis came, and rents began to fall and farmers to be bankrupt. In two years, 10% of the British farmers ... were swept away by failure.[39]

The sharp rise of unemployment in 1878-9 opened a chasm for the skilled men who, as a rule, had managed to avoid what Clapham called 'a fall into the depths'.[40]

1893 The years from 1880 ought to have been good for the working class, which might have expected a rise in the real value of wages as a result of the protracted decline in prices. There was an explosion in membership of trade unions in 1889-90, but people were powerless to neutralise government plans to consolidate the taxation of earned incomes. Historian Eric Hobsbawm noted that 'On balance, indeed, the poor paid more in taxes than they received back in social services'.[41] In 1893, the discontent exploded in the form of the lock-out of coal miners.

The cyclical expansion, with full employment, ran through to 1890 and then turned down. Unemployment trebled, peaking in 1893. The recovery began in 1895.[42] Britain was the world's maritime power at the end of the 19th century, her shipbuilding dockyards supreme in turning out the ships that were the links in an empire that spanned the world. Even so, as the workers of Jarrow discovered, there was no escaping a mid-cycle recession, with the trough in the output of ships hitting the bottom in 1893.

1911 This mid-cycle point is historically significant. Britain had just passed through the constitutional crisis of 1909-10. The House of Lords was deprived of its right to interfere with the nation's budget. The successful political outcome ought to have been the turning point in the democratisation of the public's finances. Why this was so is pregnant with lessons for chancellors of the exchequer in the 21st century.

Roy Jenkins, a former Labour chancellor who authored a book on the biographies of many of his predecessors, reviewed the budget of

1909 – what he called 'the most famous budget of the century'[43] – and then continued:

> After the budget, trade recovered strongly with a good upswing between 1910 and 1913: the budget probably had little to do with that, but at least nonsense was made of Balfour's claim that it would be 'injurious to the productive capacity of the country'.[44]

This assessment is revealing for two reasons. According to our reading of history, land speculation in the first decade of the 20th century ought to have surfaced as a mini boom bust by 1911. Instead – there was a 'good upswing'. How can we account for this in terms of our theory? Jenkins did not read cyclical significance into the terms of David Lloyd George's budget of 1909.

The Liberal Party attempted to change taxation in a way that might have terminated the booms and busts cycle at its source. Liberals campaigned for a restructuring of public finance. There were many peaks of political excitement. One was a vote in the House of Commons on March 11, 1904. The Second Reading of a Bill passed with a majority of 67, supported by politicians like Winston S. Churchill. The Land Values (Assessment and Rating) Bill was promoted by the leading municipalities of Britain, including London, Liverpool, Glasgow and Manchester. The city fathers wanted the right to focus fiscal attention directly on the value of land. *Land Values*, the journal that campaigned for tax reform in the name of American social philosopher Henry George (1839-97), editorialised in its issue of April 1904:

> The questions of employment, housing, health, and all general improvement affecting the social condition of the people come to grief daily as the necessities of the community meet the boundary line of land monopoly.

The editor of *Land Values*, however, forgot his history when, under the momentary influence of the parliamentary triumph, he added: 'There can be no going back'.[45] The aristocrats of the kingdom, with their roots in the countryside and their seats in the House of Lords, had different ideas. The concentration of land into ever fewer, larger estates had proceeded apace, from the enclosures that deprived the villagers of the commons in the 17th and 18th centuries to the amalgamation of small farms into extensive holdings in the 19th century.[46]

The landlords regarded fiscal reform as a threat to their property rights. Their defensive attack was at its most bitter in 1909 in the face of Liberal Party intransigence. There were two crisis elections. In 1910 the Liberal government appeared to consolidate its triumph at the hustings when it defeated the landlords' challenge to the democratic process. The Lords were threatened with dilution: if they did not capitulate, the Upper House would be flooded with new Members who would tilt the balance of power in favour of the people. The land owners fought a rearguard action: ultimately, through delaying tactics and the use of the courts, they defeated the fiscal reform that was promised by the People's Budget.[47] But in the meantime, there was no incentive to engage in land speculation in the turmoil years running up to 1911.

Thus, it appears that the historical evidence does lend credence to the shape of the land and business cycle that we elaborated in Chapter 5.

§3 Speculation as Causation

WE DO NOT claim that the trends that may be traced in the historical record worked with the precision that would impress a Swiss clockmaker. But the deviation by six or even 12 months on either side of the end of an 18-year period, or its mid-way point, does not discredit our theory. Its predictive success means that we have identified an economic mechanism of enormous social significance.

Economists foster the idea that each business cycle is unique. They tend to resist the notion of a recurring drama that compresses events into a pattern that offers reliable predictions. And yet, one word – *speculation* – is repeatedly used by those historians. One of them, Llewellyn Woodward, wrote:

> The growth of speculation was indeed largely responsible for the serious commercial crisis of 1866. Commercial crises had occurred in 1825, 1836–9, 1847, and 1857. The intervals between these crises appeared so regular that there was a good deal of rather vague conjecture about their causes. The memory of speculators was short; a few years after one collapse the lessons were forgotten and rash-minded men began once again to act rashly, but there were also special reasons for each crisis. In each case the nature of the speculation was different, and the 'boom' was brought to a close by different external causes.[48]

Students are encouraged to believe that the recurrence of booms and busts may be attributed to a combination of random events, short memories and the psychological weakness of individuals. The

possibility that the breakdowns result from something internal to
property rights, tax policy and the construction industry is dismissed.
Lewis, for example, after his exhaustive study of the building industry,
concluded that

> In a severe case of overbuilding, possibly made apparent by
> some other crisis which reduces both confidence and real
> incomes, the number of bankruptcies may be large; and many
> years will have to elapse before building firms once again begin
> to rise, as the shadow of speculation leading to ruin slowly ebbs
> into a past generation. This approach to the building cycle has
> been written up by a number of authors, and we shall not deal
> further with it now...[49]

Another opportunity to probe deeper into this repetitive syndrome
of boom and bust was lost. The possibility of a structural fault in
the foundations of that sector is implicitly cast aside. The focus on
individual behaviour is rationalised. The argument goes like this.
Predictable cyclical trends are inconsistent with the theory of rational
behaviour on which the doctrine of the free market rests. If turning
points in activity can be predicted, people would anticipate and profit
from them and thereby diminish their impact. Profit-seeking would
dissipate cycles. Thus, either cycles are random events (and not theoretically explicable), or we need a new theory of behaviour to replace
the version that relies on the rationality of the individual.

We are all attracted to the notion of humans as rational agents, so
why disturb the convenient assumption that the future cannot be
anticipated with accuracy? After all, to concede that damaging turning
points in economic activity can be forecasted entails an obligation to
change the rules of the game. Those who benefit from the current system would not favour such changes. Thus, it is convenient to conclude
that we cannot anticipate the future.

This self-censorship compromises our ability to match progress
with productivity. As science and technology unfolds the secrets of
how to increase wealth, so more people are imprisoned on a treadmill
of drudgery that could, in principle, be abolished. The index that most
dramatically illustrates this latent reality is the rate of increase in the
price of houses. Over the past century, these have eclipsed by far
the increases in other products or people's wages. Living standards
have been squeezed by the need to keep roofs over heads. The statistics tell the story. In 1900 British estate agent Knight Frank advertised
a 15-bedroom stone house near Bath for £9,750. Adjusting figures to
take account of inflation, 100 years later the price of milk showed an

increase of 4,900%, whiskey had risen nearly 6,000% and a similar property had increased by 82,000%.

In 1910 a 5-bedroom house in London's Chelsea was sold by Knight Frank for £1,000. Ninety years later, the same house was worth £4.5 million, an increase of 450,000%. In the estate agent's survey, luxury goods were shown to average an increase of 8,800%. The price of a basket of basic items such as bread, potatoes and coal increased by 12,200%. Compare this with the increase in a 5-bedroom house with under 50 acres whose price increased by 133,000% over the 20th century. The gap between house prices and basic products is widening by the year,[50] but remedial action is compromised by the unwillingness to factor into official analyses the role played by the alchemy of land speculation.

REFERENCES

1 Angus Maddison, *Monitoring the World Economy 1820-1992*, Paris, OECD, 1995, Table D-1a, pp.194-7.
2 Thomas Johnston, *The Financiers and the Nation* [1934], Glasgow: Ossian, 1994.
3 *Ibid.*, p.36.
4 J. Parry Lewis, *op. cit.*, Appendix 1, Table A1:1.
5 Sidney and Beatrice Webb, *English Local Government*, London: Longmans, Green, 1906, p.485.
6 Alan Booth, 'Food riots in the North-West of England 1790-1801', *Past & Present* (77), 1977, p.84.
7 Lewis, *op. cit.*, p.27.
8 Samuel Taylor Coleridge, *Lay Sermons* (R.J. White, ed.), London: Routledge and Kegan Paul, 1972, p.204.
9 George Canning, quoted in Johnston, *op. cit.*, p.2.
10 *Ibid.*, p.3.
11 *Ibid.*, p.15.
12 *Ibid.*, p.20.
13 Oscar R. Hobson, *A Hundred Years of the Halifax*, London: B.T. Batsford, 1953, pp.19, 20, 135.
14 This information is contained in the first Annual Report issued by the Leeds Permanent Building Society in 1850, which records that dwellings could be built for between £70 and £75 (exclusive of any charge for land and streets).
15 Francis Wheen, *Karl Marx*, London: 4th Estate, 1999, p.268.
16 Johnston, *op. cit.*, p.33.
17 *Ibid.*
18 Lewis, *op. cit.*, p.326.
19 *Ibid.*, p.169, Table 7.3.
20 Ellen Wilkinson, *The Town That Was Murdered*, London: Victor Gollancz, 1939, p.103.
21 Lewis, *op. cit.*, p.326.
22 Johnson, *op. cit.*, p.43.
23 Sidney and Beatrice Webb, *The Decay of Capitalist Civilization*, London: Allen and Unwin, 1923, p.107.

24   Harrison, *The Power in the Land*, *op. cit.*, pp.76-8.
25   *Ibid.*
26   *Ibid.*, p.302.
27   Stephen K. Mayo, 'Housing policy: changing the structure', *Finance & Development*, March 1994, p.45, citing Patrick Minford, 'Effects of housing distribution on unemployment', *Oxford Economic Papers*, Vol. 40(2), 1988, pp.322-45, and John Muellbauer and J. Murphy, *Why Has UK Personal Savings Collapsed*, Report prepared for Crédit Suisse, Boston and London offices, 1989.
28   Pf&D Newsletter, 'Residential', January 1994, p.10.
29   Lewis, *op. cit.*, p.26.
30   *Ibid.*, p.29.
31   *Ibid.*, p.30.
32   *Ibid.*, p.31.
33   Johnston, *op. cit.*, p.14.
34   F.B. Smith, *The People's Health 1830-1910*, London: Croom Helm, 1979.
35   *The Banker's Magazine*, London, 1854, Vol. XIV, pp.117-22, cited in Harry W. Nunn, 'Selected Documents from the Nineteenth Century', in Edward B. Hamilton, *The Law and Practice of Banking in Australia and New Zealand*, 2nd edn., London: Maxwell, 1900.
36   Johnston, *op. cit.*, p.34.
37   *Ibid.*, p.34.
38   Francis Fukuyama, *Trust*, London: Penguin, 1996, p.214.
39   J.E. Thorold Rogers, *The Industrial and Commercial History of England*, London: T. Fisher Unwin, 1909, p.84.
40   J.H. Clapham, *An Economic History of Modern Britain: Free Trade and Steel 1850-1886*, Cambridge: University Press, 1932, p.486.
41   E.J. Hobsbawm, *Industry and Empire*, Harmondsworth: Penguin, 1969, p.166.
42   Rostow, *op. cit.*, pp.25, 85, 87.
43   Roy Jenkins, *The Chancellors*, London: Macmillan, 1998, p.166.
44   *Ibid.*, p.169.
45   'The Victory in the Commons', London: *Land Values*, April 1904, p.172.
46   Arthur H. Johnson, *The Disappearance of the Small Landowner* (1909); London: Merlin Press, 1963, Introduction by Joan Thirsk.
47   William Foot, *Maps for Family History. Public Record Office Readers' Guide No. 9. A guide to the records of the Tithe, Valuation Office and National Farm Surveys of England and Wales, 1836-1943*, London: PRO Publications, 1994, p.21.
48   Llewellyn Woodward, *The Age of Reform*, Oxford: University Press, 1962, 2nd edn., p.605.
49   Lewis, *op. cit.*, pp.56-7.
50   Knight Frank, 'The cost of milk, malt and mansions over the century', London, Press release, December 16, 1999.

7

The Alchemy of Land Speculation

§1 Loot I: Nature

ISAAC NEWTON was no slouch when it came to working out what made things fall from a great height. He discovered the law of gravity. Star-gazing was transformed from an occult pastime into a scientific discipline. Unfortunately for his bank balance, however, Newton could not make sense of the laws that animated investors who were gripped with the fever of speculation. He said in 1720: 'I can calculate the motions of the heavenly bodies, but not the madness of the people'.[1] His failure to develop a theory of the motions of business cost him dearly. He bought shares when prices reached their maximum height in the South Sea Bubble. He lost £20,000 – a princely fortune at the time.

Speculation in stocks and shares became the modern equivalent of the medieval quest for the secrets of alchemy. People believed that it was possible to turn mundane metal into glowing gold. They experimented with potions to uncover the code to easy riches. They failed, but hope springs eternal. The desire for loot-without-labour is a daydream that occasionally grips most of us. We gamble even when, in our rational moments, we know that there is no chance of winning the jackpot. Sometimes we turn that passion for something-for-nothing into a social event. That is when people are swept along in a collective excitement to the point where they stake their life's savings on foolish bets.

History is replete with such episodes, but they are different in one crucial respect from the booms and busts that we analysed in Part I: the timings of the events are not predictable. They are random, occurrences driven by the frailties of individual psychology and the passions of collective mania. They lack the institutional buttresses that transform private behaviour into predictable cycles.

The mass hysteria that was beyond the grasp of Isaac Newton gripped the Netherlands in 1636. People went crazy over tulips. Prices

of the several varieties were driven sky-high. The bizarre quest for fortunes attracted gullible people to Amsterdam. The money-men smelt
the prospect of easy pickings. As brokers, credit-creators, dealers in
futures, they evolved some of the crafty arts of modern financial markets. People offered houses and land for sale 'at ruinously low prices'
to raise cash to invest in tulips. Foreign investors poured money into
the Netherlands. This raised the prices of houses, land and the neces-
sities of life. One man offered 12 acres of building land for a rare spec-
imen, such was the delirious effect that the bloom had on formerly
rational people. Prices peaked in November 1636. Slowly, they faltered,
lurched into the doldrums – the market went 'soft' – and then crashed.
The accumulated savings of thrifty people were wiped out. The leading economy in Europe was pushed to the verge of bankruptcy.[2]

Looking back, we can patronisingly view the tulip saga with
humour. It was an event that would not be repeated. Not, that is, for
tulips. No one would fall for such a pathetic dream again, would they?
Since then, people have been wiser. And so, to lure them into new
bouts of mania, it was necessary to beguile them with more sophisticated narratives if they were to be parted from their money. Conmen
and governments were sufficiently ingenious to provide the story lines
that did, indeed, drive people into destitution. While later episodes
were also random events – not orchestrated by an internal financial
logic – they provide insights that make sense of recent financial crises.
Above all, they remind us that governments are an inseparable part of
the process. They legitimise the mania by laying down (if only by
default) the culture that is an essential part of the gambling ethos
that separates sane people from their money. The events of 1720 are
classics from which major lessons can be learnt. It was the year that
witnessed the first global financial crisis.

In Britain, the South Sea Bubble originated with the issue of a royal
warrant in 1711. The government needed to raise revenue and reduce
the national debt. It was ably abetted by the shrewd operators who
were not above making money out of nothing. The illusion that easy
profits were in prospect was built on the monopoly control over the
trade in precious metals from a vast area of the globe, extending from
the west coast of America eastwards to the territory controlled by
the East India Company. Political power was manipulated to assign
territorial franchises to favoured citizens. They built a vast financial
pyramid on the back of the credit-creating system. At one stage the
authorities became alarmed. They passed a 'Bubble Act' to try and
bring events under control. The remedial action was ineffective. The
nation was in the grip of a fevered quest for easy money. In 1720 the

shares of the South Sea Company rose by an astonishing 680%. The punters who bought them paid a terrible price when the bubble burst (60% of the value was lost in two months).

In France, a similar politically-motivated sequence of events swung into action under the tuition of John Law. The Scotsman created a company whose shares reached a peak price in 1720 that was 40 times the level achieved three years earlier. France, whose monarchs had expensive tastes, was in the grip of the fortune-seekers. They, too, had fallen for the story that gold was for the taking; this time, in the vast expanses of Louisiana, where France held the territorial franchise. Law, an accomplished gambler and master of the theory of money, managed a single-handed takeover of the nation's financial system. He introduced the novel idea of paper money, which enabled the king and then the regent to expand the money supply to pay the bills. There was an initial upturn in prosperity. Law made plausible his scheme for national financial salvation and personal enrichment by securing the contracts to trade in Senegalese slaves as well as the precious minerals of Louisiana. No one would have to *manufacture* value, because it could be extracted as rent from bountiful earth.

Unfortunately, in the cases of both the South Sea Company and the Compagnie des Indes, the get-rich-quick merchants failed to deliver on their promises. The prices that investors paid for shares did not match the value of the natural resources that were landed on the quaysides of Bristol or Marseilles. Someone had to lose!

Are we now the wiser for being able to consult these sad episodes of mass mania? It appears not, for similar scams are being perpetrated today. Furthermore, they will occur again, because governments and international financial agencies are not willing to conduct inquests that lay bare the process by which people are bilked of their savings. The scam, however, is simple and neat, and intelligible to anyone who wishes to learn the lessons.

In the decade leading to the financial showdowns of 1720, the entrepreneurs behind the bubbles in Britain and France worked out that they could get rich even if they sidestepped one essential stage in the process of creating wealth. They could take golden handshakes and quit the markets without having to dirty their hands with the awful business of producing the goods and services that customers would pay to consume. What was the mechanism for achieving this delightful solution to the age-old mystery of alchemy?

The formula was unbelievably simple. You sell, today, company shares at prices that capitalise the *future* stream of rental income from natural resources. That rental income is securitised and traded on the stock exchanges, which at the time were in an embryonic form. An essential step was persuading prospective investors that the companies held the leases to valuable natural resources from which they would extract the rents. Natural resources are under the jurisdiction of kings and governments, which is why there had to be a partnership between the money-men and the power brokers. By exploiting their political connections, the merchants could publicise the fact that they had acquired leases and franchises on favourable terms.

The trick was to capture the rents immediately. The laborious task of extracting and transporting the natural resources to market would take time. If investors could be persuaded that the companies would one day be profitable, they would buy the shares today at tomorrow's prices. That would enable the original speculators to take cash up-front and run. Shareholders would be left with the business of having to deliver a value to consumers, if they wanted to recover their capital. Unfortunately for the British and French investors, gold was not strewn for the easy picking, whether approached from the east (across the Pacific) or the west (across the Atlantic). There were no rents for the taking – then. When that distressing lesson finally dawned on the investors, the markets collapsed.

It could not happen today? It did – twice – in the 1990s.

● A similar scam underpinned much of the 'emerging markets' mania that terminated in the financial meltdown in Asia. Like the South Sea and Mississippi Bubbles, the Asian bubble was (in part) inflated by people who did not want the trouble of having to deliver the goods to consumers at values that made sense of the share prices.

Entrepreneurs with political connections tied up deals to harvest (for example) mahogany trees from the rain forests of the Philippines. Because their privileged leases required them to pay low rents that bore no relation to prospective market values, the rents of valuable timber were privatised by default. But why undertake the drudgery of felling the trees and hauling them to the mills and to the carpenters who would turn them into tables for the fashionable apartments of Paris and Rome? Instead, the entrepreneurs offered shares on the Bangkok bourse. Brokers in the City of London and Wall Street worked out that these were 'under-priced'. Shareholders, not the citizens of the nations that owned the resources, would be able to capture the rents. The brokers capitalised those rents into the price of the shares which they offered to investors. The bottom had to fall out of the market. This it did with a vengeance, inflicting economic trauma on victim populations throughout south-east Asia. They were the people who had earned the title of 'Tigers' for the hard and skilled work that went into creating quality goods for sale in the world's markets.

● As the West's financial institutions were assembling 'rescue packages' for the governments and banks of the Asian tigers, yet another classic bubble was being inflated in North America and Europe: the dot.com scam was in the making.

This, too, offered dreams of unearned riches for the cunning individuals who got in at the beginning. The politicians and financiers played their part in legitimising the panic buying of the shares of companies that came to market with balance sheets that showed massive losses, no assets, and few immediate prospects, but with wild expectations about the value of their shares. The illusion could not have been pulled off if it had not been endorsed by financial analysts and the auditors who certified as accurate the accounts of the companies that were on the prowl for counterfeit profits.

America's prosperity of the late 1990s was built on that dream. So desperate were people to leap into cyberspace that share prices were pushed into vertical lift off. In 1998 the Standard & Poor's 500 index rose 25%, its fourth successive annual gain of over 20%. Families stopped saving cash for that rainy day because they believed the fructifying value of shares would secure their future. Indeed, savings were negative in the third quarter of 1998. The bubble in equities, blown up with the air from outer space, floated the US economy into new heights of euphoria. Have no fears, however, all would be well. The confidence-building Chairman of the Federal Reserve, Alan Greenspan – the Master of Economic Metaphysics – reassured the nation's governors that their economy had shifted from a 'physical' basis of production towards a 'conceptual' basis.[3] The American people were persuaded that they could live on thin air. The fall was painful.

It would be easy to censure investors who risked the security for which they had worked all their lives in the pursuit of a virtual fortune, but we should recall that they were following a precedent. The mediaeval alchemists may have failed to unlock the secret of turning base into precious metal, but the rents of land and natural resources *are* a more certain source of easy money for some people. Everyday experiences confirmed that fact.

● The shares of mines in West Australia and in Colorado aroused great excitement at the beginning of the 20th century. People became millionaires virtually overnight. That the gold was not in transit, at the time, did not deter investors from handing over money. They had a dream ... One of them, Whitaker Wright, acquired a luxury home in London's Park Lane and lived the high life before going broke. He was convicted but he avoided gaol by ending his life with cyanide.

● The nation-state is not averse to speculation in resource rents, as became apparent in the 1970s with the manipulation of oil rents. A cartel, OPEC, learnt how to manage the markets to extract the maximum oil-rents for their nations (or the elites that monopolised the power of the state).

Who do you blame if, on balance, the losses from these activities exceed the gains? If the pleasure of landing a windfall fortune is eclipsed by the pain of the many who are left destitute?

§2 Loot II: Taxpayers

THE EPISODES discussed above relied primarily on the rents that flow from the raw resources of nature. But rent is as complex as civil-isation, a multi-layered income that derives its value from the synergy of communities interacting with their natural habitats. With the progress into the post-feudal era, and the onset of industrialisation, people invested a growing share of income in capital intensive infra-structure – railways, for example, and the sewer systems that enhance public health. This intensification of investment in capital, working through the market processes such as competition to allocate resources where they could be most efficiently used, deepened and expanded rental income. And this became the primary basis for a routinised extraction of rent by speculators.

In this new era, landowners were handed Pandora's Box. This con-tained the secrets of getting rich without the risk of being swept away by the manias that inflated the bubbles of the past. It was a less exotic kind of rent which they sought. The revenue was a steady but sure flow of income from within their own communities. And it was made all the more secure by the connivance of political groups that were willing to adapt property rights in favour of a privileged few.

The technique assumes various guises. In Britain, planning permis-sion can convert a field worth £200 an acre into, say, £200,000. The landowner is enriched by doing nothing. This is the alchemy on which the greatest fortunes in history were built and continue to be nourished. That was understood by Lord de Ramsey, who was head of the British government's Environment Agency in 1998 when he sold a tract to a property developer for an estimated £300,000. With cows on it, the land was not worth much. But when the council granted planning permission for 17 houses, what was dirt cheap was transformed at the stroke of a pen into pay dirt. The Lord aroused controversy when it was discovered that he planned to sell 20 acres of Cambridgeshire farmland for what was estimated to be more than £1 million.[4] The speculators in the shares of internet companies were not, in reality, far removed from old-fashioned land speculators like Lord de Ramsey. They wanted a share of the rents of cyberspace.

TABLE 7:1

House Prices and Ownership Rates: Selected countries

	Price growth (1995-2002) *% real increase*	*Ownership rate* *%*	*Year*
Ireland	152	78	2000
UK	89	69	1999
Netherlands	83	51	2000
Spain	58	83	1998
Australia	48	70	2001
USA	27	67	1999
France	31	55	1999
Italy	8	70	1998
Canada	2	64	1999
Germany	-13	43	1998
Japan	-10	n.a.	

Source: Productivity Commission, *First Home Ownership*, Report No. 28, Melbourne, 2004, pp.19, 33.

Land values rely on taxpayers to finance public services by paying into the public purse more than they take out of it. In this way, there is a surplus that may be distributed to those with the property rights who appropriate windfall fortunes. Thus, much of the boom in Spanish property prices may be directly attributed to the European Union's funding of infrastructure such as highways, which put previously inaccessible parts of the coastline within easy reach of regional airports. In fact, the generosity of Europe's taxpayers underpinned much of the uplift in property prices throughout the Union. The country that benefited most was Ireland, into which flowed billions of euros from Brussels. The money was intended to raise the quality of people's lives in what had been a backwater of the European economy. The outcome was the transformation of tax revenue into land values, with Irish house prices increasing at rates far above any other European nation (Table 7:1).

Once the best of the capital gains had been sucked out of Ireland, the Irish speculators turned their attention to the markets in Eastern Europe. This meant projects in Ireland went short of investment. Transport infrastructure in Dublin suffers from severe under-investment. The government of Premier Bertie Ahern found that it could not afford to provide the trains and highways that the economy needed. Why not? Because the mere announcement of an intention to expand the infrastructure was sufficient for owners to increase the price of their land to levels that would capture the net benefits from the taxpayers' investment – and they wanted the money up-front, before the first section of rail track was laid. And so, at the beginning of the 21st century, Ireland's economy remained unbalanced, with exorbitantly high land prices and over-extended public services.

The Irish government declined to amend the constitution to legitimise a land value-capture mechanism, even though the case for this was powerfully championed by the Dublin Transportation Office.[5] Worse, however, the political failure to recalibrate the tax structure was aggravated by the stamp duty payable on property transactions. This was deemed to be unacceptably high by property owners, and they exercised their legal right not to sell.[6] Thus, perverse political decisions on taxation drove Irish money into the property markets of other countries.[7] Spain was on the target list of countries that would yield bumper gains. So along with British and Scandinavian investors, the Irish directed much of their profits into Iberian land deals. And as is always the case, the best deals emerge on the back of infrastructural projects funded by taxpayers.[8] This fiscal contagion does not receive attention by those who complain about property prices.

The scope for windfall gains is illustrated by the extension of the motorway along the coast between Malaga and Motril. A 50 km extension, partly funded by the EU, opened up a new stretch of coast to Europe's sun-seekers. Syndicates bought properties along the route in advance of the expensive engineering and tunnelling that was made necessary by the hilly coastline. One syndicate bought a villa on 8,000 sq. m. of land on a cliff top overlooking almond and olive tree terraces and a fishing village. The property was bought in 2001 for €200 per sq. m. With the motorway from Malaga inching its way up the coast, the syndicate could sell two building plots from their property and recover their full original purchase price while retaining the villa. Their prime land had tripled in value within three years. This was a windfall courtesy of Europe's taxpayers, and no amount of stress testing of Spanish banks could moderate the inflation of coastal land values.[9]

The alternative to removing the capital gains from land – by re-cycling them back into paying for the infrastructure – is intrusive bureaucratic and legal methods. These not only do not work, they create additional problems. That is what happened in Spain's Valencia region. A law was passed that was ostensibly intended to prevent land hoarders from obstructing urban development. The outcome was a 'land grab' in which unscrupulous developers appropriated other people's land *and* made them pay more than their share towards the costs of infrastructure, to the considerable profit of the developers! Danny Loveridge, who retired to a 130-year-old farmhouse in the town of Benissa, fell foul of this law, known as La Ley Reguladora de la Actividad Urbanistica (1994). Part of his land was appropriated. He received £8,000 compensation. He was then forced to pay the developers £12,500 for infrastructure for a proposed industrial estate, and then to sell what remained of a £260,000 property for about £100,000.[10] This was a botched attempt to recycle rises in land values to pay for the investment that caused the value in the first place. The underlying philosophy was commendable, but the implementation was crude and corrupt.

Unfortunately, politicians are not anxious to restructure the public's finances to remove the windfall gains that animate the booms and busts. So that leaves them with the problem of absolution for their own failings.

§3 Blame it on God

ONE OF the puzzles of social science is that, despite two centuries of consistent disruption to the production of wealth, governments and their advisers have not been able to abolish the speculative activity that is the basis of so much collective grief. Could the mind-sets of the experts be coloured by a purposeful streak of irrationality of the kind that is *designed* to subvert public policy? We could be forgiven for sus-pecting this possibility when we review the way in which politicians and economists – people who willingly assume responsibility for the economy – rationalise their explanations for booms and busts. The accounts of the economic failures in Britain between 1988 and 1992 reinforce the suspicion that policy-makers are incapable of thinking straight about the business cycle.

The man who presided over the Treasury in the mid-1980s was Nigel Lawson, a portly gentleman who stoutly championed Margaret Thatcher's brand of monetarism. He, like previous incumbents of the Treasury, was determined to prevent another economic catastrophe, and he was well equipped to do so. No one contested his right to regulate monetary policy on the basis of free market principles. Alas, the crash came in the early 1990s. Why? According to the mortified Lawson, it was, he concluded after deep reflection, futile to try and escape the inevitable. He wrote in his memoirs: 'There always has been, and always will be, an economic cycle'.[11]

If true, this was consolation for his bruised political pride. If boom busts are the result of a law of nature (in which case, why did its mechanics escape Isaac Newton?), there is little that vigilant guardians of the nation's finances can do about it.

But would those stewards of the economy be more effective in their counter-cyclical strategies if they could trace the problems to their origins? 'The first indicator of the recession that lay ahead was house prices,' wrote Lawson. 'These, which had been rising at a staggering annual rate of over 30 per cent at the end of 1988, had calmed down to a rather more sober 10 per cent by the time of my resignation ...'[12] Why, if Lawson realised that the housing sector provided the early warning system, did he *exacerbate* the upward trend in prices – in the Winner's Curse phase – by his financial and fiscal policies in 1988? It seems that Lawson and his Treasury economists had no idea about the *timing* or the *scale* of the looming recession; so he was not on his guard when house prices began their surge in 1986. He confessed:

> What made it all seem worse than it was was the failure of the forecasters to predict the severity of the recession, and their subsequent predictions of a recovery which did not materialize – which led Norman Lamont to make his unfortunate 1991 reference to the 'green shoots of recovery'.[13]

For the hapless Lamont, who followed Lawson into the Treasury, the devastating recession that hit rock bottom in 1992 had to be explained in terms that also exonerated him from the failures of policy. To whom could he attribute responsibility? The business cycle, it dawned on him after his bout of introspection, was what the insurance industry calls an Act of God.

> And the fact is you do have recessions, you do have trade cycles, and no amount of sophisticated twiddling knobs can avoid that; and it may be very tempting to try to blame a building [the Treasury] and a number of people in it for the fact that the sun

rises or the sun sets, but it's inherent in the world in which we live.[14]

And so the Hard Men of the nation's monetary system, spearheading the Thatcherite campaign with the steeliest of Chicago School nostrums, sought solace in Marxist doctrines: it was all historically inevitable.

True, Lawson was to write, the problem did seem to be associated with a 'pronounced credit cycle', and this was 'exacerbated by the nature of the housing sector, and the exceptionally high incidence of owner-occupation'.[15] But he could not be held responsible for the explosive increase in credit in Britain during his watch, could he? He was only the Chancellor of the Exchequer who held the monetary levers in his hands. And he could not be responsible for the high incidence of owner-occupation of houses, could he? He was only a member of the Cabinet that had privatised the stock of social housing during The Great Thatcher Asset Sell-off!

It was a pathetic performance, both in government service and in the self-serving explanations for failure. Perhaps, after all, Newton should have devoted more time to searching 'the motions of the heavenly bodies' for the causes of the business cycle, rather than being bewildered by the 'madness of the people'! Or maybe the Treasury, rather than collecting and analysing terrestrial data, should turn to astrologers for guidance? There are, after all, some who believe that the business cycle is determined by the 9-year celestial orbit of Mercury.

> [The] nine-year rhythm controls prices and the stock market, the recurrence of financial crises, building activity (18 years), and many other factors reflecting the curious waves of optimism and pessimism, initiative and depression, which mark all economic and industrial phenomena. Such a cycle is most pronounced in industrial societies. It appears very strongly in large cities, and is particularly characteristic of the United States.[16]

For those who favour more mundane, earthly explanations, I have described the financial mechanism that appears to account for the booms and busts, both as to timing and severity of the trends. For example, the theory enabled me to warn of what would happen to the British economy in sufficient time for the authorities to put up the barricades during the Thatcher years. My first red alert was published in 1983. *The Power in the Land* predicted that the economy would be in the trough of a recession in 1992. I submitted a warning in a memorandum to the Treasury in 1988. At the same time, I published the news in the hope that those with a direct interest in protecting the

housing industry – in particular, Shelter, the housing charity – would
lobby Parliament and the government in favour of remedial reforms.
In Shelter's magazine, *ROOF*, I wrote:

> Eventually, as builders use up their land banks – and currently
> they hold stocks that will last them another 20 months [until
> 1990] – they discover that it is impossible to get the raw land
> that they need, so they go out of business. All this helps to push
> the economy into a tailspin ...'[17]

Such predictions are not based on batteries of computers, armies of
economists or mountains of data, or a telescope to the stars. They rely
on a straightforward understanding of how the economy works and
malfunctions. Unfortunately, far from condemning the policy failures,
the experts seek solace in the claim that there are, after all, benefits to
be derived from recessions. So why cry over spilt milk?

§4 The Costs of Carnage

MERVYN KING, as Governor of the Bank of England, spoke with
authority when he claimed that 'productivity in those recessions did
benefit from the demise of the least efficient firms'.[18] Carnage among
entrepreneurs, apparently, raises the level of efficiency. That is what
the statistics apparently reveal to the Bank of England. The Treasury
appears to concur, because it decided to finance yet another quasi-
governmental organisation, this one with the task of dragging builders
into the 21st century. The Treasury gave £7.5m of taxpayers' money to
Construction Excellence, headed by Dennis Lenard, to propose ideas
for improving productivity on building sites. Lenard pronounced the
industry 'stuck in the 1980s ... It is an industry suffering from complacency'. Life was so easy, apparently, that companies did not need to
improve their service to customers.[19]

The doctrine that recessions might at least be condoned for their
therapeutic benefit was given academic respectability by John
Kenneth Galbraith, professor of economics emeritus at Harvard
University. As the author of *The Great Crash*, the account of the 1929
collapse that continues to be a best seller, his views are from someone
revered as a guru of the Left. Under the guise of pragmatism and a
sense of humanity, Galbraith offers his quasi-socialist interpretation of
the business cycle. We may call it the Enema Theory of Recessions.

> We've had this for several hundred years ... Good times bring
> into existence, first incompetent business executives; second,

wrongful government policies in many cases; and, third, speculators. Working together, they ensure the eventual bust, and this is part of the system ... This has been going on for several hundred years and I see no great change.[20]

The booms and busts are characterised as the failures of frail individuals from business and politics. But for Galbraith, there is a silver lining to these recessions. They offer a 'salutary cleansing process, and I can't but think that there are circumstances now that one day will require that process. As one example, does anyone imagine that we have enough financial intelligence to manage the vast number of mutual funds that now exist'.[21] After the binge, the cathartic expelling of the waste. Here we have a justification for recessions as an instrument for punishing profligacy. People needed shaking up! This thesis from the Masters of Economics warrants scrutiny. Let us consider the construction industry.

How could Britain's builders afford to ignore the technological advances that were deployed by firms in continental Europe? Administrative techniques were accelerating the production of homes out of pre-assembled materials on the residential sites of Sweden. Germany was using robotics to cut the costs of construction. Why were UK entrepreneurs relying on east European migrant labourers to undertake manual tasks that ought to have been banned as obsolete?

Blaming the construction industry is a convenient distraction from the principal reason why builders *can afford to be inefficient*. Some of them, by exploiting the alchemy of the land market, add to the general woes of the economy and curtail the risk of competition. First, the cyclical busts destroy the small and medium-sized firms that are most likely to challenge the big builders. With each recession, the vulnerable small firms are bankrupted; skills are lost as workers seek employment in other industries; and apprentices are not trained. Protected from this process are the firms that expand into speculating in land, rather than building houses for their customers. They are land bankers first, builders second.

If Gordon Brown wanted to improve productivity in the construction industry, appropriate remedial action is not of the advisory kind (at the expense of taxpayers). The solution is to restructure taxes in a way that would make everyone winners: induce the builders to build, and provide houses at prices people can afford. Such action, however, is possible only if the chancellor understood the dynamics of the land market, as manipulated by builders-cum-speculators. He could not plead ignorance. The evidence was supplied by Kate Barker, whom he commissioned to investigate why the supply of houses fell short of demand. A year of exhaustive consultation up and down the land led Barker to this account of how builders operate:

> [O]nce land is acquired competitive pressure in the industry is reduced. In some localities a single house builder may have significant market power while the site is built out. Many house builders 'trickle-out' houses, controlling production rates to protect themselves against price volatility and any adverse influence on prices in the local housing market ... this reduces responsiveness and while it may be rational behaviour for house builders, given that land is a scarce resource which society values, it is unlikely to be optimal for society as a whole. Faster rates of production may be more socially beneficial.[22]

The monopoly power intrinsic to the land market is appropriated by builders – those who can assemble strategically located sites – and used to extract rents out of the economy. To achieve this, it pays the builders not to produce all the houses that people need. Profits from land speculation are sufficient to yield the return to shareholders that makes it possible for the industry to neglect the best practices being developed in those economies – such as Germany's – where speculation in residential property is not a national pathology.

Where does this leave the claim that recessions are good for business – by weeding out uncompetitive firms?

Efficient firms are squeezed into bankruptcy not because they cannot compete for customers, but because the Bank of England, responding to the effects of land speculation, raises the cost of borrowing money. Among the victims are building firms that *can* deliver affordable properties. It is when the cost of the land, coupled with the cost of borrowing money, are conjoined to levels that neither the builders nor their customers can afford, that firms are driven to short-term malpractices that preserve antediluvian methods.

Firms that cannot make super profits out of land are among the victims. These include the manufacturers of the products that are needed on building sites. Table 7:2 traces the cyclical instability since the decade before the Barber boom of the early '70s. The trends are monitored by the Construction Products Association. The suppliers of on-site materials are obliged by competition to keep their profit margins keen and the quality of their products high. What they cannot do is ring-fence themselves against land speculation. And so, with every passing recession, more firms are wiped out; skills are cast adrift and the industry becomes less willing to invest in innovation.

TABLE 7:2

The UK Construction Industry

	1960s: Boom	1970s: Bust	1980s: Boom	1990s: Bust	Trend
Construction Activity	4.5%	-0.5%	3.2%	-0.1%	1.8%
GDP Growth	3.2%	2.43%	2.4%	1.75%	2.5%

Source: Construction Products Association, *The Next Ten Years*, London, n.d. [2000], p.1.

Among the losers are firms that manufacture products for the construction industry. That sector has an annual turnover of £40bn. When the Bank of England raises interest rates, to try and counteract 'inflation', fewer products are bought and invested in buildings. As we see in Table 7:2, the historical consequences are serious: the sector is denied the benefit of expanding in line with the rest of the economy. If the growth of output in construction during the 1970s and 1990s had matched that of the wider economy, the sector would have enjoyed, on average, an additional £15.4bn a year during the 1970s and £22.9bn a year during the 1990s. This translates, for members of the Construction Products Association, into losses of £6bn a year in the 1970s and £9bn a year in the 1990s.[23] The trends in production over the 18-year cycle – growth in the second half terminated by the recession, followed by protracted losses in the first half of the following cycle – creates a two-steps-forward/one-step-backwards tango that leaves millions of people marooned in the social Exclusion Zone.

The construction industry now accounts for less than 7% of GDP. This is a lower level of investment in construction output, as a proportion of GDP, than any other European country. One consequence is reduced competitiveness as the built environment regresses behind the UK's European partners. Following the Lawson boom of the late 1980s, the 1990s was a decade in which the UK economy grew by 20% but construction activity ended the decade below the levels it achieved at the end of the 1980s. For land dealers, the speculative process may be the next best thing to uncovering the mediaeval secrets of alchemy. But their gains are more than offset by the losses to manufacturers. One product of this cyclical havoc is the emergence of moonlighting cowboy operations. Another is that, in the boom years of the first decade of the 21st century, a shortage of labour skills constrained the output of residential and commercial properties. But why should the construction industry gear itself up for steady-state

growth when the Brown boom of the 2000s will be followed by yet
another lost decade, following the depression of 2010?

Is it surprising that, for people who earn their incomes by working,
saving and investing, land speculation is a black art?

REFERENCES

1   Quoted in Edward Chancellor, *Devil Take the Hindmost*, London: Macmillan, 1999,
    p.69.
2   This summary is based on Charles Mackay, *Extraordinary Popular Delusions, and the
    Madness of Crowds* [1841], New York: Noonday Press, 1932, pp.89-97.
3   Gerard Baker, 'Greenspan hails US labour flexibility', *Financial Times*, July 12, 2000.
4   Lucy Johnston & Jonathan Calvert, 'His job is to protect the land. Now he's
    ripping it up', *The Observer*, London, June 14, 1998.
5   *Private Property*, All-Party Oireachtas Committee on the Constitution, Ninth
    Progress Report, Dublin: Stationery Office, 2004, pp.A51-A60.
6   Lisa Urquhard, 'Emerald tiger pounces across the water', *Financial Times*, July 23,
    2004.
7   The corruption associated with planning permission and property deals in Ireland
    have been the subject of a number of sensational public enquiries. Some of the
    most senior politicians were implicated. On July 27, 2004, Judge Matthew P.
    Smith, Chairman of the Independent Standards in Public Offices Commission,
    issued their annual report in which he warned that 'we have reached a stage in this
    country where it is no longer acceptable to merely aspire to meeting the require-
    ments of openness, transparency and accountability. This is now an imperative'.
8   The Irish scandals which involved large sums as back-handers to politicians were
    closely related to transport infrastructure. See Harrison, *Wheels of Fortune*, forth-
    coming.
9   Don Riley, 'The Infrasurfer's Paradise', *Economic Affairs*, March 2005.
10 'Spanish land grabs condemned', *The Guardian*, July 13, 2004.
11 Nigel Lawson, *The View from No. 11: Memoirs of a Tory Radical*, London: Bantam
    Press, 1992, p.628.
12 *Ibid.*, p.1017.
13 *Ibid.*, p.1018.
14 Norman Lamont, Interview, *Despatches*, Channel 4, November 24, 1993.
15 *Op. cit.*, pp.1018, 1019.
16 Rodney Collin, *The Theory of Celestial Influence*, London: Vincent Stuart, 1954,
    p.285.
17 Fred Harrison 'Towards the Crash of 1992', *ROOF*, London: Shelter, September-
    October 1988, pp.42-3.
18 Mervyn King, Speech to CBI Scotland, Glasgow, June 14, 2004, p.4.
19 Jim Pickard, 'Britain 20 years behind, says building adviser', *Financial Times*, June
    1, 2004.
20 Asmina Caminis, 'Challenges of the New Millennium', *Finance & Development*,
    Washington, DC: IMF, December 1999, p.5.
21 *Ibid.*
22 Kate Barker, *Securing our Future Housing Needs*, *op. cit.*, p.13.
23 Allan Wilén, Economics Director, Construction Products Association, London:
    personal communication. All figures are in 2000 constant prices.

8

The End of Boom Bust?

§1 A Doctrine of Despair

IT WAS TO BE a revolution of the mind. As he wrote his treatise on the causes of recessions, John Maynard Keynes penned a letter to the playwright George Bernard Shaw to express his state of mind. His book, he claimed, 'will largely revolutionise ... the way the world thinks about economic problems'. He had a clear target.

> When my new theory has been duly assimilated and mixed with politics and feelings and passions, I can't predict what the final upshot will be in its effect on action and affairs. But there will be a great change, and, in particular, the Ricardian foundations of Marxism will be knocked away.[1]

The classical economists, from Adam Smith and David Ricardo through to Karl Marx, based their theories on the social laws that determined the distribution of the nation's income. Ricardo (1772–1823), a wealthy stock broker, was a key figure in the evolution of classical economics. His name has gone down in history for the contribution he made into how the rent of land emerges in a dynamic economy. Ricardo recognised that rent was not a cost of production in the sense of increasing the unit prices of products and services that were traded in the markets. Because of competition, the identical pair of shoes could be bought for the same price in a high-rent central city store as in a low-rent suburban shopping mall. The level of rents did not affect the price of the products that were offered for sale. Rent was the transfer of part of the income of the nation to people who, *as land owners*, added nothing to the sum total of wealth.

Keynes' mission, as he declared it in his letter to Bernard Shaw on January 1, 1935, was to kick the Ricardian foundations from beneath the feet of modern economists. As a Cambridge economist and consultant to the UK Treasury, Keynes was well placed to influence the way politicians thought and felt and tackled the major problems. The most pressing challenge wàs recessions. Keynes lived through the Depression that followed the Crash of '29. So *The General Theory of Employment Interest and Money* (1936) was intended to be the blueprint for abolishing mass unemployment.

Classical economists believed that the market could self-regulate itself to full employment. In the model that was specified by Adam Smith, as we argue in §4 below, this might have been possible. But something evidently went awry, because the booms and busts continued to recur with tedious regularity. For Keynes, the solution was to shift the focus away from considerations of how income was distributed and on to the mechanisms that led to the production of that income. A macroeconomic approach was required, one in which government would play a major role in ensuring steady growth over time.

Keynes dominated government economic thinking for more than 30 years. His influence remains with us today through his contribution to the Bretton Woods Conference which led to the creation of the International Monetary Fund and the World Bank. But was his project realised? Is the economy a more stable operating system thanks to grand modelling and management of the economy?

Economists now promote the view that the world has reached calm waters after the turbulent period from the First World War to the Korean War. Except for the instability of the 1970s, the past 50 years are sliced up into periods with reassuring names like the Golden Age (the decade up to 1973) and the 'Nice' decade (the 1990s). What these economists cannot agree on, however, is whether the stability they discern is likely to last. Nor are they qualified to pronounce on whether the volatility remains an endemic feature of the capitalist economy, for the good reason that 'there is little agreement amongst researchers about the main drivers' behind the stability which they claim to have perceived in the statistics.[2]

Because of this theoretical weakness, analysts are driven to developing doctrines that appear to give them authority but which fill people with despair. They champion an ideology of the market that contradicts the facts which they chronicle. This presents us with fascinating psychodramas which are worth interrogating. They illuminate some of the themes that are neglected by economics. Once again, we can do no better than refer to the metaphysics propagated by Alan Greenspan.

The doctrine of despair is sheathed in the syllogisms that offer the appearance of scientific rigour and integrity. Greenspan's analysis, which he laid before the Council on Foreign Relations in New York on

July 12, 2000, is revealing. He found it 'disturbing' that we were unable to anticipate crises such as the Mexican financial implosion in 1994 and the East Asian episode in 1997.

> Of course, something in the nature of such events may preclude their being foreseen, in that the market forces that produce a crisis would likely fend it off if it were anticipated.[3]

Having asserted the futility of identifying causes, Greenspan tantalises us with features of recent crises which he claims could not have been anticipated. Take the crises that dislocated the Asian Tigers, the US and Swedish economies in the 1990s.

- 'Net private capital inflows into emerging markets roughly quadrupled between 1990 and 1997 ... [T]here were simply not enough productive investment opportunities to yield the returns that investors in industrial countries were seeking. It was perhaps inevitable then that the excess cash found its way in too many instances into ill conceived and unwisely financed ventures, including many in real estate.'
- 'Although it might seem that the full consequences were predictable, they were not. Problems with imprudently financed real estate investments emerge with chronic frequency around the globe without triggering the size of the collapse experienced in East Asia in 1997.'
- '[W]hen American banks seized up in 1990 as a consequence of a collapse in the value of real estate collateral, the capital markets, largely unaffected by the decline in values, were able to substitute for the loss of bank financial intermediation [without which] the mild recession of 1991 likely would have been far more severe.'
- 'The speed with which [Sweden's] financial system overcame an early 1990 real estate crisis offers a stark contrast with the long-lasting problems of Japan ...'

The feature that recurs is the propensity for resources to flow into 'real estate'. That fact is uncontested. Real estate is the monitor of seismic economic disturbances. Curiously, however, Greenspan and the other central bankers who preach the need for transparency to governments of the Third World remain silent on the necessity for sophisticated statistical data to monitor the land market. There may, of course, be an ulterior motive. Greenspan's Federal Reserve Board, for example, assembled and analysed statistics on land values in such a nonsensical way that it was embarrassed into suspending the publication of its estimates in 1994. Its methodology made land values disappear! Corporate-owned land was estimated to have a *negative* value. Sites on Manhattan, according to US central bank estimates, were worthless.[4] Who bene'fits from this cavalier treatment of the rental income of the nation's most precious asset? According to Michael Hudson, 'it helps land owners and their creditors get a free ride out of asset-price inflation – The Bubble'.[5]

Having let the cat out of the bag by his review of financial crises in the 1990s, Greenspan felt comfortable about assuring his audience of Wall Street financiers that their hands were clean.

> To repeat, we do not, and probably cannot, know the precise nature of the next international financial crisis. That there will be one is as certain as the persistence of human financial indiscretion. We can be reasonably sure that it will not be exactly the same as past crises. Crises never are the same because market participants do not, as readily as supposed, repeat their mistakes of the past. Therefore, we need flexible institutions that can adapt to the unforeseeable needs of the next crisis, not financial Maginot Lines that endeavour to fend off revisiting previous crises that will not be replicated.

They do not, and cannot, know, because they turn the proverbial blind eye on the land market. Their doctrine of despair preaches the need for plastic institutions and seat-of-the-pants judgments which have to be entrusted to the guiding hands of the official experts. Defensive action cannot be taken to avoid the crises that surface with persistent regularity in the real estate sector. So, because the problems are evidently nothing to do with the laws and institutions that buttress the system, governments must shift responsibility for economic breakdown on to reckless individuals. It cannot be the system itself that is flawed, because – as Greenspan puts it – 'there are good reasons to believe that properly structured, the markets themselves can provide the self-correcting discipline that is so necessary to financial stability'. It appears that, despite three centuries of boom busts, the diagnosticians are able to persuade themselves that, *as currently structured*, the self-correcting market is a meaningful notion even though they have still not identified a self-correcting mechanism that actually works. Was Keynes' target, the Ricardian basis of classical economics, the wrong one? Or might there be a reason why the experts would wish to distract us from Ricardo's market-based theses?

The financial gurus who directed huge sums of people's savings into the emerging markets in the 1990s made conscious decisions to invest in real estate. The losses between June 1997 and August 1998 on a worldwide basis were estimated to have exceeded $1 trillion, according to Greenspan.[6] That loss was more than enough to finance all the schools and hospitals people need around the world. It was money down the drain, thrown away by highly paid financial experts who knew what *they* were doing when they chased the capital gains from land and natural resources. In the initial phase of the land boom, they were acting rationally according to the rules. When the Winner's Curse kicked in the schedule of winners and losers could be constructed. And as usual, taxpayers were the guaranteed losers. They financed the bail-out operations that are launched to rescue reckless financiers from their imprudent money-lending practices. The costs are enormous (Table 8:1).

TABLE 8:1

Banking Crises: Cost of re-capitalisation

	Period	Cost as percent of GDP
Finland	1991-3	8.0
Norway	1987-9	4.0
Spain	1977-85	16.0
Sweden	1991	6.4
United States (S&L)	1984-91	3.2

Source: I.J. Macfarlane, 'The changing nature of economic crises', Reserve Bank of Australia *Bulletin*, December 1997, p.19.

Greenspan confesses: 'Extensive efforts of recent years to bolster our international financial structure through enhanced regulatory supervision have too often proved ineffective'. Could this be because they were not looking for the source of the problem? That they had massaged the relevant statistics into kingdom come? Could it be that Keynes was wrong? That it is not possible for governments to manage the economy – *as it is at present constituted* – to remove the violent oscillations in output? How would we square this failure with their claim to have a grip on the economy conceptually, and statistically, through their massive macroeconomic models? If they are correct, then recessions must be shocks that emerge from external sources. Furthermore, those shocks must be random. If they are bolts from the blue, governments and central bankers cannot be held responsible. Inconveniently for governments and bankers, however, their *descriptions* always bring them back to the role of real estate as a central feature of economic turmoil.

§2 Economic Metaphysicians

HOW IS IT possible for eminent bankers, scholars and informed commentators to misdiagnose major events that have profound implications for people's lives? I believe the answer is to be found in the psychological condition that we may call selective amnesia. This is produced by economists and their political patrons who, in the past, fostered the conditions in which the land market and its peculiarities were erased from public and scientific discourse. Ironically, given his status as a champion of counter-cyclical theory, one of the major contributors to this void in knowledge was John Maynard Keynes. He was a master of the art of economic metaphysics.

The dearth of information about land is one demonstration of my claim that capitalism, to preserve itself in its present form, has to inflict selective amnesia on the host population. The architects of capitalism, those who intervened in the fate of the nation after 1775, abused people's right of access to information. Official statistical agencies do not compile information on land and its value in a form that suited reformers (see Box 8:1). In Britain, that data is not available to fulfil the methodological needs of science. The secrecy that is employed to shroud statistics has been documented by Kevin Cahill.[7] The British government admits that the data is seriously deficient. The Office of the Deputy Prime Minister's website states that 'there is no comprehensive and consistent information about the total amount of land devoted to different uses',[8] let alone a reliable series on rents and the prices at which land is traded in the markets.

But statistics without theory are largely meaningless. If we scour the world, we find examples of the official compilation of data that could tell a story, if the economists knew what they were looking for. Japan has no excuse for the failures of policy. The government compiles extensive information on the levels and trends of land prices in cities and prefectures.[9] Because Tokyo no longer bases its property and public finance policies on this information, Japan suffers endemic booms and busts.[10]

The void in knowledge frees governments to offer fanciful explanations for recessions as 'external shocks' over which (of course) they have no control. Thus, the recession of the early 1970s is attributed by some to the perverse behaviour of oil sheikhs rather than the outcome of domestic policies that favoured speculation in land on home territories. Furthermore, governments can displace responsibility by blaming the chaos of recession on the *failure* of social systems ('market

---

Box 8:1

The Black Hole of Statistics

THERE IS SOMETHING exquisitely absurd about economists and politicians who refuse to acknowledge that they are standing on the evidence they need to explain the problem that continually defeats them. Their resort to naturalistic models, of laws of the business cycle over which they have no control, stands the methods used by natural scientists on their head. Scientists can infer laws of behaviour even when they cannot directly detect the evidence. Economists refuse to identify laws of social behaviour even when they are walking all over the evidence.

Physicists, for example, believe that dark matter makes up about 80% of all the mass in the universe. They are confident that this heavy particle exists. It weighs about 50 times more than a proton, but it has the knack of passing through other matter without leaving a trace of itself. This achievement is made possible by its extremely weak ability to interact with other matter. Astronomers have not seen it, but ever since the 1930s they have been able to measure its gravitational pull. Not seen, but felt.

Physicists are doing their best to acquire all the evidence possible, for – we are told – without the gravitational pull of dark matter, galaxies would fly apart. Thus, dark matter holds our universe together – a centripetal force that maintains a harmony which is inclusive, the intergalactic glue on which we depend for our continued existence.

Back on earth, we find that land speculation works in the opposite direction. It deprives rent of its potential to integrate society. Land speculation is a centrifugal force that scatters the parts that would otherwise cohere. It deprives communities of their natural harmony. It is a power that is exclusive, discriminatory, expelling those who fail to monopolise a part of it.

The effects of land speculation can be observed, measured, analysed: but economists choose not to see it. But even if we could not use standard statistical techniques to measure the value, distribution, and rate of turnover of plots, we can infer its presence from its influence on our lives.

---

failure') rather than the logical outcome of the *successful* unfolding of the rules of the economic game. Such excursions into political mysticism can be traced back to the economists who obscured the role of land and natural resources.

That a significant contribution to this state of ignorance was made by Keynes is ironical. He did offer a coherent *description* of recessions. He sought an explanation in terms of the accumulation of capital to the point where it might be wasted, the pricing mechanism having failed to clear markets and ensure full employment.

If the market was sufficiently sensitive to the competing forces at work within it, people could act rationally to ensure sustainable growth. It is one of the axioms of the market economy that the expansion of supply tends to satisfy demand and cause the price that people are willing to pay to fall, or at least to moderate. This, however, often failed to happen. For an explanation, Keynes retreated into the realms of psychology. What he was not willing to do was acknowledge that land speculation may play a role in the disruption of otherwise efficient markets. He discounted land as having any significance for the modern economy at all.

Land's influence, declared Keynes, was restricted to the agricultural age.[11] His prejudice against land as an economic category stemmed from a distorted view of history. For him, capital – in the form of equipment, and even more so 'financial capital' – replaced land as the important ingredient in the economy. In the industrial age, the power of land had become obsolete. So, in 1925, just before the crisis of 1929, he pronounced that 'the land problem' no longer existed because of what he deemed to be 'a silent change in the facts'.[12] It was in 1925 that wage earners in America were persuaded to bury their life's savings in the shifting sand dunes of Florida, a speculative spree that diverted investment away from the sectors that could have created jobs and increased productivity.

Because of his doctrinal prism, the significance of land was refracted out of Keynes' sight. He focused his analysis on yields from capital which, he predicted, with the steady accumulation of savings, would eventually lead to very low interest rates. The consequence, he was pleased to note, would be the 'euthanasia of the *rentier*'.

> Interest today rewards no genuine sacrifice, any more than does the rent of land. The owner of capital can obtain interest because capital is scarce, just as the owner of land can obtain rent because land is scarce. But whilst there may be intrinsic reasons for the scarcity of land, there are no intrinsic reasons for the scarcity of capital.[13]

Keynes anticipated that, as savings were accumulated and converted into capital, the interest payments to savers would decline to very low levels such that 'the *rentier* aspect of capitalism as a transitional phase ... will disappear when it has done its work ... It will be, moreover, a great advantage of the order of events which I am advocating, that the euthanasia of the *rentier*, of the functionless investor, will be nothing sudden, merely a gradual but prolonged continuance of what we have seen recently in Great Britain, and will need no revolution'.[14]

We may disagree with Keynes' view that interest is not a reward to genuine sacrifice. Why save – if there is no compensation for doing so – when one can increase today's consumption and enjoy the benefits of the additional goods and services? This contrasts with the landowner. He did not endure any sacrifice to make the land, yet he received rent. But there is a fundamental problem with this vision of the downward trends of interest payments which ought to have alerted Keynes to the fundamental problem of land. While *income* may be on a downward trend for man-made capital, *capital gains* from the sale of land would automatically be stimulated upwards in response to the long-run decline in interest rates which Keynes predicted and commended. What looks like an unattractive drop in the yield of capital must be accompanied by sharp rises in the capital gains from land. If Keynes had acknowledged this difference, his remarkable influence on Western governments might have transformed the economic landscape of the last half of the 20th century.

Keynes ought to have incorporated into his analytical framework facts such as the immobility and finite nature of urban sites. They cannot be transported to users; users have to come to them. The scope for varying these facts of nature (such as the invention of elevators, which increased the intensity of use to which each site might be put) does not modify the principle that land is in fixed supply in the desired locations. With the important transportable natural resources (such as oil or diamonds), rents would rise if suppliers conspired in cartels to restrict the supply. They did, and still do, so conspire.[15]

In the 19th century the direct control over land was important. Speculators, mainly the aristocrats and gentry who happened to inherit their tracts from previous generations, would hoard the sites that were required for urban expansion or the construction of railways. They reaped the largest capital gains. Speculation achieved greater sophistication in the 20th century, expanding the opportunities for many more people. Most beneficiaries were passive: their savings were deposited with pension funds and insurance companies, which in turn invested in property. People traded in the shares of land-rich companies, as well as 'trading up' in the housing market. That ensured the perpetuation of the booms and busts. This history escapes the Keynesian model. Consequently, Keynes' theory of how to maintain full employment converted governance into the art of perpetual crisis management rather than crisis resolution.

The misdiagnosis by Keynes of what causes the repetitive strain on the economy persuaded him that governments needed to intervene in the markets. Order would be restored through government spending ('pump priming').

> In conditions of *laissez-faire* the avoidance of wide fluctuations in employment may, therefore, prove impossible without a far-reaching change in the psychology of investment markets such

as there is no reason to expect. I conclude that the duty of ordering the current volume of investment cannot safely be left in private hands.[16]

The problem is not with *laissez-faire*. People respond to the opportunities that are available on the basis of current laws and practices.

But remedy, in Keynes's view, lay not with the self-discipline of investors, nor by rearranging the rules that determine the rewards of economic activity. He opted for a hybrid model of market economics in which the state would function as the conductor of the orchestra. Through its monetary policies and public investment, governments would seek to manage markets. As it happens, interventionist policies failed to provide the promised stability; but they did give governments the excuse to intrude in economic activities and force up the nation's indebtedness.

The Keynesian doctrine was music to the ears of socialist and conservative governments alike. Keynes' advocacy of redistributing people's incomes 'to stimulate the propensity to consume'[17] was appealing. After the Second World War, Western governments embarked on a massive redistribution of earned incomes. They broke people through taxation (by raising the unit costs of products above the prices that customers were willing or able to pay) and made millionaires through subsidisation (as in the agricultural sector). But they failed to neutralise the job-smashing, hope-grinding business cycle.

Keynes's myopic diagnosis was designed to preserve the perpetual instability which foreclosed on the possibility of sustainable growth.

§3 A Little Local Difficulty?

ONE TECHNIQUE that is used to downgrade the significance of property in macroeconomic analysis is the claim that the value of land is uniquely tied to local markets. Thus, the awkward news that house prices are rising at an alarmingly high rate is soothingly set aside. Those price rises are 'not a source of fundamental shocks', as three Bank of England economists put it.[18] House prices are just a little local difficulty.

When experts in positions of authority reassure the public that current conditions are not risky, people can be forgiven for believing that it is safe for them to invest their money in assets such as housing. Without knowing it, however, they may be doing so just at the point when risk is about to multiply at an exponential rate.

Take the period between a mid-cycle recession (2001-2) and the take-off at the beginning of the Winner's Curse phase (2005-6). In this bridging period it is vital that people should realise that conditions move along in the cycle to the point where there is no going back to a 'soft landing'. At that point, they should be consolidating their portfolio of cash and assets to minimise the risks that will entrap the unwary who move into the land market as the manic phase of speculation launches itself (2007-8).

The importance of understanding where we are at any point in the cycle is illustrated in Table 8:2. This offers the detail which demonstrates that land markets are unique; prices do vary across regions to reflect the productivity and other attractions of local and regional economies. The data summarises the 18 years from the recession of 1974 to the recession of 1992 in the USA. The variations in house prices demonstrates a number of characteristics of the boom-bust phenomenon.

TABLE 8:2

USA Real House Price Volatility (% change)

	Recovery phase: Boom 1977-80	Mid-cycle: Bust 1980-3	Winner's Curse: Boom 1983-7	End-cycle: Bust 1987-91
Boston, MA	4.7	4.8	16.1	-5.5
Nassau, NY	0.6	10.3	15.0	-4.0
Newark, NJ	4.1	0.8	15.5	-4.0
Washington, DC	3.3	-2.1	3.5	3.6
Richmond, VA	0.4	-2.7	1.8	0.7
Chicago, IL	3.0	-4.9	3.9	3.1
Columbus, OH	3.2	-4.0	2.0	1.1
Minneapolis, MN	10.4	-3.1	1.6	-1.0
St. Louis, MO	8.2	-4.3	2.7	-1.8
Sacramento, CA	9.6	-3.5	1.4	8.5
San Francisco, CA	7.4	-2.3	5.0	7.7
Seattle, WA	13.2	-5.5	1.9	6.8
Los Angeles, CA	9.1	-2.3	3.1	7.9

Source: Data (but not the characterisation for the time slots), derived from Jesse M. Abraham & P.H. Hendershott, 'Patterns and Determinants of Metropolitan House Prices, 1977-91', Washington DC: National Bureau of Economic Research, Working Paper 4196, October 1992.

The biggest productivity gains are achieved at the economic 'centre' (in regional terms, New England and New York), and they decline towards the margins on the periphery of states like Missouri. The greatest stresses surface in regions where productivity is highest, which translates into the largest capital gains.

The biggest busts follow the largest increases in land prices. But whether the fate of a particular region affects the rest of the economy (as California can, compared, say, to New Hampshire) depends on considerations such as size and the structure of the local economy. The regions with slower economic growth rates tend to avoid the worst effects of the boom bust, but they also have smaller rental incomes to invest in culture and infrastructure. The character of the property tax can also determine whether land speculation has more or less impact on economic activity.[19]

The information on land markets – down to street level – is needed because, when correctly interpreted, it is possible to lay bare the structural buttresses that underpin capitalism. We find ourselves confronted by two distinct economic models. These coexist within common institutions. The first is based on the principles of the entrepreneur's market, in which the values and processes facilitate the production of goods and services that people wish to exchange with each other. The second model is based on the right to extract value that is created by others without the need to add any wealth to the sum total. Capitalism attempts to balance the competing, conflicting dynamics of these two opposing forces. As such, it is not a single, uncomplicated, homogenous system, much as Marx would have us believe otherwise. A full exploration of the hybrid character of capitalism will be treated in a separate volume.[20] But we do need to hold in our minds the broad outlines of the capitalist economy if we are to deepen our understanding of what motivates booms and busts.

The need for an investigation into capitalism's primary principles is attested by the consistent failure of the experts to anticipate the broad changes to economic activity: they cannot predict the turning points, despite the patterned oscillation of prices and industrial output stretching back 300 years. That weakness in economic activity is candidly acknowledged by some of its practitioners. One of them, Lord Burns, is an academic forecaster who became chief economic adviser to Prime Minister Margaret Thatcher. Sir Samuel Brittan, an informed commentator on the UK economy, reported that Burns 'has remarked that the forecasts have not become any better over the 30 or more years he has been watching them, despite improved techniques and much larger personnel'.[21] I have elsewhere drawn attention to the way in which the professor of economics (as Terry Burns then was) used *appearances* to provide diagnoses to the government he served. He was honest about the difficulties of informing social policies with reliable economic insights. For example, he confessed that there was 'no easy explanation' for the fall in the profitability of manufacturers – so he was inclined, for appearances sake, to blame wage-claiming workers.[22]

Economics, if it is to achieve scientific status, needs to improve its predictive qualities. It has failed lamentably, under the spell of neo-classical concepts.[23] It will not improve its usefulness until it retrieves the classical formulations of the land market and the difference between land speculation and the efficient use of, and payments for, land.

§4 The Pursuits of Free-Riders

THE CLAIM by politicians that they can manage the economy better than their predecessors is a cruel prospectus, for they cannot deliver on their promises. Booms and busts are built into the industrial economy's foundations. A short detour in our narrative will place this claim in its historical context.

After a century's worth of 18-year cycles, the outbreak of war with France at the end of the 18th century became the opportunity to restructure the laws and institutions of Britain in a way that would enable the building industry to make a benign contribution to sustained growth. But this outcome was not achievable because the government under William Pitt rigged the rules. From 1799 onwards they framed the public's finances in a way that would reward the free riders. Land owners were not expected to pay in full for the services which they received from the state – their services would be subsidised by taxpayers.

Adam Smith and his generation knew exactly how the system worked (see Box 8:2). We have forgotten that understanding. Economists and politicians have anaesthetised people to the painful process by which public revenue was shifted away from rent and onto wages. It was done with the connivance of those who controlled the nation's income statistics, which no longer mean what they say.

This was not a historically inevitable outcome. History took a wrong route with Pitt's income tax in 1799. This course of action was not endorsed by Adam Smith, as the historians J.L. and Barbara Hammond noted in their study of *The Town Labourer.*

Pitt was indebted to Adam Smith and *The Wealth of Nations.* On one occasion, at a dinner where Smith was a guest, Pitt insisted on standing until the economist was seated, declaring 'we are all your pupils'.

Box 8:2

The Tax Trail

ADAM SMITH formulated some of the primary laws of economic activity. In his time, the categories of income had not been distorted by government (through taxation), or by the debt-creating financial system (mortgages that extract rents as 'interest'). So Smith could trace with clarity the effect of taxes on wages and on the rents that people were willing to pay for the use of land and nature's resources.

Because rent is a surplus – the value that exceeds the cost of producing a saleable commodity or service –, reserving it to defray public expenses does not distort the ability or willingness of people to work, save and invest. Public charges that fall exclusively on land rents are, in that sense, neutral. It follows, in Adam Smith's words in *The Wealth of Nations*, that 'Ground-rents, and the ordinary rent of land are, therefore, perhaps the species of revenue which can best bear to have a peculiar tax imposed upon them'.[1]

What if government ignored this advice and taxed people's wages? Smith pointed out that such taxes would, 'in the long run, occasion both a greater reduction in the rent of land, and a greater rise in the price of manufactured goods'.[2] In other words:

- Taxes on wages are passed on in the higher prices charged for goods sold in the shops. *Governments that think they are imposing taxes on working people's incomes are mistaken.*

- As taxes are passed along the price chain, the burden finally falls on the owner of land or natural resources. *Rents are reduced by the amount of tax that government thought it was imposing on people's wages.*

The qualifications that technical economists would place on Smith's account are not important.

If we want to trace how government is harming the economy, we must deconstruct prices to identify the distortions inflicted by taxes. Remedies should be considered in the context of the economic reality that Adam Smith stressed: 'The real value of the landlord's share, his real command of the labour of other people, not only rises with the real value of the produce, but the proportion of his share of the whole produce rises with it.'[3]

1 Adam Smith, *The Wealth of Nations*, Bk V, Ch II, Pt II, Art. 1, p.370 of the Edwin Cannan edition.
2 *Ibid.*, Bk V, Ch II, Pt II, Art. III, p.394.
3 *Ibid.*, Bk I, Ch XI, p.275.

The Hammonds acknowledge that Pitt did accept, and act on, Smith's strictures against the protectionism that had privileged the merchant class. But they also explained that Pitt did not follow Smith on the need to ensure that the wages of the working class were secured by the new political economy. Why would Pitt disregard Smith's writings on the conditions of labour and side with the upper classes of the day? This was not a simplistic doctrinal contest over the distribution of income in the markets. The financial status of the state would turn on the outcome of the contest. The people in power – the landed aristocracy – knew that to raise the wages of labour would be to reduce their rents. Almost worse still, Smith had developed a conservative theory of public finance that struck at the heart of their post-feudal power.

> Adam Smith argued that in levying taxation, it was important to consider what taxes could be imposed without putting a burden on industry. From this point of view he found an ideal tax in a tax on ground rents. He recommended the taxation of ground rents for two reasons: the first that such a tax discouraged no industry, the second that ground rents owed their value all together to good government, and it was therefore reasonable that they 'should be taxed peculiarly' for the support of government.[24]

There was no doubt that ground rents provided a buoyant fiscal base. The Hammonds quoted contemporary literature as recording rents increasing in Lancashire by 3,000%. The recipients of those rents, alas, 'contributed nothing of this great unearned revenue to the expenses of the State'.[25] If Prime Minister Pitt really was a pupil of Smith's, he would not have invented the income tax.

> During the Industrial Revolution the value of ground rents was advancing at a rapid pace, and any pupil of Adam Smith would have put a tax on the immense wealth created in the new industrial towns and taken off the heavy burdens on food, clothing, and the materials of industry ... Adam Smith's teaching that ground rents ought to be taxed before the necessaries of life, received just as much attention as his arguments against Protection.[26]

The first industrial society was polarised between the twin evils of taxation (the socialisation of earned incomes) and fiscal privileges for the landed class (the privatisation of rental values that were the product of community activity and governance). The un-taxation of ground rents rewarded those who chose to speculate in the capital gains from land. At the same time, the income tax penalised those who generated profits from capital investment in industry. The booms and busts were institutionalised by acts and omissions of Parliament.

The price was paid by the working class. In 1833, for example, a labourer earning £22 10s was paying in taxes £11 7s 7p.[27] The town labourers were paying half their wages in taxes, while the rent-receivers 'were growing fabulously rich on the process that crowded the poor in dens and cellars'.[28]

Fiscal policy became the tool for the 'upper classes' which condoned the boom busts. If we want economic stability, we have no
choice but to recognise that land is the institution through which the
energies of entrepreneurs and their employees are dissipated. The
reform of policy, however, will not occur if we fail to locate the spatial
parameters within our models of the economy. Distance and area – and
the costs associated with them – need to be placed at the heart of
economic reasoning. At what point were they dropped from mainstream economics? Mark Blaug, emeritus professor at the University
of London, noted: 'Surprisingly enough, however, such problems
dropped almost wholly out of sight in the economic treatises written
after 1800 ... Here is a major puzzle in the history of economic
thought: what was it about spatial economics that prevents its recognition as an integral feature of mainstream economics?'[29]

Tax policy, today, turns landowners – involuntarily in most cases –
into free-riders. They profit by riding on the backs of taxpayers. The
negative implications of this are not ameliorated because most land
owners, as home owners, are also tax payers. They gain as owners of
land, but they lose much more in cash and quality of life: they have to
carry the deadweight losses of conventional taxes on *their* backs. Not
until we resolve this contradiction in the foundations of the capitalist
economy can we credibly pronounce the end of the boom-bust cycle.

REFERENCES

1   The extract of Keynes' letter appears on the cover of the 1967 Macmillan reprint
    of his *The General Theory of Employment Interest and Money* (1936).
2   *Will stability last?* London: UBS Global Asset Management, March, 2004, p.6.
3   Alan Greenspan, 'Global challenges', Financial Crisis Conference, New York:
    Council on Foreign Relations, July 12, 2000, mimeo.
4   Michael Hudson, 'Lies of the Land: Illusions in US property appraisal method-
    ologies', *Geo*philos, Spring 2002, 02(1).
5   *Ibid.*, p.117.
6   *Op. cit.*
7   Kevin Cahill, *Who Owns Britain*, Edinburgh: Canongate, 2001.
8   http://www.planning.odpm.gov.uk/lucs16/annex_c.htm .
9   For a review of the information up to the 1970s, see Harrison, *The Power in the
    Land*, Ch. 12. For data on land prices that span the bubble years of the late 1980s
    into the 1990s, see Fred Harrison, 'The Systemic Crisis', in Fred Harrison (ed.),
    The Losses of Nation, London: Othila Press, pp.87-91.
10 That this information is not routinely collected by the statistical agencies
    of most other countries is justified by a variety of excuses. One claim is that
    valuers (assessors in the US) have difficulty in separating the value of land from
    the value of buildings. These dishonest excuses are insulting to professionals
    in the property industry, and to land speculators and construction industry deal-
    ers who establish market values on a daily basis as they go about their routine

business of buying and selling tracts of land. For recent discussions on methods of valuing land, see Karl L. Guntermann, 'The Valuation of Undeveloped Land: A Reconciliation of Methods', *J. of Real Estate Research*, Vol. 9(2), 1994; Hans R. Isakson, 'An Empirical Analysis of the Determinants of the Value of Vacant Land', *J. of Real Estate Research*, Vol. 13(2), 1997.

11 Keynes, *The General Theory*, pp.241-2

12 Quoted in Harrison, *The Power in the Land, op. cit.*, p.300.

13 Keynes, *The General Theory, op. cit.*, p.376.

14 *Ibid.*

15 On diamonds, the De Beers group agreed to plead guilty to a price-fixing charge in the US courts following a 10-year dispute with the US Department of Justice. John Reed, 'De Beers settles US price-fixing lawsuit', *Financial Times*, July 12, 2004.

16 Keynes, *op. cit.*, p.320.

17 *Ibid.*, p.321.

18 Kosuke Aoki, James Proudman and Gertjan Vlieghe, 'Houses as Collateral: Has the Link between House Prices and Consumption in the UK Changed?' FRBNY *Economic Policy Review*, May 2002, p.163.

19 Mason Gaffney and Richard Noyes, 'The Income-Stimulating Incentives of the Property Tax', in Harrison, *Losses of Nations, op. cit.*, Ch. 8.

20 Fred Harrison, *The Pathology of Capitalism*, forthcoming.

21 Samuel Brittan, 'The naked economic forecaster revealed', *Financial Times*, January 3, 2003.

22 Harrison, *The Power in the Land, op. cit.*, p.274.

23 While most economists in the 20th century would associate themselves with the neoclassical school, a more appropriate nomenclature would be *post-classical*. I owe this point to Michael Hudson.

24 J.L. Hammond and Barbara Hammond, *The Town Labourer, 1760-1832*, London: Longmans, Green & Co., 1927, p.214.

25 *Ibid.*, p.215.

26 *Ibid.*, p.214-15.

27 *Ibid.*, p.214.

28 *Ibid.*

29 Mark Blaug, *Economic Theory in Retrospect*, Cambridge: University Press, 5th edn., 1997, p.596.

PART III

Anatomy of the First Global Cycle

9

The New Ecomony:
Selling an Anglo-American Myth

§1 Hard-Wired Hard Sell

IF I INVITED you to Las Vegas to gamble your home on the throw
of a dice, you would think that I was insane. Rational people do not
risk their most valuable asset on a game of chance. And yet, millions
of families are locked into that kind of gamble (or they provide the
sport on which others do gamble'). What makes the duel with Lady
Luck macabre is that most homeowners are passive players, onlookers
who watch as the dice is thrown by their elected representatives in
government. The value of their assets is raised and lowered as if the
game had no more significance than a Saturday night indulgence with
Monopoly money.

Politicians and their economic advisers are engaged in an unending
gamble with our prosperity. Because the dice is loaded, most of us
generally lose. Over a lifetime of working, those losses mount up to
proportions that cannot be imagined. By our work, we would all be
lottery-style winners. And yet, we are deprived of that prosperity by
our governments. How do politicians get away with it? They invent
myths that camouflage their actions. These political tales are broadcast every day to explain away their failures.

The myth for the 21st century was an elegant one. Somewhere
round about 1992 the US uncovered the secret of riches without recession. *Magic!* Here was 'the New Economy'.

Then came a 'correction'. This is a myth-maker's word that diverts
attention from a nascent recession. Deviant behaviour had to be
adjusted ever so slightly: a correction. On April 14, 2000, billions of
dollars were erased from the shares traded on Wall Street. This triggered a domino effect, with billions wiped off the assets on stock
exchanges round the world. On that day, the global economy took a
step into the mid-cycle recession of 2001. This was a staging post in

the business cycle that would end by depriving hundreds of thousands of families of their homes and clamp down on their incomes. The global economy would enjoy another seven years of growth before plunging into the depression of 2010.

As in all good detective stories, there has to be a villain. In this case, it is the democratically elected government. Responsibility for the damage that reckless taxes cause cannot be shifted onto others. The losses run into hundreds of billions of dollars every year – more than enough to pay for all the private and public services that a civilised society could possibly want. Politicians escape censure, however, because they control the terms of public debate. I will attempt to dissolve the illusions. This exercise in excavating the truth about the inner workings of the economy will make demands on the reader. The rewards for perseverance could be enormous. The first task is to determine the truth behind the claim that the global economy has entered a phase in which we can all prosper.

The viruses that kept blocking the workings of the 'old economy' are thriving in the nether regions of cyberspace. This does not mean that the reader is helpless. Armed with the basic analytical tools, *you* could avoid the worst effects of the next recession, and you might even come out richer.

The new economy was a concept with the power to bewitch, to lure investors into conspiring with media pundits to weave the fantasy of wealth sculptured on apparently solid foundations. But as every con-man knows, the secret of a good scam is the knack of co-opting victims into the illusion. And as with every previous bubble that was built on inflated expectations, there were just enough encouraging facts to conceal the rotten centre of the cycle that began in the 1990s. It was a house built of cards that would one day collapse, but in the meantime there were fortunes to be made.

The electronic age had arrived. The prospects appeared so alluring that it was not difficult to persuade people to part with their money. This propelled the US economy to new heights of activity. By the beginning of the new millennium, America had enjoyed 107 months of continuous prosperity. It was the triumph that Bill Clinton needed to rescue his presidency from a history that would focus on his personal proclivities. The president had lied about his sexual adventures in the Oval Office. He need not have worried: penal power was not on people's minds. Clinton was excused because of his apparently exemplary management of the economy. As a result of his eight years in the White House, hadn't America finally discovered the secret of sustainable growth?

Most people would accept the president's claim that he handled economic policy with integrity. The symbolic significance of the Whitewater land fraud, with which the Clinton name was linked, was not examined by the analysts for what it was – a legal get-rich-quick project which, when multiplied many times over every day throughout America, deprives people of the opportunity to earn their living in what was supposed to be the land of the free. No one interpreted that event as a symptom of the fatal flaw in the foundations of the 'old economy', let alone explained how it might still be present in a new guise in the 21st century. Instead, Whitewater was perceived as a grubby incident involving mortgages and a piece of land in a deal that went sour. The investigation into the fraud had also broken a record – for the longest probe ever into an allegation against a US president – but it was not the smoking gun that would expose the fatal weakness in the president's economic philosophy.

Whitewater could have been flagged as a metaphor for economic barbarism. It was not canvassed as such by Clinton's enemies in Congress. Why? The reformulation of language by the post-classical economists had banished land from the economic screens. If economic analysts had made the connection between a routine exercise in land speculation during the boom of the 1980s and the exponential growth of prices on Wall Street in the 1990s, alarm bells might have sounded. But the stock market gurus had inherited conceptual tools that filter out the similarities between land speculation and the novelty of speculation in the shares of dot.com companies. So why should young Bill Clinton, the Rhodes scholar and lawyer from Arkansas, be expected to anticipate that the economy over which he would one day preside would fall victim to the collapse of an old-fashioned business cycle?

The spin doctors had a free hand. They could concoct a convincing myth out of an economic stew of beguiling ingredients. Youthful characters had made fortunes – on paper – and their stories could be hyped to lure incautious investors. Few of the informed observers voiced serious doubts.[2] And for investors who were puzzled by the yawning gap between share prices and corporate profits, the myth would serve to bolster that essential ingredient in financial markets – *confidence*. The prosperity of the New Economy, reassured the politicians, was rock solid – despite its virtual character. The secret of US growth lay in harnessing computer technologies and the internet to raise productivity to a new plateau.

Keyboards and motherboards and microchips were being manufactured at ever-decreasing cost by low wage labour in the Far East. So what was creating all the value that sent the prices of dot.com shares into cyberspace? It did not pay President Clinton to ask awkward questions. In the absence of credible challenges to conventional economic wisdom, there was no need for an economic whitewash in the White House.

Dozens of new millionaires were created by the day. Even for the intuitive sceptic, the computer did offer a vision of commercial transformation. But what was new about this Information Age? Civilisation, after all, is one long series of information revolutions.

The original act of genius was delivered in the late Neolithic age. Our ancestors learnt to chisel images on stone and etch symbols on sticks. Their approach to disseminating information was cumbersome. Before the dawn of civilisation, however, it was a discovery of epochal consequence for the evolution of humans. The second revolution exploited the discoveries of craftsmen. It was based on papyrus and paper, and the information was inscribed with ink. The third revolution was the quantum leap made possible by the use of metal and the capacity to print on a press. Each of these innovations extended the spatial realm of people's lives. It enabled them to deepen their knowledge, and to enjoy enormous cultural and psychic benefits. The computer that challenged the commercial world at the end of the 20th century was no more than the step that precedes the next innovation up the information ladder.

To maximise the gains – and minimise the pains – of the latest invention, the features common to each rung needed to be extracted from each Information Age. But the basic tools for deciphering and analysing the data were not available to social scientists and investors. It was not always so. In the late 18th century, the mechanisms by which income was distributed were the central concern of the classical economists. In the two centuries of ideological warfare that followed, however, research into the way income was distributed was driven to the margins of economics. The emphasis shifted to a consideration of techniques that accelerate growth of the nation's total income. This was not a wise development in the evolution of the social science, but it did fulfil one purpose: it released politicians from responsibility for the persistent failure to confront the power that is in the hands of those who control the land and its rental income.

Thus, there was nothing to stop the internet innovation from inflating the stock markets beyond the realms of reality. The high-tech wise-guys had no reason to linger on the mundane truth that computers are just another means for cutting the costs of fulfilling people's everyday dreams. They needed a mystique that would amplify the social consequences of the virtual economy. And so the computer was sold as a liberating tool, not just another instrument that would give another twist to the riddle of persistent poverty.

The wizardry of transmitting images between screens was a gift to people who had a vested interest in *not* marrying forensic clarity to public policy. There were no votes to be garnered by acknowledging that our wonder at the achievements of the microchip would be no more profound than the astonishment of our ancestors when they first beheld symbolic images on sticks and stones. Each advance in know-how and technology had the potential to enrich lives and cut the costs of earning our daily living. Each step in the art of organising informa-tion led to the formation of new political relationships and territorial conquests. So what was new about the digital age? NATO's computer co-ordinated bombing of targets in Kosovo in 1998, and US missiles aimed at terrorist targets in Afghanistan in 2001, were symbolic. The bombs were 'smart'. But so was the arrow over the sword, and the slug of lead over the spear. The conflict was the age-old one of who had the supreme power to control land.

This assessment was not what the corporate captains wanted to hear at the World Economic Forum in Davos in the first year of the new millennium. The new myth had to be sanctified. So on January 28, 2000, the leaders of Britain and the United States lectured the world on 'the New Economy'. They had perceived the secrets of sustainable growth, and they wished to impart the good news.

In Washington, DC, the President delivered his last State of the Union message. He lingered on the prosperity that was created by Americans during his occupation of the White House. On that same day in Europe, Prime Minister Tony Blair's aircraft skimmed the Alpine peaks to descend on Davos. He brought the good news of 'social emancipation'. He urged his European partners to emulate the British model. Since May 1997, Britain had conquered the boom-bust cycle and laid the foundations for the new economy. Tony Blair wanted his party, New Labour, to receive the credit for placing the emphasis on Education, Education, Education – towards which, he would work to wire up all schools to the superhighway that was the internet.

And so was delivered the new doctrine of material prosperity driven by the Anglo-American model. Clinton reinforced the message when he spoke at Davos on the following day. The corporate leaders who had assembled, who managed combined assets estimated at $4 trillion, their minds fresh with the crises in Asia and Russia and the protracted depression in Japan, were hungry for good news. They were not inclined to challenge the claims about the New Economy.

They did not want to hear that the seeds for a global depression had been sown in Washington and nourished in London. Therein lay the danger of the powerful myth: it could distract people from the threats that lurk beneath the surface, concealed in a world of virtual prosperity.

At the outset of the new millennium, the global economy was wired to the old fashioned recession. Central bankers and government leaders were part of the problem, not the solution. One day, they would again bring the roof down on our heads. From boom to bust. Is this a harsh indictment? Do the leaders of the great democracies wilfully lure us into a gamble with our hard-earned assets? If so, how did they achieve this feat without our understanding the nature of the trap into which we were being led?

§2 The Titanic Doctrine

WE EXPECT governments to form their economic decisions by deploying the principles of reason. We also expect them to fashion policies after assessing all the information that armies of civil servants can gather. But despite the use of algebra to provide the appearance of mathematical precision, the big decisions rely on hunches rather than scientific rigour. The economy is less a scientist's laboratory and more a casino. How do the politicians conceal this reality? By shrouding their actions in a public display of *confidence* in the outcome of current trends.

Central bankers, who can make millionaires and break businessmen for breakfast, are wedded to what I call *The Titanic Doctrine*. They can't see the icebergs that threaten the ship of state, but they know they are out there. To maintain confidence, they bluff people into thinking that the treacherous obstacles can be avoided. Hold your breath, shut your eyes, keep on investing your lifetime's savings, and skim around the metal-crunching masses of solid water beneath the surface.

Is this an unfair characterisation of people like Alan Greenspan, the respected head of the most powerful central bank? Greenspan's pronouncements on economic prospects could move global markets. Arguably, he became the single most influential economic manager in the world. Could he really be bluffing us? Who better to ask than Lawrence H. Summers?

After a distinguished academic career, Summers entered the US Treasury and was appointed Secretary by President Clinton in 1999. When he was professor of political economy at Harvard University,

Summers had assessed with brutal frankness the approach to monetary policy employed by chairmen of central banks. In 1988 he delivered his views on the way in which monetary policy was formulated and implemented. His verdict flowed from the startling confession that 'the absence of convincing models supported by both logic and evidence is a discouraging commentary on the state of macroeconomic science'.[3] This was a damning indictment of economic practise. Economists, hired by Wall Street and the City of London, are paid fabulous salaries and bonuses because they are believed to be masters of the tools of their trade. The confession by Dr. Summers casts serious doubt on the reliability of their prognoses, let alone their prescriptions.

In the view of Dr. Summers, the use of fixed rules to manage the economy was an unreliable approach to ensuring stable growth. People comply with rules that produce predictable outcomes. But in the casino economy, the rules offered by economists are more akin to those employed by punters at the Las Vegas roulette wheel: keep staking money on black 17 and your number is bound to come up at some point in time (*though not necessarily before* you *are cleaned out*).

Dr. Summers favours the gambling model. He reminds us that some people *can* succeed in poker by bluffing their opponents. They 'win consistently at poker ... they are able to bluff effectively and to appropriately manipulate the expectations of others. The fact that economists do not have insightful models of how some people consistently win at poker should not blind us to the fact that they do'.

In the Summers doctrine this model of the poker player is the one that investors should use to decode the words of people like Greenspan and Sir Edward George, who served as Governor of the Bank of England until 2003. For 'it is at least possible that successful central bankers possess the same ability to manipulate expectations and bluff that good poker players do'.

Central bankers regulate interest rates to forestall what they choose to call inflation, the index that is supposed to forewarn of crisis in the markets. A dose of higher interest rates is the medicine prescribed to cool exuberant behaviour which, in the medium term, puts jobs at risk. Unfortunately, higher interest rates also weaken prices on the stock markets. Good news for employees can be bad news for stockholders. We need the best information possible on what is actually happening if we are to make rational decisions about our portfolio of investments. So when the central bankers offer their advice, are we not entitled to believe that they are playing fair: that they are not holding their cards close to their chest, depriving us of the maximum available information on which to base judgments about what is in our best interests?

Central bankers bluff to maintain confidence even when the evidence does not warrant that glowing feeling of assurance. Their task is to persuade us to continue to invest. To achieve that, they must deny their fallibility. According to Dr. Summers, bluffing is the name of the game. Drawing on the evidence, he concludes that 'it seems clear that history judges some Federal Reserve Chairmen to be more successful than others and not only because they were more inflation-averse. Success in contriving the right sort of expectations must be part of the reason why'.[4]

When he moved out of the lecture theatre and into the political arena, Dr. Summers found himself driven to play the game of bluff. Even as Wall Street was inventing stratospheric values for loss-making dot.com companies, he flew to Tokyo to admonish finance ministers of the other six leading industrial nations on their 'complacency of diminished expectations'. He wanted the G7 nations to bolster confidence in their ability to accelerate economic output. They were too willing to accept growth of around 1%, which, apparently, was not within the confidence-building range of Washington's expectations.

True, there had been a leap in productivity in the US in the late 1990s. The most important source of those gains – computer science and technology – did cause a rise in efficiency. The costs of production were redistributed. But the net gains would ultimately cascade down into the old economy's rent of land. *Nothing had changed to override the forces that cause booms and busts.* The shift of income away from working people is a predictable outcome, for the beguiling delights of the internet favour those who appropriate the rents of natural resources. This development was not anticipated, which is why politicians misled people into thinking that good governance had delivered sustainable growth.

The cold facts tell a different story. In the US since 1974, the productivity of labour, which had formerly grown at about 2% per annum, dropped to 0.8% p.a. The economist who documented the trends since 1945 asked: 'Isn't it paradoxical that at a time of massive technological advance resulting from the introduction of information technologies and the like, the advance in a worker's productivity should stall?'[5] 1974 was also the point at which wage inequality began to increase, even as the costs of new computers began to plummet.

But if labour's share was apparently declining, along with the costs of computers, who was benefiting from the latest techniques for making money? The *net gains* from the new economy (the surplus after paying for all the costs of production) followed a well-worn path out of the hands of people who produce wealth and into the pockets of those who sit back and are enriched without lifting a hand. The old problems have been carried over into the post-industrial age because the ground rules remain the same.

Thus, the puzzles today are those that bewildered governments in the past. Why, for example, are we not able to provide decent accommodation for everyone? The technology is available. So is the sand and cement. And we have not yet reached standing room only in Europe or North America. Why is there a persistent problem with putting roofs over people's heads? The honest official answer is that we don't know the answer. (In 2002, the output of houses in Britain dropped to the level that had been achieved in the 1920s.) And why do we not know the answer? The problem is not being correctly diagnosed. Governments take 'corrective' action while wearing blindfolds. That was the conclusion of the head of the British government's economic service. Gus O'Donnell (who was to become Permanent Secretary at the Treasury) set out to improve the way government makes its decisions, but his report turned into a devastating critique of official information and the tools of the governing trade. Why, despite the expenditure of vast sums of taxpayers' money on housing policies, were thousands of people still vulnerable to the state of homelessness? O'Donnell discovered that the government's model of rents was such that 'the real-world impacts of policy change are un-modelled – and unknown'.[6] If entrepreneurs managed multi-billion dollar budgets without knowing what the effects would be on their balance sheets, or on their customers, they would be lynched from the lamp posts of the financial districts. But in politics, people get away with murder. In Britain, they are often rewarded by elevation to the House of Lords.

But someone has to pay the price of failure. Joe Public is the fall guy, and he – or she – will remain the loser for as long as the fog is allowed to disguise how government malpractices are multiplied by the land market, that conduit through which the errors are magnified and inflicted on everyone.

§3 The Theory of Public Property

UNIVERSAL LAWS are at work. That is why history repeats itself. Recall the great land rush in the New World in the 19th century. There was a similar land rush at the beginning of the 21st century – for the possession of sites in cyberspace. Early in 2000, more than 1.3 million sites had been registered by the owners of computers in the UK alone.

Rent is determined not just by qualities of nature, but also by the laws that regulate the use of those resources. What makes the two square kilometres of land wedged between the French hills and the Mediterranean Sea which is called Monaco much more valuable than equivalent tracts further along the Riviera in the direction of Spain or Italy? The answer, as everyone knows, is the tax regime that lures millionaires to this intensively occupied location. The principality has built as many skyscrapers as it can onto every available plot, and then burrowed down into the ground. It has now turned the land beneath the sea into valuable real estate, by constructing a giant concrete container extending 30 metres below sea level. Most of the Grimaldi Forum, an amphitheatre that accommodates 2,500 people, is beneath the sea. The extraordinary costs of building a modern conference and exhibition facility below the salt water line would be uneconomic practically anywhere else in the world. But in Monaco, because tax rates are low, land values are high. Taxes come out of net income, or rent. If the state fails to capture that income, it surfaces in the land market and is pocketed by landowners. So the price of land is determined not only by the level of science and technology, or by the cultural requirements of a particular society, but also by the revenue-raising policies of government.

Armed with the knowledge of the distinction between land, and the man-made improvements on, in and under land, we begin to perceive how the 'New Economy' is no more than a new gloss that contributes to the old business cycle. This knowledge is the prerequisite for defensive action, which means we have to be able to interpret the consequences that arise from the conjunction of two facts.

- The driving force that shapes the business cycle is the pursuit of capital gains from land.
- Governments stealthily intervene in our lives through the medium of rent. The size and distribution of rent is manipulated through the tax system.

Should we, as a community, care? To reach a sound judgment it is important to emphasise that *rent is the primary source of revenue on which we rely to pay for shared services.* The larger the rental income, the more we can spend on those services that we cannot provide for ourselves as individuals.

Appreciating the interactive process in the triadic relationship – the individual, society and nature – is critical if we are to formulate moral judgments about the nature of reforms that we ought to demand of democratic governments. The historical perspective which we offered above is a good starting point, but it makes sense only if we use the correct theory of *public* property. In the past, politics operated without respect for the property rights of the community that matched the respect for the theory of the individual and his private rights and private property.[7] That was why, as new layers of rent were peeled off nature, material progress was associated with new rounds of political confusion, military conflict and private grief.

The original manifestation of rent was the surplus that was generated from the organic powers buried in the soil. That was the first social revolution in the history of mankind. The second revolution, 6,000 years ago, was based on the rents of location. The synergy of urban communities had an electrifying effect on people's ability to multiply their community's net disposable income. But because moral philosophy failed to keep pace with material progress, technological, scientific and managerial advances were not an unmitigated blessing.

Water-borne trade expanded productivity, first in the Mediterranean Sea and then around the oceans. This continued late into the 18th century. That was when the slave trade, which was based on the rents extracted from Africa, was at its height. This is a reprehensible use of the term rent, which is not generally employed to include human beings. But slave-traders regarded the beings whom they captured (or purchased from African traders) and auctioned to New World plantation owners as working animals. The burghers of Bristol and Liverpool enriched themselves by treating people as a free resource of nature that could be harvested from the soil of Africa and sold in the markets of America for the price of sending sailing ships back and forth across the Atlantic under the power of the wind. The bulk of the fortunes that they accumulated was 'rent'. The state of Virginia even passed a law classifying slaves as real estate. This was not offensive to the economics of the slave trade. The people of Africa were not 'produced' as a cost in the balance sheets of the traders. They were 'free' for the taking, and therefore a 'natural resource' whose value could be classed as rent.[8]

Alternative forms of rent were uncovered in the late 18th century. The raw energy of water, for example, was combined with wood and steel to generate hydro rents. In the 20th century, with the advent of the combustion engine, the oil rents flowed. With costs of extraction at, say, $5 a barrel, and prices reaching $20 a barrel in the second half of the century, the $15 a barrel oil rent laid the foundations for massive private fortunes and a measure of public prosperity in countries like Norway and sheikhdoms in the Near East. In the 1990s, the electro-magnetic spectrum came into its own. People had listened to the wireless and watched television for 50 years, but it was the microchip that multiplied the economic value of the radio spectrum.

These advances in science and technology would have been associated with greater happiness if society had employed a coherent theory of public property, which is inextricably bound up with public finance based on rational principles.

Instead, confusion arose over policies that were the legitimate responsibility of the public domain. Who, for example, owns the secrets of nature that are buried in our genes? President Clinton and Prime Minister Blair issued a joint appeal in March 2000 for information on the gene sequence to 'be made freely available to scientists everywhere'. Is the gene pool in the public domain, or is it private property? Wouldn't you think this was an issue that philosophers, lawyers and politicians would have resolved long ago? Apparently this was not the case, because the statement by the leaders of the USA and UK wiped billions of dollars off the value of biotechnology companies. Investors had banked on being able to privatise and securitise the latent stream of rents that could be anticipated from the genetic code.

Public policy suffered, bedevilled by misinformation. For example, by the late 20th century, farm rents were no longer a measure of natural fertility. The subsidies transferred to farmland owners ostensibly to help them produce food (much of which, in Europe, was then stored because consumers did not want it), was more a measure of the aesthetic and recreational value of the countryside to urban dwellers. Nostalgia for green fields was exploited by the landowners' lobbies to persuade governments to be generous with taxpayers' money. That transfer of money was capitalised into land values. In Britain, that process was explicitly based on misinformation, in which statistics about farm incomes were used to pervert political discourse and the redistribution of taxpayers' money.[9]

To disentangle the complex web of emotions, financial commitments and public policies that complicate discussions about the ownership and use of land, we must be alert to the developments that loom in the new millennium. One of these unexpected challenges is rents from the moon. The extraction of lunar minerals is part of the forward planning of some corporations. But on September 8, 2000, the first project in Britain to squeeze rents from the moon was launched from a website. For £10, a punter could buy an acre of the sunny side of the moon, complete with a deed of ownership. MoonEstates.com Ltd. advertised itself as having the franchise to sell the sites from one Dennis M. Hope, who claimed to have filed his ownership rights at

the San Francisco County offices in 1980. If the purchase of land on
the moon sounds a foolhardy exercise for investors, it will prove no
more so than for the speculators who were persuaded to buy shifting
peat fields in the Scottish Highlands during the land boom of the early
1970s; or those who bought the shifting sand dunes on the Florida
coast during the land boom of the 1920s. While the purchase of title
deeds to land on the moon was no doubt a humorous gesture, the exercise in lunar speculation had begun. Someone was going to reap rich
rewards through cyberspace-sponsored speculation. One day prospec-
tors will extract minerals from the moon and lunar location rents will
be ferried back to earth. If that sounds like fantasy, we should remind
ourselves that cobalt is mined from the ocean floor: a UN convention
has already designated the rents of those resources as the income that
must be used for the benefit of mankind rather than appropriated by
the shareholders of the corporations.[10]

To advance our narrative, however, we must return from the bright
side of the moon to the dark side of earth.

REFERENCES

1   In August 2004, spread-betting firms in the City of London reported a surge in
    gambling on a house-price crash in the South East of England. Spread betting is a
    derivatives-based form of gambling that enables punters to 'buy' or 'sell' the move-
    ment of a market. Joe Morgan, 'Bets soar on London and South East crash', *The
    Times*, August 27, 2004.
2   An exception was the internet insider Tony Perkins (see his *The Internet Bubble*,
    London: Harper Business, 2000).
3   Lawrence H. Summers, 'Comment on Postwar Developments in Business Cycle
    Theory: A Moderately Classical Perspective', *Journal of Money, Credit, and Banking*,
    20(3), August 1988, Pt. 2, p.472.
4   *Ibid.*, p.476.
5   Jeremy Greenwood, *The Third Industrial Revolution: Technology, Productivity, and
    Income Inequality*, American Enterprise Institute, 1997, p.3.
6   Nicholas Timmins, 'Modelling a new approach to social reform', *Financial Times*,
    January 31, 2000.
7   Tanya Roskoshnaya and Fred Harrison, 'The dangerous myth: Methodological
    individualism as a tool of ideology', *Geophilos*, 01(1), Spring 2001.
8   In 1781, Britain was shocked by the actions of the owner of the slave ship *Zong*. He
    threw 132 sick slaves over board and claimed the insurance. He argued that he was
    entitled to take this action 'to jettison some cargo to save the rest'. Legal support
    for this interpretation came from Lord Mansfield in the ensuing court case, when
    he compared the fate of the slaves to the disposal of a cargo of horses. Cited in
    Jenny Uglow, *The Lunar Men: The Friends Who Made the Future, 1730-1810*, London:
    Faber and Faber, 2002, p.410.
9   Duncan Pickard, *Lie of the Land*, London: Shepheard-Walwyn/Land Research
    Trust, 2004.
10 D.R. Denman, *Markets Under the Sea?*, London: Institute of Economic Affairs,
    1984.

10

Launched in the USA

§1 Debt and Destruction

FOR SIX MONTHS in 2001 an illusion was widely broadcast: the grief in the US would be confined to Wall Street. People did not want to heed the warning that was issued by the financial gnomes in Zurich. As early as June 5, 2000, the Bank for International Settlements (BIS) warned that the global economy faced a 'hard landing'. Consumers were freely spending cash on the back of rises in asset values, especially their homes. Eleven months later the World Trade Organisation announced that the growth in global trade would be half the 12.5% achieved in 1999. The nearly $6.2 trillion merchandise traded on the world markets in 2000 – twice the annual average for the previous decade – was a peak that would have its top lopped off. Who – or what – was to blame?

The recession could not be blamed on inflation. Higher prices for energy were offset by declines in the costs of manufactured goods. In fact, in 2000, prices of manufactured goods recorded the fifth consecutive annual decline. Average prices fell to their lowest level in 10 years. Employees, the favourite whipping boys of politicians, could not be treated as scapegoats: wages had not caused products to be priced out of the reach of consumers.

The first ripples of the recession that radiated out from the core American economy headed in an easterly direction, across the Atlantic to the shores of Europe. Could one of the coastal countries serve as a buffer against the recessionary tide? With a GDP of £836bn, Britain had overtaken France to become the fourth-largest economy behind the US, Japan and Germany. France still had higher levels of productivity and a trade surplus with Britain, and a higher GDP per person than Britain, but she also had an unemployment rate about twice as high as Britain's. France lacked the institutional flexibility to challenge the negative forces emanating from the US.

Nor could Germany serve as a buffer. She was weakened by the struggle to absorb the costs of unification with her erstwhile communist half. The rent-seeking motive had undermined the honourable effort to transform the former command economy of East Germany. Symbolising the flaws in the development strategy was Bankgesellschaft Berlin, the new capital's biggest financial institution. Ten years after the notorious wall had been taken apart brick by brick it was forced to fend off bankruptcy in the summer of 2001 with the quest for €2bn (£1.2bn.) in new funds. The bank was severely exposed by the bad loans advanced to the property market by its mortgage lending subsidiary. But it was not only the big-time financiers who were suffering. Reporter Haig Simonian summarised the crisis in a single telling sentence:

> From lawyers to Lufthansa pilots, the list of wealthy West Germans who have lost money investing in Berlin property since 1990 is about as long as the wall that once divided the city.[1]

The consequences of globalisation began to feed into Europe from the USA. One hundred years earlier, when the sun never went down on the British Empire, international trade was as global as the exchange of goods between countries could get, but the onset of business cycles has now changed. The distinctive development, today, is the synchronisation of cycles into a single gigantic trend.

In the 19th century, national business cycles worked according to their own timetables. Because they were not synchronised, they conveniently served as countervailing influences on each other. A recession in one country would partially compensate for an unsustainable boom on the other side of the world. This cushion effect helped to moderate the peaks and troughs. A boom in the United States could attract unemployed workers from a Britain that had plunged into recession.

Each cycle operated on the 18-year timeframe, because the internal financial mechanisms, property laws and fiscal policies were similar. The starting point for the cycles varied, however, for historical reasons. It would take a power of awesome proportions to deflect those trends. That did happen in the 20th century. Two world wars exerted sufficient reverse thrust to prevent the cycles from unfolding to their programmed timetables. Those wars were to exert a fatal impact on the world for years after the guns were silenced. They helped to shake out the differences and weld the industrial giants of Europe, North America and Japan into a single cycle.

Because Europe and Japan lost their sanity in 1939-45, it was not business as usual for a full decade after the termination of hostilities. Consequently, all the leading industrial nations were ready to jump-start their post-war cycles at about the same date – on or around 1955.[2] Coincidentally (see Table 6:1 on p.101), that put the British economy back on its historic track. The outcome was 18-year cycles that converged in time: 1956 to 1974, and 1974 to 1992. These had not fully matured into global cycles, however, because governments continued to try to preserve economic autonomy. But at the same time they were driven by political and economic forces to harmonise their interests into a few giant blocs.

Sovereignty, of the kind associated with the 19th century nation-state, came to an end with the onset of the 1992-2010 cycle. Europe and North America consolidated their free trade blocs, and computer technology meant that territorial borders did not have to be formally demolished – they were rendered obsolete, leapfrogged with the aid of satellites. Thus was launched the first integrated global cycle, economic life in every corner of the world carved up to suit the dynamics of the over-arching 18-year cycle.

The United States was the driving force. It was the first to go into the recession at the beginning of the 1990s, and was the first to recover. Its leading role was due to other factors, most importantly its pre-eminent size. This was where the recovery from 1992, the depth of the recession, would begin. The rocket launchers that fired the long run of growth under the Clinton presidency came in several guises.

● The demise of the Soviet Union left no one in doubt that capitalism reigned supreme. The USA was the leading champion of the market model, invincible both economically and militarily. The dollar was the global currency. Even the Russians preferred to keep their meagre savings in greenbacks rather than in roubles.
● The 'new economy' had the power to beguile: fortunes were made out of thin air. Or, at least, that was the mounting belief as computer technology progressed and the price of PCs crashed. Here was access to a new flow of rental income (from the electro-magnetic spectrum) that would spice up people's get-rich-quick expectations.

The BIS, in its annual report issued in June 2000, compared the US with Japan in the late 1980s. A combination of high-productivity growth, low inflation and an explosion in the price of assets ended in an economic implosion from which Japan failed to recover during the

1990s. That collapse had been driven by speculation in the land market, which drove prices to astronomical heights. *It was on the back of these prices that banks had expanded credit beyond sustainable limits.*

There are two approaches to analysing the underlying trends that culminate in a recession. The first is an analysis of institutions and market processes. The second is offered by trends in income distribution. My account of the first half of the 18-year cycle that began in 1991 in the US begins with market institutions.

The US economy was in recession in the second half of 1990. Growth could not begin until the glut of commercial and industrial buildings was cleared. The property market was dead in the years up to 1993. During this period, the collapse of office values was of the order of 40% to 50%. In 1994, entrepreneurs began to absorb some of the overhanging vacant properties, but the rate of take-up was slow. New construction began with vigour in 1997. Despite brief hiccups during the Asian financial crisis, followed by the Russian crisis in 1998, real estate was back in favour. The boom was fuelled by money that was poured into Wall Street, and poured back out through the real estate investment trusts (REITs). The managers of pension funds were not anxious to buy directly into property; they wanted the freedom to play with highly liquid stocks (their way of maximising trading fees). So they purchased shares in REITs, whose prices enabled them to set the pace for bidding up the price of real estate in the central business districts and around the suburban shopping malls.

In 1998, the construction industry supplied 1bn square feet of new offices – more than the record achieved at the peak of the previous cycle (1987). The market was 'overheating'. Then, in 1999, vacancy rates in office blocks in the suburbs began to rise. The output of industrial space was more than doubled during 1997 and 1998, and it remained at that level of production in 1999. Supply was eclipsing demand. The Wall Street analysts ought to have sounded the alarm bells.

In the first quarter of 1998, land sold for commercial development accounted for about 30% of real estate investment nationally. The flow of funds into the land market between the final three months of 1997 and the beginning of 1998 raised the average price increase of an acre of raw land by an annualised rate of 39%. The real economy, where productivity anchored the rise of wages and profits to between 3% and 10%, could not cope with such an increase. The numbers being reported by monitoring organisations such as the Commercial Investment Real Estate Institute ought to have revived memories of the historical parallels. Instead, the analysts were largely silent. Why was the real estate sector once again allowed to play the leading role in the progression to the next bust? Anthony Downs, a Senior Fellow at the Brookings Institution in Washington DC, a distinguished commentator on real estate, offered an explanation.

> [I]t was not lack of information that caused overbuilding in the 1980s. Two other factors were more important. One was the egotistical attitude among developers, each believing he should build his project, even if the total market would be overbuilt, because he would surely out-do the competition. That egotism is an essential ingredient in any successful developer's personality. But it leads to overbuilding when all developers are viewed together. The second factor was the strong incentive among financial institution officials to put out money in order to make fees. That incentive still exists today.
>
> I have not noticed a great welling up of humility among developers I know. Their propensity to overbuild is still there. And sources of capital are still pressured to make deals to get the money out, even when the money is coming from Wall Street.[3]

Dr. Downs, the author of a number of major books on economics and political theory, based his observations on a lifetime study of the property market. He has been consulted by many real estate investors, and his expertise has been tapped by federal government agencies. So when he wrote, in September 1999, that 'I do not expect an overall recession in 2000', his reassurance to risk-averse investors was worth a lot of money. Unfortunately, it was in the middle of 2000 that

● the growth of earnings reversed and went into a nosedive;
● first-time unemployment insurance claims began to rise;
● business investment in equipment and software began to decline.

Dr. Downs was not alone in his reassuring prognosis. In May 2000, the OECD also pronounced itself convinced that America had, indeed, unwrapped the secrets of a 'New Economy'. Close observation of the real estate sector had failed to arouse anxieties about the recession that struck manufacturers before the year was up. The US found itself locked into recession in 2001.

But if the institutional approach was failing to alert investors, diagnosis of economic prospects on the basis of trends in the distribution of income could fare no better. For this approach is complicated by the fact that we have to know how to unpack the influence of government on income before the statistics can disclose the hidden realities. Unfortunately, governments are not willing to allow us to understand how income is actually distributed between land, labour and capital. We need to know this, if we want to trace the influence of rental income on the business cycle. But to monitor the ups and downs of income – how much we produce, and whether there are variations in the trends between the factors of production – we need reliable statistics. But the rents of land and nature's other resources are not accorded respect in the nation's accounts. In the 19th century, disguising the scale of rents was turned into an art form by governments that were obliged to camouflage the bias in their financial policies.[4] The formal obliteration of rent was confirmed in the 20th century. In the UK, for example, in 1956, it was decided that, for the purpose of national income statistics 'rent might better be regarded as a form of trading profit – the surplus on operating account derived from the business of hiring real estate – than as the earnings of a specific and distinguishable factor of production'.[5]

Honest tax jurisdictions can calculate land values and rental income. An example is to be found in Canada, where British Columbia has an efficient procedure for assembling the information. Table 10:1 tracks the annual increase in values since 1979. From this, we can see the ups and downs in values. The column that discloses the percentage changes in land values identifies the mid-cycle boom of the early 1980s which was followed by the downturn in 1983, when an annual increase of 40% was followed by a 20% drop in values. The Winner's Curse phase was between 1989 and 1991, when the annual increase in land values topped 60%, followed by the recession of 1992.

The administrative infrastructure for valuing land separately from buildings in British Columbia was established by an American assessor, Ted Gwartney, who was hired in 1973 as a consultant to the Finance Minister. He employed the tools provided by professional bodies. He recommended the policy that was adopted by the legislature to revalue real estate annually. In 1975, he was appointed Assessment Commissioner. He successfully implemented a province-wide revaluation of all real estate. A data file was created that allowed the annual update of all real estate values. British Columbia has seen the number of properties increase from 879,130 (1975) to 1,623,097 (2000). The market value of property increased from $42 billion (1975) to $403 billion (2000). Land values increased from $29.6 billion (1979) to $221 billion (2000). Using computer technology, the work is performed with a reduced staff in spite of increased workloads.

Table 10:1

Property Assessments in British Columbia (1979–1998)

	Value ($ billions)			Annual increase (%)		
	Total	Land	Buildings	Total	Land	Buildings
1979	81.5	29.6	51.9	5.57	N/A	N/A
1980	94.1	39.1	55.0	15.46	32.0	5.9
1981	123.1	53.7	69.9	30.84	37.23	26.30
1982	157.1	75.3	81.7	27.59	40.22	17.62
1983	138.3	59.5	78.8	-11.97	-20.97	-3.50
1984	140.8	59.9	80.9	1.81	0.73	2.62
1985	145.7	62.2	83.5	3.48	3.86	3.20
1986	147.7	62.5	85.2	1.37	0.42	2.08
1987	135.5	61.5	74.0	-8.26	-1.54	-13.19
1988	140.4	63.6	76.8	3.62	3.39	3.81
1989	163.3	78.2	85.4	16.52	22.95	11.20
1990	170.0	79.7	90.3	3.91	1.96	5.70
1991	238.3	127.7	110.6	40.18	60.20	22.49
1992	245.6	128.9	116.7	3.06	0.95	5.51
1993	304.9	169.5	135.4	24.14	31.48	16.04
1994	343.2	196.7	146.5	12.56	16.00	8.25
1995	373.2	215.2	157.9	8.73	9.44	7.77
1996	384.4	218.7	165.7	3.02	1.60	4.95
1997	395.2	223.9	171.3	3.81	2.39	3.37
1998	403.0	222.7	180.3	0.02	-2.42	3.21

Source: 1978-2000 Annual Reports of British Columbia Assessment Victoria, British Columbia

Figure 10:1

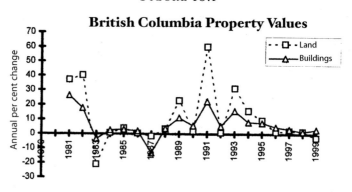

British Columbia Property Values

Over the 20 years to 1999, the value of land in British Columbia increased by 652%. This compared with a 247% increase in the value of buildings. Might such land value data of the kind available in British Columbia be relevant to governments that are charged with delivering sustainable economic growth? Not, it seems, according to conventional economic theory. The land market is strangely absent from the theories of economists. This, consequently, exposes people to the creative inventions that suit each period of feverish speculation. A new language is devised to beguile investors into parting with their money. In the digital age, the carrot held out to the mug punters was the 'new economy'. Yet another new way had been found to create wealth.

If, in the 'old economy', the mechanisms for financial speculation were opaque, they were even more so in the 'new economy', in which money could apparently be made out of thin air. As Greenspan anguished over 'asset prices', the US government and the Federal Reserve presided over the creation of the largest credit bubble in history. People borrowed to buy the shares of dot.com companies. The working population in 1999 paid income taxes of $450bn, which was how much the federal government needed to finance the $6 trillion national debt. The public burden was matched by a private debt of equally fearsome proportions. The driving force behind this credit bubble was the impatience of wealth-seekers.

In the past, the dreams of instant fortunes were built on land speculation. The rental income was *capitalised* into a tradeable asset. As people's expectations began to exceed the capacity of the economy, they embarked on the illusory process of deceiving themselves. They abandoned arithmetic in favour of gambling on the prospect that suckers would pay them prices that were higher than their land was worth. In the 1990s, people or companies that owned (or claimed to own) natural resources were too impatient to wait for rents to accrue. Through the stock markets they could *securitise* the rents by selling shares or other wondrously constructed financial instruments. This produced capital gains without having to deliver the goods.

Money and credit were expanded. At the beginning of the decade, total financial sector borrowing stood at $2.4 trillion, ballooning to $7.6 trillion by the end of 1999. Commercial paper provided the means to expand borrowings from $526bn to $1.4 trillion, an increase of 166%. Commercial paper that was supposed to be 'asset-backed' increased in value by more than 1000% in seven years. The commercial paper was the device employed by banks to expand lending which they did not have to chronicle in their balance sheets. This meant that they could sidestep Federal Reserve regulations that are supposed to ensure the stable supply of money to the economy.

But with Western governments preaching to Asian countries on the need for financial prudence and transparency, new methods had to be developed to cover the tracks of banks that were fuelling speculation through the credit pyramids. Enter the quasi bankers and the money market innovators. They could find ways around the constraints imposed on banks, which were supposed to relate their loans to the size of their capital base. Now, the divide between banks and non-banks was blurred almost beyond recognition. Thus was the 'money supply' multiplied to the point where it could no longer be defined, let alone grasped. The 'new economy' took off like a NASA rocket, fuelled by nuclear power in the form of perplexing financial instruments that were beyond the comprehension of the people whose savings and pensions were at stake.

Internet insider Tony Perkins warned that this speculative investment would be the undoing of the Wall Street stock market. He calculated that as much as half of the $400bn (£243.9bn) combined valuation of US dot.coms was due to market hype and the naivety of investors. Perkins was well informed, as co-owner of Red Herring, the California bible for dot.com investors. He flew into London to launch his book *The Internet Bubble* and in an interview he warned investors not to follow the herd.

But follow the herd they did. The temptations were too great. People on average wages were transformed into millionaires. The number of households with a net worth of more than $10m grew four-fold in the last decade of the 20th century, rising from about 67,700 to almost 350,000, according to New York University economics professor Edward Wolff. Households with net worth of $1m or more totalled 5m in March 2000, more than double the figure for 1983. The average age of the millionaires dropped: among those households holding the top 1% of assets, 5% were headed by someone 35 years of age or younger, compared to only 0.7% in 1983. *Forbes* magazine identified 267 Americans with a net worth of more than $1bn in 1999, up from 13 in 1982. The geographic shift in the fortunes identified the source of the wealth: in the 1980s, the rich usually were the product of Hollywood or Wall Street. Now they were concentrated in Silicon Valley.[6]

A measure of the precariousness of this 'wealth-creation' is margin debt – the borrowing of money to purchase stocks – which accounted for 1.6% of total stockholdings in 1999. This was the highest ratio since 1994. The financial authorities were correct to worry that, with so many citizens sinking such a high proportion of their assets into stocks, a Wall Street crash would suddenly dry up their willingness to consume goods. This would trigger a cut-back in the inventories held by retailers and a collapse in manufacturers' order books.

The crash at the end of 2000 was unavoidable, as manufacturers reported a weakening of demand for their goods. The final blow against the 'New Economy' came when the Conference Board, the New York-based business research group, announced on January 30, 2001, that their survey of households had shown a drop in consumer confidence to levels last seen in 1993, at the end of the recession of 1991/2. That word *confidence* was back in the news. The arch-confidence manipulator Alan Greenspan claimed that a recession would be averted even though the US economy was now growing at a rate 'probably very close to zero'. The critical issue, he insisted, was 'whether the degree of contraction is enough to breach the fabric of consumer confidence'.

Greenspan's analysis was presented to the Senate Budget Committee. The media confidently forecasted a further cut in the rate of interest as a desperate bid to bolster people's confidence. But a cut would encourage people to get even deeper in debt. Aligned with this would be a recovery of land prices (in locations where real estate markets had weakened), pushing them even higher (in locations where land prices continued their upward trajectory). So the tools used by the Federal Reserve to counteract the mid-cycle recession of 2001 – lower interest rates – would exact an even heavier price on the population during the recovery, as the economy launched itself towards the Winner's Curse phase of the speculative bubble.

§2 Predatory Finance

IN 1999 the level of credit creation indicated the exhaustion of economic potential within the US under the existing economic rules. US households expanded their mortgage debt by more than 10% in that year – far in excess of the increase in median wages and salaries. Corporate debt was increased by more than 11%, and the financial sector expanded debt at a rate of 17%, adding more than $1 trillion to its indebtedness, which was the second year of debt expansion exceeding the $1 trillion mark. Financial sector debt at the end of the millennium exceeded $7.6 trillion, an increase of over 75% during the previous five years. Additional debt in 1999 exceeded the additional growth of GDP by a ratio of 5:1. The housing market saw the average price of a dwelling nearly hit the $200,000 benchmark. Despite the decline of prices in nine of the 31 major housing markets which are surveyed by the Federal Housing Finance Board, nationwide the picture was one that commentators portrayed as 'healthy' growth. San Francisco remained the most expensive market, with its average price topping the list at $347,200.

One index measured the degree of stress among American families as a result of the rapid decline of affordability of homes. What HUD calls 'doubly burdened' cities tracked the crisis. One in eight cities fell into this category in 2000. They had an unemployment rate more than 50% higher than the US rate, and had either lost more than 5% of their population since 1980, or had a poverty rate of 20% or higher. Forty eight of the 67 doubly burdened cities were actually 'triply burdened', in that they suffered from all three characteristics.[7]

The dry figures disguise suffering on a mass scale, but the analysts failed to link the social malaise to its roots – the land market. As the prosperous section of America pressed ahead with the purchase of houses, this had the effect of 'driving increases in rents more than one-and-a-half times faster than inflation – and creating staggering jumps in home prices as well'.[8] Over the three years to 1999, the Consumer Price Index (CPI) rose 6.1% (2% p.a.), rents rose by 9.9% and house prices by 16%. US citizens were generously endowed by nature but despite its vast expanse of unsettled lands, the high average price of $194,300 (1999) reflected the universal truth in the 'old economy' adage: what matters is location, location, location.

The tax system promotes the swallowing up of land in a way that abuses the locational principle. The result in the US was 'accelerating growth in land consumption ... [which] threatens to undermine the quality of life in both cities and suburbs'.[9] While population was growing at 1% a year, land use for single-family housing was increasing at twice that rate – 2% a year, or 2.3 million acres a year since 1994. The rate of use of land increased, with more than a threefold increase since the 1950s.[10]

With the wasteful absorption of land came, in a very real sense, the gobbling up of people's lives. As home ownership expanded, the predators emerged from the woodwork. The culprit was what the US government called 'predatory lending'. This occurs when

> lenders ... are able to engage in lending abuses such as charging excessive up-front fees, high interest rates, and prepayment penalties. Such practises contribute to skyrocketing foreclosures ... especially in minority and low-income communities.[11]

Between 1993 and 1998, those loans increased ten-fold, from 80,000 to 790,000. With prosperity came the poverty on which the financial vultures could feed – 'the most vulnerable home owners – the elderly, minorities, and low-income families – loading them down with debt and stripping them of equity. In a growing number of cases, these predatory loan terms are too much to bear, and, as a result, the family loses its home to foreclosure'.[12]

By 2000 the strategies of home-buyers divided into the classic dualism of the late phase of speculation. High prices forced some Americans to buy their homes by borrowing to the hilt, and putting down minuscule deposits on the purchase price. But others paid cash representing more than half of the purchase price, as they traded up: selling their houses for top dollar and sinking the capital gains in more expensive homes in more desirable locations in the expectation of even higher capital gains in the future.[13] It appears that these families were not willing to comply with the psychological profile that Greenspan defined for them, as victims of 'transaction costs'.

> ... sales in the real estate market incur substantial transaction costs and, when most homes are sold, the seller must physically move out. Doing so often entails significant financial and emotional costs and is an obvious impediment to stimulating a bubble through speculative trading in homes.[14]

The reply from the 'victims' would be that, when land prices are soaring, transaction costs are viewed as trivial.

The last year of Bill Clinton's presidency saw the noose tightening. As consumers, the confidence among America's families slumped to a 7-year low. This timing fitted with the theoretical model described in Chapter 5. The seven years of growth completed the first half of the 18-year cycle. As home owners, families were saddled with mortgage burdens that achieved the highest levels on record. Even as more Americans were buying their homes, they owned less equity in their properties. The impact on spending power was crippling. Consumers paid debt service equal to 14% of their disposable incomes in the third quarter of 2000. This was the highest level since 1987, the peak year of the previous cycle. This helped to accelerate the appreciation of house prices. In real terms, the amplitudes of the price increases were on a rising trend through successive cycles: the year-on-year percentage changes were 13% for 1976 to 1979, 17% (1984-9) to 36% (1995-2003).[15]

Although the emerging evidence confirmed that the land market was the principal determinant of economic health, the way in which economics was personalised rebounded on the reputation of Alan

Greenspan. As George W. Bush took control of the White House, the whispering began. Greenspan's name was linked with the recession of the early '90s, when Bush Snr was the occupant of the White House. George Bush blamed Greenspan for raising interest rates and triggering recession before the elections that saw the first Clinton victory. Was Greenspan now responsible for contributing to another recession just as Bush Jr was assuming responsibility for the economy?

The first half of the 18-year cycle had been a phase of fabulous growth. The financial gurus who make megabucks out of pretending to predict what they claimed were random events had lionised the Chairman of the Federal Reserve. The share speculators justified the prices they paid for stocks on the basis of their confidence in Greenspan's handling of monetary policy. And then, suddenly, it all went sour. By April 2001, $4 trillion was wiped off stocks. And, inevitably, the knives came out. A scapegoat was needed and the 75-year-old hapless Chairman was the prime candidate. Now, he was blamed for encouraging unrealistic expectations. His warning of 'irrational exuberance', issued four years earlier, counted for nothing. The speculators assumed Greenspan knew what he was doing and that he would bale them out with cuts in interest rates.

As the price of shares achieved astronomical heights in 1999, Greenspan ought to have been raising the cost of borrowing money to cool the ardour of the dealers in Wall Street. He failed to do so, and that became the basis of the indictment against him when the big-time losers went searching for excuses. But despite the crash in the Spring of 2001, US stocks were estimated to be overvalued by $3.5 trillion, according to Professor Marcus Miller of Warwick University, whose preliminary analysis had been examined by the Federal Reserve early in 2000 – too late to take remedial action.

As the US stock market crumbled, the pundits who make their commissions by talking up the price of stocks and shares battled valiantly to claim that it would be a 'soft landing'. Even the international financial institutions were reluctant to analyse the downturn as the beginning of a full blown recession. But the analysts were misled. This was a recession like none of the previous ones. It was the first termination of growth within a globalised landscape, and the national statistical agencies lacked the macroeconomic tools with which to capture the impact on their computer screens.

As the transnational corporations were reporting a loss of profitability, the human consequences were not restricted to the United States. In the age of the portable corporation, with its outsourcing of production spread across the globe, a balance sheet crisis

---

Box 10:1

The Debt Trap

SOCIAL REFORMERS campaign for debt cancellation or relief in the developing world, but debt also achieved critical levels in Europe and North America. As the US boom popped in 2001 like soap bubbles in a windstorm

- investment-grade companies floated a record $582bn of bonds;
- household debts averaged 73% of GDP, compared with 63% in 1990-1, at the end of the previous business cycle; and
- corporate debts soared to over 47%, compared with 42% in 1990-1.

The regulatory authorities lost track of this debt mountain, because it was quickly repackaged in new financial instruments and sold to institutions. So instead of a clean-out of the debt, the excesses of the dot.com bubble were concealed in opaque accounting practices and laundered through the world's financial markets. The banks transferred the risks to others; and that, ultimately, meant it was carried by working people through a reduction in the quality of the investments held by their pension funds.

- In 2001, according to Standard and Poor's, there was a record worldwide default: 216 companies defaulted on $116bn of debt.
- Over the previous six years, collateralised debt obligations had been pumped up to between $300bn and $400bn on the global scale.
- The Bank of England estimated that the combined size of the credit transfer markets had quadrupled to $2,000bn since 1995.

This indebtedness in the rich nations had no equivalent in the developing world, and yet it was largely regarded with equanimity. But the post-industrial economies had lost the knack of manufacturing value of the kind that consumers wanted, so how were they to pay it off as they recovered their poise in 2003?

---

in Chicago or Baltimore would translate into a downsizing of workers in Delhi or Manila. So the initial reports that alarmed financiers in Wall Street failed to capture the human tragedy that was emerging in the first half of 2001. The global economy was locked in a debt trap (see Box 10:1).

By the end of 2000, growth had dropped to 1%, and bounced along at 1.3% in the first quarter of 2001. House sales dropped as firms slashed their stocks of goods for fear that consumers would reduce their spending. Manufacturing was in a depressed state, with lay-offs beginning to shatter people's belief that prosperity had come to stay. The decline in the sales of new single-family homes was evident in all major regions, but the decline was notably severe in the Mid West and South-East, which are heavily dependent on factory-based employment.

§3 The Risk Makers

AMERICA IS represented as the model of the future. Elevated levels of productivity, the dynamism of the digital age, are said to be products of the free market economy. The real dynamic of the 'New Economy' is more disturbing. It is driven by debt, which has become a primary mechanism for extracting rent from society.

The financial, insurance and real estate (FIRE) sector was investigated by Michael Hudson. He contrasts the financial sector with the 'real' economy that produces tradeable goods and services.

> A major reason for treating the financial sector separately is that its assets – and revenues – grow by a different mathematical dynamic from that of the production and consumption sector. Debts accrue interest while stocks earn dividends. These revenues are recycled into new lending to earn yet more interest and dividends, along with a rising flow of amortization payments to pay off the rising principal.
>
> This means that as the volume of debt increases relative to national income and production, more and more revenue must be diverted to pay interest to the financial sector. As this revenue is re-lent, about 70% is channelled into mortgage lending. This is used to bid up property prices. And the higher prices rise for real estate, the larger the loans grow that buyers take out to pay interest. This accelerates the ratio of debt-service to wages and profits...[16]

The 'interest' accumulated by the FIRE sector is, increasingly, rent. People who take out mortgages to buy their homes add to this accumulation. Syndicates of investors that use debt to buy commercial properties are willing to yield the flow of rents to the FIRE institutions (as 'interest') because they expect to reap capital gains when they sell their assets. Thus, financiers and property speculators are united in bloating the debt burden, to the neglect of production. As the economy's capacity to deliver consumer goods and services diminishes, it becomes vulnerable to its competitors – now, principally, in the Far East – which are specialising in factory-based enterprise. As the debt mountain accumulates, so the lives of an increasing number of people are exposed to the vagaries of currency flows over which they have no control.

In this system, risk is no longer the abiding discipline for capitalism. Bankers believe they can transfer risk to others. But they have short memories. The anxieties that mounted during the banking crisis in New England in the run up to the crash of 1992 – a classic result of real estate speculation – vanished as the new business cycle began in 1994. But this was not a paradox, for bankers are not risk-*takers*. They are risk-*makers*, by the recklessness with which they pour money into land speculation.

Bankers are not overly concerned with their appalling record as shamefully disclosed in the bankruptcy courts. First, their insistence on taking land as collateral for loans demonstrates that the risks, if there are any, will not fall on *them*. But when, eventually, under the overwhelming weight of reckless lending, some of them do collapse, they expect the federal government to come to their rescue.

In 2004, as the US headed for its next peak in property prices, two experts from the Federal Reserve of New York asked the pertinent question: Are home prices the next 'bubble'? Jonathan McCarthy (senior economist) and Richard W. Peach (a vice president) trawled through the data and concluded that the scare stories in the media were unwarranted. They sought to dowse the alarm bells being rung by journalists who feared that a housing bubble would lead to a collapse in prices. They claimed that 'the marked upturn in home prices is largely attributable to strong market fundamentals: home prices have essentially moved in line with increases in family income and declines in nominal mortgage interest rates'.[17] This confidence-building analysis came as the chief economist of bankers Morgan Stanley reported that 'America's asset economy is a house of cards'. Stephen Roach traced the upheaval in the US, which had switched from an income-generating economy to one that relied on asset-driven wealth effects.[18] The old rules were disparaged as obsolete, as consumers rejected the habits of thrift – based on how much they earned – to go on a spending spree. The 'wealth effect' delivered the ability to draw cash from the rise in asset values – such as one's home – and consume to one's heart's desire. Then, as interest rates began to crawl up, the Consumer Federation of America warned of the 'time-bomb'. Low-income earners were locked into mortgages that would become insupportable round about 2007.[19]

Americans sleepwalked into a debt trap, but the grief would not stop at the US borders. The globalisation of business means that the costs of the policy errors in America are automatically transferred to the rest of the world, most immediately through the financial markets. The US enjoys unequal power with Africa, Asia and South America, so it offsets a large part of its losses by borrowing from others, and through a deficit in trade. The unemployment that ought to fall on American families will be shifted to these regions in the Depression of

2010. But one man was hoping to avoid that fate for his country. Gordon Brown was relying on his magic mantra to protect the UK from the recession at the end of the first global cycle.

REFERENCES

1 Haig Simonian, 'A troubled city', *Financial Times*, May 30, 2001.
2 Harrison, *The Power in the Land, op. cit.*, p.79.
3 Anthony Downs, 'Where are we now in the real estate cycle?', September 1, 1999; www.anthonydowns.com .
4 Kevin Cahill, *Who Owns Britain: The Hidden Facts behind Landownership in the UK and Ireland*, Edinburgh: Canongate, 2001.
5 *National Income Statistics, Sources and Methods*, London: HMSO, 1956, p.332; cited in Phyllis Deane and W.A. Cole, *British Economic Growth 1688-1959*, Cambridge: University Press, 1962, p.241, n.1.
6 Laura M. Holson, 'Nothing Left to Buy', *New York Times*, March 3, 2000.
7 HUD, *op cit.*, p.31.
8 *Ibid.*, p.iii.
9 *Ibid.*, p.61.
10 *Ibid.*, p.63.
11 *Ibid,* p.viii.
12 *Ibid.*, p.60.
13 Edwin McDowell, 'Mortgages: Up, Down and Sideways', *New York Times*, June 25, 2000, Section 11, pp.1, 6.
14 Alan Greenspan, Testimony to the US House of Representatives' Joint Economic Committee, April 17, 2002.
15 Jonathan McCarthy and Richard W. Peach, 'Are Home Prices the Next "Bubble"?' Federal Reserve Board of New York *Economic Policy Review*: forthcoming, p.2, Chart 1.
16 Michael Hudson, 'Saving, Asset-Price Inflation, and Debt-Induced Deflation', in L. Randall Wray and Matthew Forstater (eds), *Money, Financial Instability and Stabilisation Policy* [Edward Elgar, forthcoming].
17 Jonathan McCarthy and Richard W. Peach, 'Are Home Prices the Next "Bubble"?', FRBNY *Economic Policy Review*, forthcoming, p.1.
18 Stephen Roach, 'America's asset economy is a house of cards', *Financial Times*, July 20, 2004.
19 Jenny Wiggins, ' "Time bomb" signals end of US house party', *Financial Times*, July 26, 2004.

II

Gordon Brown's Magic Mantra

§1 Miss Prudence, I Presume?

THERE WAS TIME to pre-empt the Depression of 2010. In writing *The Chaos Makers* in 1997, I warned: 'There was no need for the market economies to be caught unawares in 1974, 1982 or 1992, or by the next mid-cycle crash in 2000 which will be followed by the major economic collapse in 2010'.[1]

The backwash from America hit Britain's shores in February 2001. Manufacturers were the victims. Order books shrank, exports fell and the stockpiles of unsold goods started to rise. The Confederation of British Industry (CBI) read the results of its survey and forecast a further loss of 188,000 manufacturing jobs. Over the winter months, commentators remained optimistic that Britain could weather the storm. One man was less sanguine. Sushil Wadhwani, then a member of the Bank of England's Monetary Policy Committee, warned: 'I believe that standard econometric models do not adequately capture the link between the UK and the US economies'.[2]

If mantras had magical power, Gordon Brown's chant would have saved Britain. During his stewardship at the Treasury, he chanted the phrase 'no more booms and busts' on countless occasions. Then, weeks before the election in June 2001, the bad news about the haemorrhaging manufacturing sector delivered embarrassing headlines. The scriptwriters were called in. Shrewdly, the chancellor dropped his favourite incantation. He needed a new sound-bite. One was ready to hand: he adopted the rationalisation proffered by his predecessors. The chancellor was suddenly converted to the Natural Law theory of the business cycle. For 'booms and busts' – which he had insisted he would not countenance – he now substituted 'ups and downs'.

> The economic cycle has its ups and downs – to fight for a better platform for stability is not to say that the economy does not from time to time face ups and downs. But I think we are

better placed through having low inflation, our fiscal position in
order, and through avoiding some of the problems we had in the
late Eighties.[3]

He absolved himself. Those ups and downs were inevitable – acts of
God. Certain familiar themes were indeed recurring. Shopkeepers
were being driven out of their high street premises by rent increases
that they could not afford, according to the retail consultancy Verdict.
Only businesses in high-margin sectors such as mobile phones, coffee
bars or fast food restaurants could afford the space. These are features
of the 'ups and downs' of business; but they are not driven by a law of
nature. The culprits are the tax system favoured by Gordon Brown,
the laws of the land, and an economic wisdom that distracts people
from the realities beneath their feet.

If Brown's mantras had worked, his legacy would have been an
historic accomplishment. The mantra did appear to possess the
powers of self-hypnosis for the chancellor, but its influence was too
weak to overcome the public actions of the custodian of the nation's
economic welfare. Brown affirmed and reinforced policies that would
terminate with an old-fashioned boom bust. His infatuation with
Miss Prudence, the Lady of Whitehall whom he courted in the belief
that she would deliver stable growth, was sending Britain straight
into the downturn towards the end of the decade. Brown was steering
the economy with his version of the Titanic Guidance System. As
passengers gaily danced to the lyrics of 'openness, accountability and
transparency', the ship of state was blindly steered on its ill-fated
course.

The goal was unambiguous: 'The government's macroeconomic
framework has been designed to avoid a repeat of mistakes which led
to boom and bust cycles and relative underperformance'.[4] To avoid
this fate, Brown declared that he would not manipulate the economy
for short-term political purposes. Unfortunately, his tools would prevent him from fulfilling his promise. His list of famous last words will
include this promise and prediction:

> This cycle of boom and bust has been enormously damaging
> to the UK economy. Each downturn has led to more people
> becoming detached from the labour market, often giving up
> on finding a job and becoming economically inactive. That
> is why the Government has put macro-economic stability at
> the heart of its economic policy, ensuring that there will be
> no return to the boom and bust of the past. The
> Government's ambition is that by the end of the decade

there will be a higher percentage of people in employment
than ever before – not through an unsustainable boom, but
through sustained policies of macro stability.[5]

According to the statistics, he achieved this goal in seven years.
Britain had an unemployment rate of 4.8% in 2004, half the rate of
some EU partners. But Britain also had more than 2.7m people out of
work who were declared sick or receiving disability benefit: one in
every 22 Britons without jobs, many of them able and willing to work.
As the *Financial Times* editorialised (July 28, 2004), if people who were
willing to work were taken into account the unemployment rate would
be double – taking the figure up to the worst EU levels.

Brown was not on a course for sustainable growth, but the crash
that loomed at the end of the decade could not be anticipated by
those who relied on conventional wisdom. The Treasury does not forecast beyond the short term. And so, if it is correct that 'three years is
too short to establish a trend',[6] it is difficult to see how the Treasury
could claim that it had established the conditions for continuous
growth. In fact New Labour had set the dials on the control systems
so that the economy would head straight for the hidden icebergs. This
was exemplified in the market for houses.

Gordon Brown triumphantly told the House of Commons, time
and again, that his economic philosophy was 'prudence for a purpose'.
His decision to relieve himself of the power to set interest rates had
been vindicated.

But the economists who were steering the monetary course had
to abandon their official measures and fall back on *ad hoc* hunches, to
take into account something that was happening to the cost of buying
houses. For there was one seriously imprudent feature of the inflation
target: it did not formally focus the minds of policy makers on the
signals emitted by the capital gains being reaped in the property
market. Brown and his team of ministers in the Treasury, who had
their hands on the levers of taxing power, operated with a guidance
system which told them that the economy was on an even keel. And if
it hit an economic iceberg the Treasury could shift responsibility away
from itself.

> The inflation target applies at all times, and the MPC is
> accountable for any deviations from it. The framework recog-
> nises, however, that any economy can at some point be subject
> to unexpected events which can cause inflation to depart from
> its desired level. In such cases, the onus is on the MPC to
> explain how it proposes to return inflation back to target.[7]

By defining the target, and transferring responsibility to economists and financiers who had not been elected by the public, a further erosion of democratic accountability was executed with triumphant fanfare. If a crash came, the politicians would not carry the blame.

But why did the Treasury place such importance on inflation as the key indicator? According to its own assessment: 'Inflation outturns have been a poor guide to prospects in previous cycles'.[8] Why was inflation a poor indicator? The evidence offered by the Treasury emphasised the cost of acquiring homes: 'Past housing cycles have been characterised by stronger and more persistent over-shooting in activity and prices relative to longer-term sustainable levels'.[9] An inflation target that excluded vital information on what was happening in the housing market was bound to offer misleading signals!

Brown, while persisting with the habit of his predecessors – lecturing people on the need to be responsible for the way they bargained over wages – remained imprudently vague about the need for responsibility in the deals that were struck in the property market. Did this matter? Towards the end of 1999, with an annual growth in real household disposable incomes of 5%, house price increases escalated by 15%. The Treasury hedged its bets. It claimed that 'While the new macroeconomic framework provides a more credible guard against speculative behaviour, policy will need to remain alert to the risks'.[10] That speculative activity, however, would be inadequately analysed. Remedial action was not likely because the chancellor's inflation target myopically downgraded the one source of instability that would signal risks to people's hopes of providing shelter for themselves that they could afford. If the economy was to steer a course around the concealed icebergs, it would be due to luck rather than the prudence of Gordon Brown.

During the first New Labour administration, a chance for an authoritative challenge to the orthodoxy of the Treasury occurred when the government established a new statistics commission in June 2000. This was part of the biggest overhaul of official data in 30 years. The economic secretary to the Treasury, Melanie Johnson, explained: 'Our aim has always been to raise the public's confidence in official statistics'.[11] The watchdog commission would be able to challenge the government if it sought to twist statistics to serve partisan political purposes. But there was one piece of information that the Treasury decided it would not transfer to the commission – the inflation index.

Was this exclusion perverse, or was it consistent with Brown's promise of transparency in economic policy? When he was appointed

Chancellor of the Exchequer in May 1997, he promised to behave in a 'prudent' manner. All his actions during the first two years in the Treasury were tailored to 'get rid of boom and bust from the economy', he recalled after introducing his budget on March 21, 2000. The outcome, he claimed, was a balanced approach between enterprise and fairness, in which taxes were amended to encourage capital formation, research and development and the 'tough love' approach to forcing unemployed people back into work. Despite the public confidence with which he boldly proclaimed these policies and objectives, however, he would not tolerate the searching challenges of independent statisticians. Inflation would remain a political concept. Gordon Brown would retain control of the public's perception of what counted as a relevant price rise.

That was one reason why the three waves of land price increases that engulfed Britain in the 1990s did not attract public alarm. The third wave, the monster of the decade, began in 1998 – during the economic stewardship of Gordon Brown – and roared into the first three months of the new millennium at an annualised rate of 50%, according to the market evidence monitored by FPDSavills. The growth in the price of residential building land over the 12 months to June 2000 slowed, but was still 33.4%. This gain in price dwarfed the wage and salary increases that people were achieving. There was nothing in the government's data on price inflation to match the trends in the land market, and yet – for the purpose of formulating inflation-containing policies – these numbers were off the radar screen.

The annual rate of 33% had not been seen since 1994. Average land values were raised to £607,000 per acre, which was 23% higher than the record levels achieved in 1988, the peak in property prices that triggered the slide into the recession of 1992. With prices at that level, it was not surprising that FPDSavills registered a weakening of prospective visits by home buyers to the development sites of builders in the second half of 2000. Then, as the bad news from the United States seeped into the financial expectations of people in Britain, land prices dropped to an annual growth rate of 13.2% in the first quarter of 2001.

Builders need to be eternal optimists in the face of the volatility that is endemic in their industry. But that optimism exposes them to the trap of paying too much for land. FPDSavills warned:

> The danger is that competition for land and upward pressure on land prices means that developers rely on high projected sales values in order to buy land. It is vitally important that developers make sure that projected sales values bear some relation to the fundamentals of the local market ...[12]

Was the cost of buying land so insignificant as to warrant the Treasury's cavalier treatment of the statistics? According to Yolande Barnes, the Director of Research at FPDSavills: 'In real terms [house prices] have only risen by 36% in 20 years, while land prices have increased by 307% over the same period'.[13] This astonishing good fortune for landowners received no official attention during the 1990s. Two paralysingly simple pieces of logic enabled statisticians to gloss over the land market's macroeconomic significance. Since the same logic is employed in all industrial countries, we can summarise the practise by referring to the summary offered by the United Nations in a document that was compiled in association with international financial agencies such as the World Bank.

The first step is the use of fiction to achieve a zero effect in the nation's books. 'By convention,' says the UN, 'all owners or purchasers of land located within the economic territory are resident institutional units.'[14] Thus, if I sell you land, and if we both live in England, so far as the statistics are concerned the effect is zero: we exchange money for land of equal value, so the transaction can be ignored for statistical purposes. But what if the owner is a foreigner who might take his money abroad? The problem is solved by fabricating a fictitious entity: 'A national resident institutional unit has to be created that is deemed to own the land, while the non-resident unit is deemed to own the national unit'. In this way, we keep the land transactions within the territorial borders, and the financial effect– as far as the statistical chronicles are concerned – is zero. Zero is a more reassuring number than a 30% rise in prices!

The second issue is both conceptually and morally important, but its practical significance is cheerfully ignored by the crystal ball gazers in the national treasuries and central banks. Rent is acknowledged as a transfer payment. It is not a reward to the owner for a value added to the sum total of goods and services in the economy. Rents 'accrue to the owners of the assets [land or other natural resources] in return for putting them at the disposal of other institutional units for specified periods of time'.[15] This contrasts with the 'rentals' payable for the use of buildings, which are treated as purchases of services (someone, after all, had actually to build those structures with materials that were manufactured). Land, as 'a non-produced asset', is metamorphosed into something less interesting than buildings. While ideally the value of land should be recorded separately from the value of buildings in the national accounts, 'if it is not possible to determine whether the land or the structure is the more valuable, by convention, the transaction should be classified as the purchase of a structure, that is, as gross fixed capital formation'.[16] *Hey Presto!* Because nearly all countries decline to value land as a separate entity, and they use faulty methodology to under-value land even if they do, they have no reliable data to feed into the book-keeping exercise. So the unique characteristics of land are levelled out into the averages that are achieved from buildings. The staggering volatility of prices in the land market are screened out. This enables governments to ignore the cyclical eruptions beneath their feet.

The levelling of the impact of land to zero allows governments to employ arbitrary tools for diagnosing the economy. The computer models in the UK Treasury and the Bank of England cannot cope with 50% annualised rates, which is what surfaced in the land market in 2000. And so, the state of health of the nation is left to the tender mercies of monetary policy.

§2 The Tax-Funded Hoax

THE PERVERSE logic of Gordon Brown's monetary policy can be understood in terms of the analogy of a fire. Assume that you are the leader of a fire brigade that is called out to combat a blaze located in the roof of a 20-storey apartment building. Everyone can see the flames going through the roof. There is a risk that the fire will spread to the apartments on the 19th floor. Time is against you. What would people think if you gave the order to douse every apartment in the building with equal amounts of water? Saturation soaking of the apartments on the 18th and the 17th floors might be warranted. The judgment might be that the speed with which the flames were spreading was such that containment required desperate measures, including the spraying of apartments on the levels which had not yet been damaged. But why also train the hose pipes on the tenth floor, the fifth floor and all the way down to the ground floor? These would be self-defeating tactics indeed. They exhaust the defensive measures that might be taken on the floors where the conflagration was concentrated, and they maximise the water damage to furniture on the floors where the fire need not reach.

The authorities responsible for the fire brigade would censure you for wasteful tactics. The water concentrated on the ground floor would be at the expense of dealing with the heat where it was at its maximum – and going through the roof. That is what governments and central banks do when they raise interest rates. In the British residential land market, the conflagration of prices is always red-hot in the

South East. Here, prices achieved £600,000-plus an acre in 2000, compared with £400,000 in South Wales, and £250,000 in Scotland and Northern England. So why douse Wales or Scotland with the same vigour as England's South East?

The single-bore interest rate policy demoralises workers and investors and corrupts the political system. When aligned with taxation, the implosion in the urban economy is fatal. Wales is one of the victims.

Most people in Wales live in areas that exist close to or below the economic margin. Many of these communities would not be habitable at current levels of acceptable living standards without the infusion of aid from taxpayers in regions that generate a taxable surplus. But the Welsh are still required to pay taxes such as VAT on the goods they consume even though many of them cannot afford to do so. So out of a population of about 3m people, 2m live in areas that benefited from £1.2bn transferred to them in 2001 by the European Union under a scheme known as Objective One. But communities in the valleys and West Wales would receive this money not as a net addition to the income they can generate for themselves. For even as the money flows in from public agencies to be spent on projects approved by government, at least an equivalent amount flows out of the local economies as tax payments to the exchequer in London. This process is akin to the sleight of hand of the cardsharp: giving money with one hand and taking it back with the other hand. In between these two hands there is a leakage of value. Bureaucracies have to be supported that serve no function other than to recycle taxpayers' money. This creates the illusion of enlightened government generosity. In fact, it is one grand political hoax.

Occasionally, under pressure, the truth is leaked. That is what happened as the high exchange rate of sterling – buoyed by the relatively high interest rates – caused problems for exporters. Manufacturing industry lost 400,000 jobs in 1999, and the sector's output fell three months in a row up to February 2000. But the two key economic power brokers were helpless. As BMW pulled out of its operations in the West Midlands, the then Governor of the Bank of England, Eddie George, was confronted by members of the British Chambers of Commerce. George replied: 'The question for me, sympathise as I do, is what the hell can we do about it, and I'm afraid the hard-hearted answer is not an awful lot'.

Both Sir Edward (as he was to become) and Gordon Brown were imprisoned by their doctrines. Inflation was their key barometer. Nothing would be allowed to jeopardise their commitment to a 2.5%

target rate. A callousness similar to the one that had last been experienced under Margaret Thatcher was expressed by Brown in a statement to the Treasury Select Committee in the House of Commons: 'I appreciate the concerns of exporters, but they themselves would say that the last thing they want the government to do would be to put at risk the stability of the economy by pushing us back to boom bust. That's not something we are going to do'.[17]

The boom bust was in the making, but Brown did not fear the threats. He was busy building the image of Macho Man – of being able to take what he called 'tough' decisions – to bolster his interpretation of economic prudence. But the price of political virility was paid by the teachers and nurses who were locked out of the market for homes in the regions where land prices rocketed beyond their ability to finance mortgages. Industry in south-east England discovered it could not hire workers. This was reflected on the stock market, for example, where the shares of Stagecoach, a bus and rail operator, fell 42% after it reported a shortage of qualified drivers. Stagecoach identified 'rising house prices and the high cost of living' as the cause of a shortage of employees.[18] The high cost of living, in this period, had everything to do with taxation, and little to do with people's demands for wage increases. Government policy manifested itself in various guises, including the subsidies it paid to compensate people for the damage inflicted by its taxes. For example, the inflow of workers from higher-unemployment areas was obstructed by the shortage of affordable homes. The government's solution was to suggest subsidising the cost of borrowing money to buy houses for teachers and nurses. Such announcements encourage land owners to raise their prices even further. When the housing market is subsidised by taxpayers, the subsidies are capitalised into land prices. That makes it even more difficult for low-income families to acquire homes.

Another perverse strategy was Brown's use of stamp duty on housing transactions. These were levered up in each of his budgets. In March 2000, the rate remained at 1% for properties over £60,000, but was raised to 3% for properties over £250,000, and 4% for properties over £500,000. But despite the doubling of the two higher tax rates, the housing market boomed. The general agreement of property professionals was that the stamp duty would not deter people from 'trading up' in a market where they paid to the government a small fraction of the capital gains. But that tax helped to price low-income families out of the housing market.

While preaching prudence and fiscal rectitude, Brown unwittingly encouraged people to participate in the culture of deception. The stamp duty could be avoided by vendors whose properties were worth more than the benchmark prices. For example, a house worth £525,000 could be sold for £499,000. This would make the seller liable for the lower stamp duty. The vendor, however, would also sell fixtures and fittings for £26,000, to achieve the full market price for his property and enjoy a rewarding victory over the taxman.

Compounding the impact of the housing crisis, in the run up to the first election to be faced by the Blair government, was the overvalued currency. This punished industries that exported their products. British goods cost more compared with the products of foreign competitors. But appeals to the Bank of England for a shift in policy fell on deaf ears. Sir Edward declined to reduce interest rates to weaken sterling. Between them, the Treasury and the Bank of England were boxed in by their theories.

Investors from Japan added to the pressure on the British government. Their domestic economy moved deeper into depression. Businessmen searched abroad for opportunities, and Britain offered a safe haven for their investments. That outlook changed when the value of sterling began its rise against the euro. Japanese entrepreneurs did not conceal their intentions. They warned that their earlier contribution to the inflow of capital into Britain was jeopardised by the high exchange rate.

Even the leading British 'blue chip' companies were losing out in the capital markets. The fashionable dot.com companies hoarded the cash that would have been invested in traditional value-adding/ profit-making ventures such as breweries and construction firms. The internet companies were awash with cash as a result of the gamble in their shares. Investors persuaded themselves that they would reap fortunes from the new locations of the 21st century – the 'sites' in cyberspace.

The micro chip had made it possible to peel back another of nature's layers of rent, but the process was camouflaged by economic theories that distracted the analysts from the realities of the 'new economy'. All the publicity was aimed at downgrading the significance of land in favour of the latest fads. *The Sunday Times*, for example, identified the richest man of the past millennium as William of Warenne, a Norman noble who was rewarded by William the Conqueror with land which by 1088 stretched across 13 counties. At his peak, he was worth about £57bn in today's terms – about £4bn more than Microsoft's Bill Gates before the value of his shares fell in March 2000. But cyberspace had replaced terrestrial space as the medium of analysis.

[L]and no longer dominates. Finance, computers, banking, information, media and entertainment are now quicker ways to making a fortune than being a knight in battle.

But *The Sunday Times* then failed to reanalyse its verdict on the basis of its concluding observation: 'Mind you, what do the new billionaires do with their wealth? They buy the sort of estates Warenne once enjoyed and employ a good tax lawyer'.[19]

§3 Building in the Crisis

GOVERNMENTS ARE the architects not only of their own downfall. Many innocents are victimised along the way. As private incomes are plundered for taxes, elected representatives pour money into activities that elevate the price of land. The outcome is a culture impoverished by self-defeating policies. One of the conduits for routing failure into the wider economy is the construction industry. It is used to spread taxpayers' money in a way that exacerbates the business cycle. This may be illustrated by the need for decent schools for the children of Scotland.

There was plenty of work for the construction industry in Scotland, where schools were in such disrepair that it would cost £1.3bn to bring them up to standard, according to the Convention of Scottish Local Authorities.[20] The construction industry would welcome this work, but the opportunity is denied because of the violent roundabouts driven by land speculation. The construction industry itself could not pronounce against the forces that were disrupting its activities, because it, too, lacks a theory of why its entrepreneurs are repeatedly bankrupted. The industry complained of 'land assembly problems', but blamed planning procedures. And so the industry deluded itself with a forecast for the 10 years up to 2010. 'Encouragingly the economy and government policy now appear set on a more stable course for many years.'[21] That verdict was published as the Land Registry reported house prices in some areas leaping by more than 30% over the previous 12 months.

The mid-cycle housing boom came on time. It was to be anticipated. In 1990, I warned that unless the structure of fiscal policy was shifted away from wages and profits, and onto the annual rent of land,

the UK economy will be afflicted by another mini boom/slump caused by land values before the end of this century, and will tailspin into another horrendous depression by the end of the year 2009'.[22]

The first half of the boom in land prices exploded in 1998, with the ratio of house prices to earnings soaring in 1999. Personal indebtedness began to climb as people took out larger mortgages to acquire homes. The Financial Services Authority launched an inquiry in March 2000 to establish whether banks were once again embarking on reckless loans to home owners. Indebtedness rose to proportions last seen at the height of the land boom of the late 1980s. People borrowed more as the market price of their homes rose, but in 1999 this increased personal insolvencies in England and Wales to a five-year high.

The exuberance lasted until the middle of 2000, by which time the damage covertly inflicted by land speculation on Britain's manufacturers had been done. The OECD tracked what it called 'the recession that wasn't'.[23] Manufacturers suffered recession for two consecutive quarters in 1999.

With house prices overheating in London and the South East, the Bank of England decided to ratchet up the cost of borrowing money. Higher interest rates did not cool the ardour of people who wanted to own their homes. The victims were the investors in manufacturing enterprises and their employees. The output of GDP flattened at the end of 1998, but the manufacturing sector felt the worst effects. The OECD noted: 'While the economy as a whole did not record a recession, in the conventional sense of two consecutive quarters of negative growth, some sectors did, notably manufacturing'.[24]

As the people who added value to the economy suffered, home owners sitting on piles of equity went on a spending spree. They re-mortgaged their properties to spend cash in the shops. Equity withdrawal (as a proportion of post-tax income) reached its highest level since the previous peak in 1991. Even though the high street was assaulted by deflationary pressures, which prevented retailers from raising prices, the Bank of England reacted by hardening the cost of borrowing money. Employment in manufacturing fell by 3% in 1999, continuing the hollowing out process that began in the Thatcher era.

Better news appeared to come thick and fast by the summer of 2004. The economy was diagnosed as in a good state of health by the commentators, and the global economy was recovering after the mid-cycle recession. Growth was now on the agenda, and there was tax-payers' money to spend on health and education. The government having weathered the scandal of the Iraq War, New Labour was set fair to face the voters at a general election. There was just one little problem. It was spotlighted in the back of the financial pages of the press, the vaguest hints in such obscure terms that they would even have escaped the attention of the intelligence officers of Her Majesty's Secret Services.

House builders had monitored the signs, and some of them decided to wind down their output of dwellings. Land had become so expensive that the economics of construction no longer made sense. As builders with shrinking land banks but high brand recognition, like Wimpey, outbid family-owned firms that are driven to the margins,[25] the housing market braced itself for a return to difficult times.

- The UK's largest volume house builder, George Wimpey, decided to be 'selective' – a euphemism for putting the brakes on its plans. Chief Executive Peter Johnson identified the increase in interest rates as bearing down on house prices while land prices remained high.[26]
- One of Britain's quality house builders, the Berkeley Group, decided to cash in its chips. It was time to sell about half its 26,000 plots and distribute £1.4bn to investors. Why the pull-out? The firm announced that the cost of building houses was eclipsing the prices at which the properties could be sold. That meant the price of land was outstripping people's ability to match the expectations of land owners.

The market shuddered with anxiety as analysts noted: 'Berkeley has said it is not buying land at today's prices [which] implies that it is not confident that today's house prices are sustainable'.[27] The inancial analysts recalled that Tony Pidgley, who ran the Berkeley Group, had sold most of his land at the top of the market in the early 1990s. In 2004, did he know something that had escape the attention of others?

For its part, the Bank of England sighed with relief as estate agents noted a hesitancy among buyers. The market in houses paused. Having exploited the low-value properties in the peripheral markets of Wales and the North of England, the centre of action gravitated back to the South-East. The property market would revive in 2005, after the general election. The speculators owed their emerging fortunes to the policies of one man: Gordon Brown.

The Treasury was convinced that it had to boost the output of houses. But pouring public money into construction while failing to neutralise the impact of the capital gains from land would drive Britain into the grasp of the Winner's Curse in 2006. Public sector spending would lead the dash into the Depression of 2010.

Brown wished to help low income families, but spending taxpayers' money to subsidise housing was like throwing petrol on a bonfire. This was what happened when the government decided to spend £250m on low-cost housing for key workers. The intention was to provide an extra 56,000 homes by 2004; but that public money gave another upward twist to the price of land.

The government's urban strategy was calculated to subvert its plans. For example, it placed a premium on the evolution of compact urban environments. Its spending plans, however, by raising land values, would encourage owners to retain their sites in a vacant or under-used state in the expectation of even higher capital gains. Brownfield sites would not be brought forward for use in the volume required to meet the government's targets for the building programme.[28]

The new frontier was to the east of London. This was where the government decided to take its stand. It announced a massive expansion of construction of affordable homes. The Thames Gateway project would be the bonanza for land owners. The minister in charge of planning – Deputy Prime Minister John Prescott – announced that they would ease the guidelines to cram hundreds of thousands of houses onto their acres. This added a new level of expectation which translated into an increase in the rate of growth of land prices. In 2004, the prices of farmland without permission for development increased by 30%.

People were desperately in need of homes at affordable rents. At the same time, in London alone, 70,000 properties in the private sector were vacant for more than six months, according to the Empty Homes Agency. But instead of realigning property rights and public finance to eliminate the incentives that encourage such waste, the government announced its intention to spend up to £1bn in the two years up to 2006 to help 12,000 public sector workers to buy homes. Such piecemeal policies could not possibly compensate for the costly legal and institutional flaws in the system.

Britain needed a simple but fundamental reform that would liberate people and their communities to take a grip of their own destiny. Instead, with the blessings of the Treasury which provided the funds, Prescott announced that spending on housing would rise to £1.3bn in 2008. The money would be spent not just on houses but also the supporting infrastructure. What's more, the big-hearted Prescott had identified nine areas in the North and the Midlands where housing markets had collapsed and were trapped in negative equity – the owners had mortgage debts which exceeded the value of their properties. So he nominated these as renewal areas in which spending would be nearly trebled from £160m in 2004 to £450m by 2008.

Thus, by government edict, money was flushed into the property market at an accelerating rate. That process would reach its crescendo in 2008 – the peak of the property cycle.

§4 Back to 5%

GORDON BROWN had ample opportunity to analyse these processes and to adopt effective remedies, but he declined to confront the realities. When he was questioned by parliamentarians on December 17, 2002, he refused to describe the housing market as being in a 'boom'. Instead, he preferred to describe it as experiencing 'a very fast rise' in prices. His tough language was reserved for the labour market. He called for discipline among public servants who should not seek 'excessive wage rises'.[29] The labour market, unlike the land market, was not privileged.

As the pressure cooker gathered steam, Brown sought refuge in his magic mantra. He would remain prudent, but he was not averse to a little help. He reassured the House of Commons Treasury Select Committee that 'income tax revenues are rising because bonuses are returning to the City'.[30] Those bonuses would pump up the top end of the London housing market in the second half of the property cycle. What is more, the chancellor offered a bonus to the property market: he decided to sell £30bn of public assets by 2010.

But the chancellor's rosy view of the world was not shared by the people who earned their living in Birmingham, the birthplace of building societies. Here, Brown's doctrines were causing grief. To hit the 2% inflation target which the chancellor had set in December 2003, the Bank of England had to raise interest rates to 5%. The inflation rate was predicted to hit 2% in 2006, but a collateral consequence would be the halving of the economy's growth rate from 4% to 2%.[31]

The Bank of England considers 5% to be the neutral interest rate. But under the policies which it and the Treasury employs, 5% is anything but neutral. It was calculated to impose an artificial constraint on the productivity of private enterprise. This became apparent as the Bank of England expressed its satisfaction with trends in the economy as it raised the interest rate to 4.75% in the summer of 2004. In Birmingham, raising the cost of borrowing money to influence house prices was a catastrophe for small and medium sized businesses.

According to a survey conducted by the CBI, orders received by small and mid-sized factories had contracted. While the Bank of England claimed to be concerned about inflation, manufacturers found it all but impossible to raise their prices as profit margins came under pressure from foreign competitors. The confidence of entrepreneurs drained away in response to the five quarter-point rises in borrowing rates in the eight months to August 2004.

One of the victims was K. & S. Plating, a Birmingham firm that coats manufactured products with layers of corrosion-resistant materials. It employs 32 people with sales of £1.5m. Linda Evans, managing director, reported that trading conditions had been made difficult by the rise in interest rates. Her firm's customers, many of whom rely on substantial overdrafts to conduct their businesses, were suffering. As a result, one of the biggest risks to her company was that her customers would redirect their business to lower cost countries in the Far East.

The haemorrhage of orders could be measured in terms of the outflow of jobs. According to analysis in the technology sector by Forrester Research, more than 1m European jobs would move offshore over the 10 years to 2014. Nearly two-thirds of those jobs would be at the expense of UK employees.[32] For Linda Evans, such forecasts confirmed her worst fears. She saw 'nothing but doom and gloom'. But there was one bright element in her life. Interviewed in August 2004, she said that she had just sold her home for five times more than she had paid for it.

> When I bought it 14 years ago it was for the right market price. When I sold it, it was worth double what I had paid, but not five times more. In 14 years, to get five times more is ridiculous.[33]

She believed that the increase in interest rates would not make much difference to investors in the housing market, where capital gains had been leaping at the rate of 20% per annum, but they were 'devastating' for manufacturers.

The single-tool strategy employed to guide the UK economy did not make sense to employers in Birmingham. The solution, for entrepreneurs like Linda Evans, was to expand the output of houses at prices people could afford. 'If property was not overpriced in the first place we would not have the problem with the interest rate, because it would be low enough for people to buy houses and for manufacturers to run their overdrafts. It is good to have a low interest rate, but it needs to be kept low because we cannot compete with the Far East or Eastern Europe whose costs are lower than ours.'

2004 was supposed to be in the upswing of the business cycle. But official policy imposed an artificial ceiling on productivity. The Bank of England disguised its cap on capitalism with dense terminology. Raising the interest rate towards 5% would deliver Gordon Brown's 2% inflation target, but at what price? The Bank in its August 2004 *Inflation Report* said that inflation would flatten by 2006, 'reflecting the attenuation in capacity pressures resulting from the slackening in demand growth during the second year of the projection'.[34] In plain English, the productive potential of the UK was to be sacrificed to achieve the doctrines fashionable in the Treasury. The anvil on which the economy would be hammered was traced by the red line on the Bank of England's Chart 1.1.[35] This projected interest rates flattening off at 5%.

The restraint on trade was to accommodate the orthodox view of what was the tolerable rate of growth for the UK. While China could register double-digit growth rates, UK growth was to be officially obstructed to control 'inflation'. According to the data, inflation was barely more than 1%, which fell *short* of the Bank's 2% target. But with manufacturers and retailers recording the fact that they could not raise prices even if they wanted to do so, the Bank clamped down on the entrepreneurs with increases in the cost of borrowing money.

The overriding pressure to level the interest rate at 5% was driven by the housing market. But while using monetary policy to damage Britain's manufacturers, the Bank of England remained in a fog over the trend in house prices. According to Governor King:

> In the view of the [monetary policy] committee there will be a slowing of the house price inflation over next two years. We simply don't know whether it will involve falls in house prices themselves or merely a much longer and slower adjustment of house prices to earnings in which house price inflation remains low for an extremely long time.[36]

The Governor made a virtue of their ignorance. In stressing that the Bank could not be confident of the future trends in output, inflation and interest rates, King wanted people to be in no doubt that they were not being modest: 'When we say that, we mean it'.[37] Such frankness disarms critics, but the knowledge void was wilful and therefore inexcusable. An example of the deadly consequences of this ignorance was provided by the Bank's analysis of the link between house prices and consumption. That link 'has been less apparent in recent years', it pronounced, a link that apparently broke down in 2001. While house prices continued to roar up by more than 20% a

year, consumption continued to grow at about 3% a year.[38] The interpretation of the statistics was prejudiced by the absence of a coherent
theory of the property cycle. In 2001, both house prices and consumption *ought* to have nosedived – in the mid-cycle recession. They
failed to do so (Chapter 1, §2). That they did not drop in tandem was
truly remarkable, because house prices and consumption had simultaneously collapsed prior to the three previous recessions – 1973, 1979
and 1989. Where was the Bank of England's robust explanation for the
missing 2001 recession? In particular, why did house prices continue to
rise when (going by past performance) they ought to have dropped
dramatically? And why did people continue to spend money in the
shops when they ought to have retrenched? Here was a continuity of
association, even if it was in the reverse direction to the one that we
would have predicted going by events of the past. Did the Bank, which
loudly proclaimed its lack of confidence in its own expertise, expect
people to believe that *it* had wrought this miracle by manipulating
interest rates?

Having misread the past, what about the future? Was the Bank of
England better equipped to alert people to the looming dangers at the
end of the decade? Not if it cannot anticipate the course of output,
house prices and inflation. Could Britain's European partners come to
the Bank's aid? In 2004 Eurostat, the EU's statistical agency, revealed
that it would include housing costs in its definition of inflation (the
Consumer Price Index). Would this be the comprehensive economic
compass to replace the Bank's crystal ball? Unfortunately, the EU's
expanded definition of inflation 'excludes the price of land'.[39]

Doubts about the competence of the Bank of England did not
serve the political interests of the man who coveted the top political
job: Gordon Brown. He had built his reputation on the back of the
claim that it was his stroke of genius – to make the Bank responsible
for setting interest rates – that had delivered stability to the UK economy. That was a message that the media, by and large, had swallowed,
but was it *really* a plausible explanation for the missing 2001 recession?
Did the Bank's policy independence, *per se*, make the slightest difference to the outcome? The lessons from the USA, from which Brown
imported the policy (he was advised by Alan Greenspan), is revealing.

The Federal Reserve has enjoyed rate-setting independence for the
best part of a century, and it has presided over one boom bust after
another. Why hasn't it learnt from past errors? Its part in the Crash of
'29 is revealing. The Fed's policy on interest rates 'seesawed' between
high rates (to deter speculation) and the need for low rates (to encourage American industry). Instead of publicly exposing the tensions in

government-ordained policy – which placed an impossible burden on monetary policy – the Fed chose to rationalise its position by promoting the idea of a 'new era'.

> The feverish atmosphere of the financial markets was intensified during the early months of 1929. Financial writers and even some economists accepted the theory that this was a 'new era' and that earlier rules no longer applied.[40]

Instead of telling the people that they needed to reform governance, the wool was pulled over their eyes with talk of a 'new era'. And the Fed pulled the same red herring out of the hat in the 1990s. Alan Greenspan, instead of providing a comprehensive account of why the dot.com fever was bound to end in tears, distracted people with the idea of a 'new economy'. Once again, *the rules had changed.* Until, that is, the stock market crashed and ruined the small investors.

Central bank independence is not, by itself, the formula for economic stability. We should not forget, however, that the Bank of England's struggle to make informed decisions on monetary policy was matched by the Treasury's perverse decisions on fiscal policy. Like the Bank's, the Treasury's policies were biased in favour of imposing an artificial cap on productivity. Britain's entrepreneurs and their employees could increase output by an enormous factor (see Chapter 14). But to realise the full potential, it would be necessary to amend the way that government raises the public's revenue. Fiscal policy could be made to harmonise with monetary policy. The correct reforms would enable people to be the self-regulating agents who determined the economic destiny of the nation. Would the people of Britain countenance such a reform? We have measures of the failure to do so. In the recession of 1991-2, more than 75,000 homes were repossessed per annum. That number will be dwarfed in 2010.

REFERENCES

1   Frederic J. Jones and Fred Harrison, *The Chaos Makers*, London: Othila Press, 1997, p.28.
2   Charlotte Denny, 'CBI says jobs to go as output slows', *The Guardian*, February 23, 2001.
3   Faisal Islam, 'All the world to play for, says Brown', *The Observer*, April 15, 2001.
4   HM Treasury, *Budget 2000. Prudent for a purpose: Working for a Stronger and Fairer Britain*, March 2000, London: Stationery Office, p.16.
5   HM Treasury, *The Goal of Full Employment: Employment Opportunity for All Throughout Britain*, London: HM Treasury, February 2000, p.2.
6   National Audit Office, *Audit of Assumptions for the March 2000 Budget*, London: The Stationery Office, March 2000.

7   Treasury, *The Goal of Full Employment, op. cit.*, p.17.
8   *Ibid.*
9   *Ibid.*, p.178.
10 *Ibid.*
11 Charlotte Denny, 'Politics taken out of statistics', *The Guardian*, June 8, 2000.
12 FPDSavills, UK Residential Research Bulletin No. 35, Spring 2001, p.4.
13 'Demand for Building Land Expected to Ease', FPDSavill's Research Press Release, London, 30 August 2000, p.1.
14 UN, *System of National Accounts 1993*, New York: UN, 1993, p.234, para. 10.123.
15 *Ibid.*, p.182, para. 7.133.
16 *Ibid.*, p.234, para. 10.125.
17 Mark Atkinson, 'Eddie George 'powerless to help' manufacturers', *The Guardian*, April 5, 2000.
18 Dan Bilefsky, 'Low paid labour at a premium', *Financial Times*, April 5, 2000.
19 Richard Woods and Dipesh Gadher, 'The Fortune that Lasted 1000 Years', *The Sunday Times*, March 26, 2000.
20 Stephen Fraser, 'Scottish schools' repair bill soars to £1.3 billion', *Scotland on Sunday*, May 21, 2000.
21 Construction Products Association, *The Next 10 Years*, London, n.d., p.2.
22 Fred Harrison, 'Twenty-first century tailspin', *ROOF*, London: Shelter, July-August 1990, p.18.
23 OECD, *United Kingdom: June 2000*, Paris, OECD 2000, pp.23-38.
24 *Ibid.*, p.24.
25 George Wimpey became the biggest house builder in Britain in 2002 when it purchased Laing Homes for £297m. Analysts claimed the deal was driven by the need for Wimpey to access prime land in south-east England. That land bank would last for little more than two years.
26 Maija Pesola, 'Wimpey to focus on growth in US', *Financial Times*, July 29, 2004.
27 Maija Pesola, 'Investors to receive £1.4bn as Berkeley quits housebuilding', *Financial Times*, June 26, 2004.
28 The number of families housed in bed and breakfast and other temporary accommodation almost doubled between 1997 and 2002, reaching 85,000. John Carvel, 'Labour "failing" on targets to reduce poverty', *The Guardian*, December 12, 2002.
29 Ed Crooks, 'Brown rejects prospect of housing crash', *Financial Times*, December 18, 2002.
30 Larry Elliott and Charlotte Moore, 'Brown banks on city bonuses', *The Guardian*, July 16, 2004.
31 Bank of England, *Inflation Report*, August 2004.
32 Chris Nuttall, 'Europe set to move 1m jobs abroad in decade', *Financial Times*, August 16, 2004.
33 Interview with author, August 16, 2004.
34 Bank of England, *Inflation Report*, August, 2004, p.iv. For the projections for GDP and inflation, see Charts 1 and 2.
35 *Ibid*, p.3.
36 Anna Fifield, 'Bank slows down to reach finish line first', *Financial Times*, August 12, 2004.
37 Mervyn King, Opening Remarks, *Inflation Report* Press Conference, November 10, 2004, p.3.
38 Bank of England, *Inflation Report*, November 2004, pp.12-13.
39 Scheherazade Daneshkhu, 'House prices expected to be included in inflation measure', *Financial Times*, November 10, 2004.
40 Margaret G. Myers, *A Financial History of the United States*, New York: Columbia University Press, 1970, p.304.

PART IV

The Automatic Stabiliser

12

Counter-Cyclical Action

§1 The Language of Failure

THE EPITAPH for the 'new economy' was written by Alan Greenspan. America's population was aging and productivity gains could not be sustained. Many people would have to postpone retirement and work until they dropped dead.

> If we have promised more than our economy has the ability to deliver to retirees, as I fear we may have, we must calibrate our public programs so that pending retirees have time to adjust through other channels.[1]

The message was stark: the Tax State would not be able to take care of old people. Medical care and pension provisions would have to be diminished, which would oblige people to work for more years than they had expected. President George Bush's tax cuts for the rich had turned Bill Clinton's budget surplus into a deficit of over $400bn (2004). In his testimony to the House of Representatives on September 8, 2004, Greenspan warned of the dangers of an unbalanced budget. The bursting of the dot.com bubble had restored the dynamics of the old economy.

As the aged were told to curb their expectations, so the young were nurtured into a social system in which an increasing number of them were consigned to destitution. In George Bush's first three years in power, 4.3m people fell into poverty, the total growing to almost 36m people (2003), according to the annual Census Bureau report. Children, in particular, were vulnerable. There were 12.9m living in poverty in 2003, nearly 18% of the under-18 population. That was an increase of 800,000 from the previous year. On health, 5.2m lost their medical insurance, taking the total without protection to around 15.6% of the population.

The New Economy of the 1990s did not alter the historic trends. Millions of people in the richest nation on earth were institutionalised into poverty, and there was little they could do about it. The situation was similar in Europe.

Under the pressures of globalisation, the old industrial countries have two choices. In slow motion style, they may contract economically. Alternatively, they may embark on a renaissance driven by the democratisation of public finance.

Tony Blair understood the need for a radically new approach. He and his colleagues shared a sincere commitment to social justice. But the levels of child poverty continued to exceed those in other European countries. The percentage of wealth held by the richest 10% of the population increased from 47% to 54%. There was no way to reverse those trends because the causes were embedded in the foundations of the system. The rules were functionally designed to mass produce social exclusion; rules with which no one had tried to tamper for more than 50 years. Transferring income between winners and losers had not worked, and something new was needed. Crosspollinating two antithetical philosophies – socialism and capitalism – would merely perpetuate the history of failure.

New departures from old ways of governing the country are necessary. Tony Blair's Third Way was supposed to break the bonds of the past, but seven years of New Labour government did not reverse the deterioration. Blair groped for a new political grammar but it was an exercise doomed to failure. It relied on a confused economics. Evidence for this was to be found in the financial crises faced by low-income people, both those who had mortgaged their lives and those who paid rent to landlords. The human costs are reflected in the statistics, such as the inability of adults to establish families. Increasing numbers return to parental homes, unable to marry and have children because they could not afford to build family nests of their own.

The catalogue of failures ought to inspire radical questions about the fundamental principles that underpin the economy and the government's role in defeating people's aspirations.

Productivity   According to the Economic and Social Research Council (ESRC), Britain's productivity continued to lag behind competitors. Output per worker is 39% below that in the US. The productivity gap with France and Germany remains around 20%. The explanations, according to the ESRC, included 'a relative failure to invest, failure to innovate, poor labour relations, trade distortions attributable to Empire, antagonism towards manufacturing, 'short-termism' among business leaders and financial institutions, techno-logical backwardness, lack of entrepreneurship, over-regulation of business, an overly-instrumental attitude to work among employees, and the rigidities of the class structure. The list is not exhaustive'.[2] Since few people consciously wish to degrade their living standards, the roots of these obstacles to prosperity need to be sought in the rules that shape people's lives.

Unemployment The formidable array of problems confronting Britain is such that Gordon Brown might have concentrated his ener-gies on dealing with domestic challenges before preaching to the finance ministers of Europe. And yet, he lost no opportunity to berate Europe's governments for failing to create more jobs and reduce unemployment. With France and Germany reporting unemployment rates of more than 9% (2004), the UK's figure of 5% looked impres-sive. But the UK disguised the facts by labelling 2.7m people sick and disabled. The number of men under 50 who claimed to be incapable of working rose to more than 700,000 in 2004. When the 'sick' but able and willing to work are added to the unemployed, the comparison with France and Germany leaves nothing for Britain to be smug about.

Investment Over the 10 years to 2003, construction investment in the UK as a percentage of GDP was less than any other major European country – 7%, compared with the European average of 12%. Ireland, Portugal and Spain managed to invest sums equal to more than 16% of GDP.[3] Without adequate capital investment Britain cannot compete in the global markets. Improved productivity depends on the willingness to upgrade the built environment. The UK has less physical capital per worker than the US and considerably less than France and Germany. Significantly, the British are more attracted to pouring money into residential property than in capital equipment: the speculative mentality has a greater influence over the economy than on the continent. The 'short-termism' explanation for the UK's relatively poor performance may have less to do with the comparison of relative returns to plant and machinery and more to do with the higher capital gains from speculation in real estate. This hypothesis does not form part of the research agenda in the UK.[4]

Transport Despite its grand plan for enhancing mobility and cutting the costs of transportation, the government's targets for roads and railways proved unachievable. Of the eight targets set for roads in

the 10-year transport plan in 2000, just one – to build 40 new roads –
was met by 2004. One target – to cut congestion to 5% below 2000
levels by 2010 – was abandoned. The same sad story unfolded in
the railway sector. The burden of blame was placed on the lack of
funds. Those funds, as we shall see in Chapter 14, are readily available
– if the government agrees to reform its defective policies on public
finance.

Housing   Gordon Brown staked his reputation on his ability to
raise the output of houses. This increase in output was supposed
to defuse the 'bubble' in house prices. Weakening house price rises late
in 2004 had nothing to do with an increase in output. Brown's expert
on how to build more affordable houses – Kate Barker of the Bank of
England – warned: 'Influences like short-term falls in house prices
could divert us from where we need to go'.[5] And sure enough, as the
housing market paused, major building companies announced that
they were cutting back on their output. There was no reverse of
the downward trend in output since the Thatcher era of the 1980s.

Pensions   The deterioration in the amount of money people saved
delivered a pensions crisis. The Parish-based OECD warned that the
retirement age would have to be postponed. The think-tank also
censured the British government's method of recording the jobless
figures, urging that it should 'take further steps to prevent disability-
related benefits being used as a '*de facto*' early retirement scheme'.[6] As
people sank deeper into mortgage debt, the prospects of a comfortable period of retirement receded into the unreachable future.

Europe   Meeting in Lisbon in 2000, Tony Blair played a leading
role in persuading Europe's governments to accept the need to make
the EU the 'most competitive and dynamic knowledge-based economy in the world' by 2010. Within four years, it became clear that this
was impossible. That was the verdict of the European Union's internal
market commissioner,[7] and a similarly pessimistic prognosis was
offered by the German Finance Minister, Hans Eichel. Germany was
particularly vulnerable to the erosion of people's economic expectations, with the return to popularity of neo-fascist groups which could
exploit the discontent among the unemployed and those who feared
the loss of their jobs.

Overcoming these crises requires the constructive engagement
of many people, but their energies will not be mobilised until

government reforms the way it raises revenue. Taxes are not just about paying for public services. They also affect the willingness of people to work, save and invest. The attitudes and practices that prevail today will not dissolve in the face of empty rhetoric from politicians. If people's behaviour is to be modified *en masse*, the incentives for this would spring from the removal of taxes that damage private interests and the welfare of people's communities.

Evidence of the urgent need for this lesson to be learnt surfaced in Europe in 2004 when the EU admitted 10 East European countries to membership. Some of them cut taxes on corporations to attract investment and raise productivity. France protested vigorously. This was unfair competition! The former Soviet countries were expected to obstruct their people from working and investing by penalising entre-preneurs who were willing to create jobs in regions of high unemploy-ment. Finance Minister Nicolas Sarkozy – while cutting his country's taxes to encourage the return to France of business operations that had moved offshore – censured the lower-tax eastern countries. The European Commissioner for external relations, Chris Patten, ironic-ally asked: 'Should we regard poverty as a form of comparative advan-tage, for which the poor should be penalised?'[8]

The dream faded. The Third Way was not a doctrine that would lead Europe to a new Promised Land. When the EU's political leaders convened in conference in Budapest in October 2004, the talk was about why the Third Way did not work and what should replace it.[9] For some of the clues, there was no need to look further than the activities of their host, the supposedly left-wing Prime Minister of Hungary. He had become a multi-millionaire through property specu-lation, and his government was intensively engaged in privatising the state's assets.

Europe needs rescuing. The careers on which people relied for life-time employment are disappearing as jobs migrate to the lower wage economies of the Far East. By 2025, China's economy will eclipse Europe's in size; and India is expected to overtake Europe in about 2040. As these eastern economies move into overdrive, so they will suck capital out of Europe, leaving behind a culture in retreat, locked into diminished expectations. In economic terms, there is one way only to turn this looming catastrophe into a win-win situation in which everyone gains: by raising Europe's productivity above its historic trend. That cannot be achieved within the framework of policies on which the boom-bust economy rests. Those policies, quite simply, are self-defeating.

§ 2 Self-Defeating Strategies

IN JUNE 2004 the Governor of the Bank of England and his deputy began to make ominous pronouncements about house prices. The responsibility was on them to deliver stable prices, but they had one problem: Gordon Brown had tied their arms behind their backs.

In common with other countries, Britain relied on an 'inflation' index to provide the guiding mechanism for the economy. Fine-tuning is performed by adjustments in the rate of interest paid by people who borrow money. This locked the market economies into what Marx would have called a capitalist contradiction. The policy certainly had the appearance of perversity.

- When the UK and the USA went into the 2001 recession, interest rates were slashed to help industry. But lower interest rates, through the capitalisation process, meant that land prices were increased at a time when the profit margins of entrepreneurs were being squeezed.
- When the economies recovered from recession, the central bankers turned their attention to escalating house prices. They raised interest rates, which penalised industry which needed to borrow and invest for growth.

These ding-dong decisions amount to contradictory rewards and punishments that defeat the proclaimed aims of government policy.

Mervyn King, to celebrate his first year as Governor of the Bank of England, admitted in an interview with the *Financial Times* that house prices – racing upwards at more than 20% a year – had affected their judgement when they raised interest rates to 4.25%. He had already admitted in evidence to the House of Lords Economic Affairs Committee that he had 'no idea' what would happen to house prices, a confession which suggested that the reverence with which the media treats pronouncement by the Bank of England may be misplaced (see Box 12:1).

Despite being bereft of the knowledge that would enable the Bank to guide the economy to the path of sustainable growth, the MPC felt sufficiently bold to raise interest rates. Its members suspected that house prices relative to earnings were not sustainable.[10] King ought to have been sure that one response to the Bank's record low interest rates over the previous four years would be the capitalisation of land at very high prices. This was the first step in the interest rate trap of

---

BOX 12:1

The Future? Toss a Coin ...

MERVYN KING, when he was Deputy Governor in charge of monetary policy, held in his hands the rudder used to stabilise the nation's economy. What the bank did not know about economics was not worth knowing – you might think. In reality, what the bank does not know is what we ought to know.

In November 2002, King, a former professor of economics at the London School of Economics, announced that escalating house prices of between 20% and 30% over the previous 12 months would most likely drop to zero in two years time (2004). Unfortunately, he was obliged to confess that he did not have confidence in this prediction. In fact, the Bank of England was clueless: there was a 50/50 chance that prices could be higher or lower than zero. This was not much good for people who were trying to plan their family's futures. 'No one knows what will happen to house prices,' King claimed. 'The probability that the outturn will be close to the central view [zero] is zero.'[1] In fact, prices rose by an annual 13%.

The Governor would not be drawn on the housing crisis. 'The best way to destroy the credibility of the Monetary Policy Committee is to lecture people about house prices,' he said, revealing his concern to protect the reputation of the Bank. But ignorance did not constrain Professor King from lecturing his students at the LSE. In his co-authored textbook he forayed into the question of taxing the economic rent of land. He claimed that 'it is apparent that the total of economic rents, of all kinds, is not now a sufficiently large proportion of national income for this to be a practical means of obtaining the resources needed to finance a modern State'.[2] Alas, there were no worthwhile statistics on which to base that claim about the rent of land, any more than King had a theory on which to predict trends in house prices.

The Bank's doctrines would permit the ship of state to inflate into the land price bubble that was looming round about the time that its economic model was predicting a zero rate of increase in house prices.

1 Ed Crooks & Scheherazade Daneshkhu, 'House price movement baffles and concerns the Bank', *Financial Times*, November 14, 2002.
2 J.A. Kay & M.A. King, *The British Tax System*, 5th edn., Oxford: Oxford University Press, 1990, p.179.

---

the mid-cycle recession. But instead of encouraging capital formation during the growth phase, the Bank – not knowing where its inflation dial was leading it, so far as house prices were concerned – began to bump up interest rates. This caned the building industry and the manufacturing sector. King's deputy, Rachel Lomax, claimed that their strategy was designed to ensure that 'the party remains under control. We don't want to encourage binge behaviour'.[11]

But the binge had begun and Britain's housing market was getting ready for the phase (in 2006) that would lead to the mania of the Winner's Curse (2007/8). This could not be staved off by penalising industry with higher interest rates, hindering Britain's ability to catch up with the incomes enjoyed by other economies.

Monetary policy, by itself, does not provide the tools for stabilising the market economy. It was no comfort to the captains of Britain's industries to learn that the administrative controls employed by Communist China's Politburo were equally ineffective when it came to dealing with its overheated property market. In 2004, the Peking government applied bureaucratic curbs on investment in real estate and stricter enforcement of land-use rules in their version of a counter-cyclical strategy. Not only did it not work, it prejudiced investment in the sectors where growth was vital if new jobs were to be created for the peasants who were displaced from the countryside.

Both East and West, having fought a Cold War to decide whose ideology was superior, found themselves locked into combat with a common enemy from whose grip they could not release themselves without inflicting losses on millions of their citizens. Neither had worked out the terms that would automatically stabilise a growing economy. Such a policy did exist, but the Marxists and monetarists were united in their blind spot. Neither of them factored effective land-and-tax policies into their doctrinal equations.

How the opposing schools of economic thought are able to share the same selective amnesia on the unique characteristics of land is an issue that needs to be understood. We are assisted by an important insight offered by American psychologist Dr. Irving Janis. He coined the term *groupthink*.[12] This was a mode of thinking in which people engage when they strive for unanimity. Such is the need to achieve consensus that they override realistic assessments of the advantages of alternative courses of action. In essence, *groupthink* is a collective technique for achieving self-delusion in the pursuit of a predetermined goal. In America, *groupthink* delivered a catalogue of political disasters, such as President John F. Kennedy's decision to endorse the invasion of Cuba. The Bay of Pigs could never have succeeded: but the political, military and intelligence communities got together to convince themselves that it would work, and they were not willing to scrutinise critically the evidence that would challenge their aspirations.

More recently, the US and UK secret services associated with their political masters to override the evidence that weapons of mass destruction were not at the disposal of Saddam Hussein. The facts undermined the ideological ambitions of the Bush administration. By a collaborative process of imagination, the Bush and Blair governments persuaded themselves that Iraq was a present and real danger to their citizens. This dictated the need for a pre-emptive strike. When a congressional investigation interrogated the way in which the Washington intelligence community assembled its evidence, the conclusion was that the spies had suffered from 'collective group think' in its assessment of the threat. A similar conclusion was reached by the Hutton enquiry into the failings of Britain's spies. This was a classic case of *groupthink*, in which the participants rationalise and moralise their positions and ignore competing views. Disastrous outcomes were predetermined because minds were closed.

A similar process is at work in economics, and it operates on a global scale. Governments and their advisors have persuaded themselves that the most efficient way to stabilise the market economy is through monetary policy. A tolerable rate of inflation is selected as the target for management techniques. Changes in the rate of interest become the means to achieve the desired outcome. The conceptual and statistical foundations of this doctrine are indefensible, yet contrary views are not allowed to disturb the consensus. The political establishments and their central bankers really believe that they can smooth the business cycle by altering the cost of borrowing money. Silence prevails on the one fiscal alternative that would work.

§3 The Counter-Cyclical Strategy

WHAT ARE the problems to be solved 'and the goals to be achieved by a counter-cyclical policy?

On the supply side of the economy: as population and incomes grow, there is a continuous need to increase the construction of houses. Speculation in capital gains from land ought to be removed because it shrinks the supply and raises the price of land above levels that deliver efficiency in the use of all resources – land, labour and capital.

On the demand side of the economy: people ought not to bid house prices up above what they can afford. The balance needs to be struck to maximise the achievement of the aspirations they have for themselves and their communities.

To achieve such outcomes, the buttresses in the foundations of the economy need to be re-sculptured.

- The credit-creating financial system must work in harmony with the productive economy to support people who produce wealth rather than those who extract the value created by others.
- Burdens that damage income-earning and saving incentives need to be eliminated, to balance short-term needs to produce wages and reproduce families with the long-term need to pay for health, education and retirement.

This complex set of goals cannot be secured by monetary policy alone. Nor can it be delivered through regulation from a command centre. People need an efficient market framework to aid correct decision-making. That means we need a democratic consensus behind a yardstick with which to test the efficacy of both private decisions and public policies. For example, most people would agree that the corrective mechanism(s) should not cause artificial increases in prices.

This combination of guidelines and goals places a heavy burden on policy instruments, which must synthesise the cumulative energy of all individuals, who are both self-serving competitors and community-creating co-operators.

The tool that can deliver these outcomes is to be found in fiscal policy. Taxation arouses animosity, but the key to reform is to understand that the problem is not with *how much* is taken from people to be spent on common services. What matters is *how* that revenue is raised to provide the support services which we cannot, or choose not, to provide for ourselves. Cambridge economist Alfred Marshall, who contributed much to the refinement of the science of political economy, defined the public's revenue base in terms of the rent of land and natural resources.   '

> For the net income derived from the inherent properties of land is a true surplus, it does not directly enter even in the long run into the normal expenses of production, which are required as rewards for the work and inventive energy of labourers and undertakers. It thus differs from the incomes derived from buildings, machinery, etc., which are in the long run needed (in the present state of human character and social institutions), to sustain the full force of production, invention, and accumulation.[13]

Income tax, VAT, payroll taxes (such as the national insurance contributions levied in the UK), and most of the other taxes favoured by government, raise the general level of prices and distort the way that people work, save and invest. The payment of rent to fund shared services is free of these negative private and social consequences. This fiscal strategy is grounded in the principles of fairness and efficiency. But by themselves, these two values have singularly failed to persuade governments to deliver the reform. That is why we need to deepen the philosophy of the individual and of the community, to enable government to secure a public mandate for tax reform.

It is important not to demonise rent (in the way that Marx did for 'profit'). The rent of land and nature's other resources is not, in itself, evil. Land's rent is the measure of the success of economic activity.

It is the proof of productivity. The greater the skill with which people apply their labour and their capital, the higher the surplus above wages and profits that is available to pay as rent for the benefit of the exclusive use of amenities at any given location. Rents become a problem only when they are privatised. When they are capitalised and sold in the private markets, society's community-created income is misdirected. This does not necessarily mean that government *per se* must appropriate and spend the rent revenue, if alternative forms of community cooperation are possible (which they are not, for national defence, law and order and governance). So we need to review the philosophy of property rights.

No revolutionary departure from the liberal doctrines of Western philosophy is required, and no forcible reallocation of assets is entailed by the property rights that are consistent with the sustainable growth of incomes. The solution is shockingly simple. It merely requires that people should apply the principle which they accept in their everyday transactions in the markets for consumer goods, when we hire people and when we borrow other people's savings. *People need to pay for the benefits that they receive when they occupy the locations of their choice.*

That this is a conservative proposition will be understood when we reflect on what happens when we buy property. When we negotiate the price of a house, for example, we do fully pay our share of the cost of the amenities that we wish to access. The problem, of course, is that the money we pay is not handed over to the agencies that provide those services. We transfer that value, instead, to people who do not have responsibility for providing the amenities of our choice. That is perfectly legal on the part of the property seller, but the collateral consequence of failing to pay the money to the service providers (transit authorities, hospitals, schools, and so on) is that government is obliged to raise revenue by taxing wages and savings. This places a cap on capitalism that prevents people from enjoying the standard of living to which they are entitled by their work.

This misalignment of public finance policies is the reason why we need to stress that our problems are the result of political – and not market – failure. The land market is legally sanctioned to deliver perverse outcomes. It devours the basis of its existence. Speculators – which, today, includes families who view their houses as investments rather than homes – are free to gamble on land. The edifice which they inflate has to crash. It may take 14 years from start to finish, but when land values are pushed too far beyond people's earning power, the crash becomes inevitable.

The solution is to re-balance the public's finances by raising revenue directly from the rent of land. At the same time, people would be compensated with an equivalent reduction in income, capital and consumption taxes. Government would be able to continue to meet its financial obligations until people decided which public services they wanted to privatise, if any.

If distortions in the land market are to be avoided, the public charge on rents needs to be at a uniform rate on all land. The charge needs to be payable annually as an obligation for the services received by whoever derives the benefits. The charge needs to be levied on the current market values that are freely determined by the users of land.

This reform reduces the flow of rents that can be privatised. The level of the rental charges – if these are to be effective for counter-cyclical purposes – will be discussed in Chapter 13. Here, we need to establish the principle that such public charges are consistent with people's ethical sensibilities, and that they reduce the artificial con-straints on the enterprise economy. This agenda should not come as a surprise to Gordon Brown, for it was the core of the politics of the era which he and Tony Blair found eminently attractive to their political sensibilities.

§4   The People's Budget

IN JUNE 2004 Gordon Brown's incumbency in the Treasury broke a record set by David Lloyd George, who was the Liberal's Chancellor from 1908 to 1915. Commentators wrote glowing profiles: they accepted Brown's self-assessment that he had bequeathed a unique period of stability to the UK. The chancellor celebrated his record in his speech to high financiers at his annual Mansion House lecture. In this, he thrice repeated one of his favourite accolades – his willing-ness to take 'tough' decisions. And he reminded guests at the Lord Mayor's banquet that he was still wedded to prudence, who had helped him to 'lock in long term stability'. There was, however, one domestic fly in the ointment:

> Let us recall that most stop go problems that Britain has
> suffered in the last 50 years have been led or influenced by the
> housing sector. Forty years ago we built 400,000 homes a year,
> by the mid 1990s it had fallen to just 200,000 so we will press
> ahead with resolution ... to tackle the large and unacceptable
> imbalance between supply and demand in the British housing
> market.[14]

Brown forgot to mention that the output of houses had declined by a further 20,000 a year during his stewardship at the Treasury.[15] This sad record was partly due to the failure to restructure the public's finances to favour construction and penalise land speculation. That the chancellor had not reflected on the economics of the property market is suggested by the accolades which he bestowed on himself for the changes that he had introduced. He drew special attention to the fact that 'we have cut capital gains tax from 40 pence down to 10 pence for long-term business assets and in budget after budget I want us to do even more to encourage risk takers, those with ambition, to turn their ideas into reality and make the most of their talents'.[16]

His actions achieved the reverse of his aspirations. Capital gains contain more stored up rent than stored up labour or ploughed-back capital.[17] Honda, the Japanese car maker, discovered the reality of this when it re-valued its plant site in England. It made more from its land than from the cars which it manufactured. Since establishing its factory in Swindon in 1985, the value of its land rose from £6m to £200m. This capital gain was a 3,333% return.[18] Even as the Japanese firm was notching up its windfall, with the bonus in prospect from Gordon Brown's cuts in the capital gains tax, the chancellor was raising the cost of hiring labour to operate the car-making machines.

- Brown's cuts in capital gains tax were a public subsidy to the land market and a penalty on the jobs market.
- To fund his favoured welfare projects, he increased the payroll tax (National Insurance Contributions). This bias against the labouring class is evident in Conservative as well as Labour periods of government, but it is curious that Brown, the champion of the workers, should perpetuate a class-based system of public finance.

How does this record match with his forebear in the Treasury of a century earlier? Lloyd George, in his 1909 budget, wanted to restructure the finances. The Welshman was one of a coterie of radical Liberal politicians which included Winston Churchill, who supported Lloyd George with fighting speeches in the House of Commons. This is what Churchill said on May 4, 1909:

> Roads are made, streets are made, services are improved, electric light turns night into day, water is brought from reservoirs a hundred miles off in the mountains – and all the while the landlord sits still. Every one of those improvements is effected by the labour and cost of other people and the taxpayers. To not one of those improvements does the land monopolist, as a land

monopolist, contribute, and yet by every one of them the value
of his land is enhanced. He renders no service to the community, he contributes nothing to the general welfare, he contributes nothing to the process from which his own enrichment
is derived.[19]

Today it would be incongruous to single out landlords as villains.
Major beneficiaries from investment in the community's infrastructure include home owners. The economics so clinically
denounced by Churchill remains with us to this day, but there have
been many additions to the usual suspects.

To counteract the injustices that were built into the distribution of
the nation's income, Lloyd George proposed three levies. Roy Jenkins,
a former Labour chancellor, summarised them.

- A 20% tax on the unearned increment in land values, 'which was to
  be paid either when the land was sold or when it passed at death'.
- A capital tax of a halfpenny in the pound 'on the value of undeveloped land and minerals'.
- A 10% reversion duty 'on any benefit which came to a lessor at the
  end of a lease'.[20]

Jenkins assessed Lloyd George's 1909 plans 'as a whole hardly revolutionary'.[21] That is not how the landed aristocracy interpreted the
budget. That class suffered collective apoplexy. The absolute opposition of the peers was played out in the House of Lords, which blocked
Lloyd George's Finance Bill. This created a constitutional crisis. The
Liberals turned to the electorate and secured a new mandate. The
aristocratic landowners lost the first round: the budget was turned
into the law of the land. But their lordships were not going to give up
without a vigorous rearguard action, which they prosecuted, in part,
through the courts. If they could block the valuation of land, there
could be no tax on rents! Lloyd George's attempt to finance provisions
for the unemployed, the sick and the widows and orphans of the
nation out of the rents of the nation's land was scuttled.

In 1919 the landed lobby was ready to deliver the death blow. And
in one of those ironic twists of fate, Lloyd George's principal adversary
of 1909, Austen Chamberlain, was the Chancellor of the Exchequer
who used Commons procedures to temporise until he could kill the
land taxes by 'euthanasia in the following year's budget'.[22] The Prime
Minister who was made to preside over this humiliation? Lloyd
George himself.

The revenge was sweet for their lordships. History had gone against the Welsh Wizard. The Conservatives had maintained their campaign, guided by the strategy articulated by Austen Chamberlain.

> It is certain that if we do nothing the Radical Party will sooner or later establish their national tax, and once established in that form any Radical Chancellor in need of money ... will find it an easy task to give a turn of the screw.[23]

Against this budget's philosophy, which we are told Gordon Brown so admires,[24] there is nothing to compare with what the New Labour chancellor delivered a century later. But if Edwardian history did not provide a template for Brown's fiscal philosophy, what about the lessons from his own party's origins?

The emerging Labour Party had within its ranks a reformer from the Yorkshire Dales. Philip Snowden (1864-1937) described himself as a socialist. He worked tirelessly on behalf of the labouring classes but he believed in free trade and was hostile to the Bolshevik experiment in Russia. He was convinced about the need to restructure the public's finances after listening to a speech by Henry George, who visited the UK on lecture tours in 1882 and 1884.[25] Snowden found himself moving to the right of his colleagues in the Labour ranks, and this was reflected in his brief tenure as chancellor in 1924: landowners were relieved when they heard the contents of his budget. It was to be a different story when he returned to the Treasury in 1930.

As unemployment swelled in the depression years following the 1929 Wall Street crash, Snowden introduced a budget on April 14, 1930. It was assessed in these terms by Roy Jenkins: 'Snowden scuppered the hope not only of the Labour government producing a counter-cyclical expansionist policy but also of its using direct taxation for a sustained egalitarian drive'.[26] From Snowden's philosophical viewpoint, he *was* pursuing exactly such a course of action. The macroeconomic and social implications were beyond the comprehension of a mind tutored in neoclassical doctrines.

What was the radical heart of the 1930 budget? Jenkins summarised them.

- All taxes on food would be removed in the lifetime of the Parliament.
- Legislation for land valuation was announced to begin the process of phasing in public charges on the rents of land.

According to the Jenkins interpretation, Snowden served notice that his modest increases in income tax and surtax 'sealed off any further attempt on the part of that Labour government to produce socialism by redistributive taxation. It was a direct contributory cause of the decision of the rump of the ILP [Independent Labour Party] effectively to detach itself from the Labour Party'.[27]

The profound implications for the economy and society were not perceived by the revolutionary Left, which weakened Snowden's hand by its hostile reaction. But the implication of the order to value the land was not lost on the landowners, who still held sway over the British Establishment. Five hundred years earlier, Henry VIII dissolved the monasteries and began The Great Land Sell-off. Snowden's agenda, if it was successfully implemented, represented the beginnings of a non-catastrophic restitution of the people's private and community rights. The goal was to allow people to retain the income they earned by their labour. The policy would have simultaneously removed the temptation to speculate in land, by removing the windfall gains: people would pay for the benefits that they received from their possession of land. The land market, once stabilised, would lay the foundations for sustainable employment and production, a by-product of which would have been a sufficient supply of affordable homes. By his two measures, Snowden proposed to build into the market the egalitarianism which capitalists recognise as the level playing field. This fairness in the rules of the economic game cannot exist when socially-created rents are privatised and privately created incomes are socialised.

Jenkins characterised Snowden's strategy as 'the most orthodox of financial policies'.[28] For good measure, he condemned what he called 'an elaborate and irrelevant scheme of land taxation'.[29] Jenkins' assessment is revealing for what it tells us about the mindset of today's economists. Snowden's enemies in the ranks of the landed Conservatives were not fooled. They regarded the budget as subversive.

Neville Chamberlain, the half brother of Austen – whose claim to public notoriety lies with his attempt to appease Herr Hitler in 1938 (another example of *groupthink*) – knew that it would be folly to underestimate the social consequences of this fiscal reform. He succeeded Snowden in the Treasury in 1932. In his budget of that year he suspended the land value tax, which was due to take effect in 1933. And in 1934 he repealed the legislation.

Snowden did have one success during his ill-fated second term. He managed to reform the nation's debts, which reduced the cost of borrowing money. The high interest bearing debt had obstructed a move to lower rates of interest. His success in 1932 with the debt-conversion scheme moved the economy 'towards the cheap money which was one of the best features of the British economy in the 1930s, and a major factor in the private-house construction boom which gained momentum a year or so later'.[30] Cheap money and a housing boom: a sure recipe for a recession (the next one was due in 1938) if the automatic stabiliser was not allowed to operate in the land market! Snowden's fiscal agenda was designed to deliver growth that was sustainable: in 1934, land owners would not have the incentive to speculate in the capital gains from the enhanced productivity of the working population. Chamberlain thwarted that agenda and ignited the land boom that followed.

Both Lloyd George and Philip Snowden faced up to the 'tough' challenge of the 20th century: reforming the public's finances so that equity in all its forms – property rights and the distribution of earned income – would prevail. If they had been allowed to succeed, they would have originated the historic process of neutralising the dysfunctional features of the land market. They failed, but not for the want of trying.

Chancellors of the Exchequer have a special obligation to promote the new political economy of efficiency and fairness, if only because that is what they routinely claim to be doing in their budgets. Unfortunately, it is not until they write their memoirs that they display the courage to deliver intelligent insights. This was demonstrated by Nigel Lawson in his discussion of the economics of North Sea oil.

> It was common ground that a special tax regime for the North Sea was justified because its low extraction costs, relative to the world price, gave rise to exceptionally large profits known technically as economic rent, a term used by economists to describe a systematic excess of revenue over the minimum required to maintain the activity in being.[31]

If the Treasury had used this knowledge during Lawson's stewardship in the 1980s, policies could have been developed to prevent the boom of 1988/9 and the bust that followed.

The challenge is to synchronise the tax-take to the costs of production so that – as Lawson noted in relation to North Sea oil – the government's share would 'not make fields that are economic pre-tax uneconomic post-tax'. The Institute of Fiscal Studies noted that a resource rent charge should take more of the rent as the costs of production declined, but the revenue-take should decline to zero 'if a field

is close to the margin of profitability'.[32] Philip Snowden had a
layman's way of explaining what this meant: the state 'has no right to
tax anyone, unless it can show that the taxation is likely to be used
more beneficially and more economically'.[33] And as a believer in
Parliamentary democracy that meant laying all the facts before the
people so that they could judge what was in their best interests, rather
than leaving it to the patricians who direct the affairs of state.

This was the economics which I elaborated in *The Power in the Land*
and with my co-authors in *The Losses of Nations*. Copies were supplied
to HM Treasury, but to no avail. In an assessment of public charges on
resource rents, an economist in the Treasury's Environmental Tax
Team wrote in August 2000: 'Mr. Harrison's book contains some interesting and controversial views on the nature of taxation ... while such
issues are in themselves interesting, they do not accord with the
Government's overall economic strategy ... the views of Mr. Harrison
are also somewhat at odds with those of most economists'.[34] And so,
aware that 'most economists' continue to fail their clients, as a result
of their special brand of *groupthink*, we now try again.[35] We begin our
assessment of the rent-as-public-revenue policy by considering the
political viability of this strategy in a continental setting: Australia.

REFERENCES

1   'Remarks by Chairman Alan Greenspan', Symposium, Federal Reserve Board of
    Kansas City, Jackson Hole, Wyoming, August 27, 2004.
2   ESRC, *The UK's Productivity Gap*, Swindon, 2004, p.1.
3   Construction Products Association, *Achievable Targets? 2004. Is Government deliver-
    ing?* London: 2004.
4   ESRC, *op cit*, pp.15-16.
5   Jonathan Guthrie and Scheherazade Daneshkhu, 'Fall in property prices could
    affect plans for building affordable homes', *Financial Times*, September 24, 2004.
6   David Turner, 'OECD says pension policy puts growth at risk', *Financial Times*,
    September 24, 2004.
7   Peter Norman, 'Further expansion will make EU impossible to run, Bolkestein
    warns', *Financial Times*, October 18, 2004.
8   Chris Patten, 'What Sarkozy can learn from eastern Europe', *Financial Times*,
    September 23, 2004.
9   Anthony Browne, 'After the Third Way, where next?' *The Times*, October 16, 2004.
10 Ed Crooks, 'King repeats warning that house prices could fall', *Financial Times*,
    June 30, 2004.
11 Ashley Seager, 'Bank's Deputy governor warns house buyers to sober up', *The
    Guardian*, July 2, 2004.
12 Irving L. Janis, *Groupthink: Psychological Studies of Policy Decisions and Fiascoes*, 2nd
    edn., Boston: Houghton Mifflin, 1982.
13 Alfred Marshall, *Principles of Economics*, London: Macmillan, 1898, 4th edn.,
    Vol. 1, pp.717-18.

14 Gordon Brown, Speech, Mansion House, London, June 16, 2004, transcript, p.3.
15 Steve Wilcox, *UK Housing Review 2003/4*, Coventry: Chartered Institute of Housing, 2003, Tables 19h and 19i, pp.96-7.
16 Mansion House Speech, *op. cit.*, p.5.
17 Mason Gaffney has called ploughed-back rents 'geogenic capital', and ploughed-back capital he designates 'autogenic'. Mason Gaffney, 'Toward Full Employment with Limited Land and Capital', in Arthur Lynn, Jr. (ed.), *Property Taxation, Land Use and Public Policy*, Madison: University of Wisconsin Press, 1976.
18 James Mackintosh, 'Land makes more than cars for Honda', *Financial Times*, February 7, 2003.
19 Barker, *op. cit.*, p.116.
20 Roy Jenkins, *The Chancellors*, London: Macmillan, 1998, p.167.
21 *Ibid*, p.6.
22 *Ibid*, p.137.
23 Roy Douglas, *Land, People & Politics: A history of the Land Question in the United Kingdom 1878-1952*, London: Allison & Busby, 1976, p.150.
24 Larry Elliott, 'Brown sidles past Lloyd George's milestone', *The Guardian*, June 16, 2004.
25 Henry George (1839-97), the author of *Progress and Poverty*, 1879. An economic historian recorded that George's book went through an astonishing 10 London reprints between 1881 and 1884. J.H. Clapham, *An Economic History of Modern Britain*, Cambridge: University Press, 1932, p.483.
26 Jenkins, *op. cit*, p.289.
27 *Ibid*, p.290.
28 *Ibid*, p.288.
29 *Ibid*, p.294
30 *Ibid*, 351.
31 Lawson, *op. cit.*, p.187.
32 Institute of Fiscal Studies, *North Sea Oil Taxation*, London: IFS Report Series No. 6, December 1983.
33 Jenkins, *op. cit.*, p.281.
34 Letter from Piers Bisson to Geoffrey Lee, August 25, 2000.
35 Janis formulated this psychological state in terms of a *'temporary* group derangement' (*op. cit.*, p.3, emphasis added). For the self-delusion to persist for a long period of time, and for its contagious effects to be transmitted to people in other circles (or countries) it is necessary for the condition to be reinforced in institutional terms. Some of the academic buttresses are discussed in Gaffney, *The Corruption of Economics, op. cit.*

13

Australia:
The Pathology of Taxation

§1 A Land of Riches

VOLATILE HOUSE PRICES in Britain are blamed on an inadequate supply of new dwellings and an inadequate supply of useable land. Australia is an embarrassing affront to this wisdom. There, the trends in house prices since the recession of 1992 have been vigorous, even though the supply of new residential units is broadly balanced with demand. This was established when the Australian government, concerned that increasing numbers of people could not afford to buy homes, instructed its advisory Productivity Commission to investigate. The Commission concluded that 'given the small size of net additions to housing in any year [2%] relative to the size of the stock, improvements to land release or planning approval procedures, while desireable, could not have greatly alleviated the price pressures of the past few years'.[1] There is no shortage of land in a huge continent with a population of 20m people. And yet, prices more than doubled over the decade to 2003. Despite its rich endowment, Australia has suffered the same boom-bust cycles as the UK.

The costs of those episodes were grievous. At the end of the 1974-92 cycle, the banks alone lost A$25 bn.[2] Because of this history, Australia decided to take a grip of the credit-creating activities of the banks. The Governor of the central bank, in identifying problems with credit creation, noted that 'the main players are companies and banks, or financial institutions generally'.[3] An inflow of foreign capital may help to bid up asset prices but

> Domestic banks do not sit idly by – they join in to lend money
> for all sorts of promising projects and asset purchases ... it looks
> as though everyone can make money ... but much of it is
> inevitably invested unwisely. A lot of it goes into property or
> is invested in industries which are already over-supplied.[4]

The government decided to take pre-emptive action to prevent a recurrence of reckless credit-creation. Prudence was the benchmark. The Australian Prudential Regulatory Authority (APRA) was established in 1998. Preventative action was in the interest of taxpayers, because they were the mugs of last resort who were expected to foot the bill when things went wrong. Common practice throughout the world was explained by Ian Macfarlane, Governor of the central bank, the Reserve Bank of Australia (RBA).

> The government has to step in and close down the insolvent lenders, and take the bad loans off the remaining banks so they can start with a relatively clean slate.[5]

Has Australia learnt the lesson of how booms and busts in the property market can devastate migrants who hope to escape the economic vicissitudes in the Old World? Despite the historical evidence, the Australian authorities managed to persuade themselves that they had arrested the propensities in the real estate sector. True, property prices forged upwards at the turn into the 21st century. But, according to Graeme Thompson, the Deputy Governor of the central bank,

> while asset prices are rising, there is no sign of the bubbles we saw in the 1980s; commercial property prices are up only modestly from their low points of 1993.[6]

Because they lacked a coherent theory of the property cycle the stewards of the economy had dropped their guard. It made no sense to treat the bubble of the late 1980s as comparable with what happened in the late 1990s: these were different phases of the 18-year cycle. The 1980s were the end of the cycle, so prices would be far more volatile than midway through the following cycle. Price rises in the late 1980s, for example, were concentrated in a two-year period (the Winner's Curse phase) which ended in the first half of 1989. This contrasts with the price rises up to 2002, which were spread evenly over five years.[7] The differences in the magnitudes of the changes in prices are illustrated in Table 13:1. In Sydney, in the five years up to 1989, house prices rose by 140%. The following mid-cycle increase was 45%. Flowing against the historical tide was Brisbane, which took the lion's share of the inflow of people into Queensland (Victoria and New South Wales experienced a net outflow).

TABLE 13:1

House Prices: Percentage Change Over 5 Years

	5 Years to March 1989	5 Years to March 2002
Sydney	140.4	45.4
Melbourne	122.2	89.3
Brisbane	47.9	62.0
Perth	142.0	37.1
Adelaide	43.9	42.3
Canberra	42.8	49.8
Darwin	N/A	14.0
Hobart	N/A	27.3
Australia	*114.1*	*56.9*

Source: 'Recent Developments in Housing: Prices, Finance and Investor Attitudes', Reserve Bank of Australia *Bulletin*, July, 2002, p.2, Table 1.

TABLE 13:2

Dwelling Wealth as Percentage of Household Disposable Income

	1980	1990	1998
Australia	248	281	355
Canada	123	118	129
France	172	218	227
Germany	n.a.	331	301
Italy	133	170	166
Japan	' 380	641	381
UK	343	361	293
US	169	173	163
Sweden[1]	208	245	198
New Zealand	185	243	283

1 Includes non-financial assets as well as dwellings.

Source: 'City Sizes, House Prices and Wealth', Reserve Bank of Australia *Bulletin*, December 2001, p.2, Table 1.

How do we account for volatile house prices on a continent where you can travel for days without seeing another soul? Australians invest a larger proportion of their wealth in housing than do people in countries with greater population densities (Table 13:2, which shows Japan as the exception). Australia has nearly 8m dwellings valued at over $2,200bn (including land). In what is an active market, about 500,000 dwellings are traded each year. An average of just under 150,000 new dwellings are commenced each year, with an efficient residential construction industry generating an annual turnover of nearly $50bn. The 2% addition of new houses to the stock is not sufficient to ameliorate the economic impact of this activity. This was described by the Productivity Commission:

> Rapid growth in demand for an asset stock that can only be expanded slowly will almost inevitably lead to increases in the value of housing land, and therefore to higher house prices – particularly in premium locations.[8]

Australia, for all its continental-wide expanse of land, was locked into the same economics as land-poor countries. Sites suitable for homes and offices are limited by the intense demands from a heavily-concentrated population, as in the case of Japan. In 1990, the value of dwellings held by Japanese households was 641% relative to disposable income. The huge increase in the price of residential property during the 1980s meant that Japan would have to suffer a protracted period of penance. The economy was consigned to a decade-long doldrum.

Japan, where land suitable for settlements between the mountain ranges is scarce, at least has an apparent excuse for its high prices. In Australia, houses are well endowed on large plots. Families occupy a greater proportion of detached dwellings than other countries, and yet the size of the structures are smaller than in the USA where the population is more than ten times larger. Intuitively, one would have thought that houses would have constituted a smaller proportion of family wealth. The explanation for the realities on the ground stresses the importance of the supply of land in places where people want to live and work. Demographic concentration is what gives strategically located sites their value. For policy purposes, the total land mass of a country is irrelevant, a reality which continues to elude governments in large countries like Russia. In Australia, 54% of the urban population lives in Sydney and Melbourne.[9] This is well above the average of most countries. The equivalent number living in the two largest cities in the UK is 19%, 15.7% in the USA and 20% in Germany.

But house prices are also the result of bankers' practices. In Australia, despite the creation of the regulatory agency, banks were quick to make credit available to borrowers in the 1990s. A study by the RBA found that investor activity grew exceptionally quickly during 2001-2 when the economy was in its mid-cycle phase.[10] But the bald numbers mean little without theory to interpret their significance. And for all its prudential provisions for the credit-creating bankers, the central bank was ill-equipped to deal with the debt acquired by households. It did know what lay behind the trends. In 2004 the Deputy Governor, Glenn Stevens, analysed prices and pronounced that 'it was hard to avoid the conclusion that strong speculative forces were at work over the past couple of years. That was not a healthy state of affairs and the sooner it passed, the better'. Were the speculators acting irresponsibly? The view prevailed that prices would not come down. The psychology that is inextricably associated with the pursuit of unearned capital gains fostered the willingness to gamble against the historical odds.

- In June 2003, the median house price was equivalent to six times the average annual household income, compared with four times income at the peak of the 1980s boom.
- Household debt rose faster than in any other country apart from Spain and the Netherlands. Loans to investors doubled from 15% to over 30% of banks' outstanding housing loans.
- Families increased their vulnerability to the vagaries of the property market. The number of households with an investment property increased from 8% to 12% (2001).

TABLE 13:3

Annual Pre-Tax Returns on Investments: %

		2000[1]	2001	2002	2003
Shares:	Australian	15.5	9.1	-4.7	-1.7
	International	12.6	-6.0	-23.5	-18.5
Australian Bonds		6.2	7.4	6.2	9.8
Cash		5.6	6.1	4.7	5.0
Residential Property:	Melbourne	12.1	20.9	17.3	25.3
	Sydney	13.1	6.3	22.0	20.0
	Australia	11.8	14.7	21.3	18.2

1 Data for June of each year.
Source: Productivity Commission, *op. cit*, p.53.

Across the continent, people were enticed by a burgeoning property seminar industry. They were beguiled with the prospects of making fortunes. Adventurous investors could use debt to become landlords. And the numbers certainly appeared to suggest that investing in real estate made sense. As we see in Table 13:3, with the collapse in share prices as the dot.com bubble burst the best returns were from residential property. Property speculators were apparently behaving rationally from the point of view of self-interest. But what would come of all this? It was pointless turning to the central bank for guidance. Deputy Governor Stevens was no better informed about the direction in which prices would move than the Governor of the Bank of England. He admitted: 'It is just about impossible, of course, to predict with any precision how all of this will unfold from here'.[11]

The property market paused for breath in 2004, settling down for two years before launching into my predicted Winner's Curse phase (2007-8), which will consolidate the conditions for a recession in 2010.

But if, as we claimed in Chapter 12, a shift in the structure of public revenue in favour of land rents is the effective counter-cyclical policy, how can we explain the coexistence of booms and busts on a continent where the land tax has featured for 150 years? Australia has a comparatively efficient administrative system of land taxation; so why was she afflicted by boom busts that originated in the land market? Is our advocacy of fiscal reform misplaced?

§2 Land Values as Public Revenue

AS EARLY AS the 1850s some Australian settlements levied a tax on the rent that would be yielded by land. The practice spread throughout the continent by 1890. In 1910 the federal government introduced a graduated land tax to break up the large estates.

The wisdom of exempting capital improvements from the property tax becomes apparent when we compare the different rate of development between colonies which strongly favoured a public charge on site values (Queensland, New South Wales and West Australia) and those that tended to tax both land and buildings. Table 13:4 identifies the trends in the agricultural sector. During the depression years of the 1930s, the states that tended to exempt buildings and fixed equipment achieved strong growth, expanding the acres under cultivation. This compares with the contraction in the three states that penalised people with a tax on the savings which they invested in capital improvements on land. These trends continued in the recovery years after the Second World War. There was a remarkable expansion in the states that encouraged capital formation compared with those that penalised it with the property tax on improvements to land.

A similar difference in impact is observed in the housing sector. Construction in the 40 years up to 1958 was markedly more buoyant in the states that exempted houses from the property tax. Measuring

TABLE 13:4

Comparative Performance of Property Taxes: Agricultural

Depression era

Land value rating states

Change from 1929 to 1939	Change in Acres	%
Queensland	688	68
New South Wales	1,548	22
West Australia	153	3
Group	*2,389*	*213*

Improved value rating states

South Australia	-243	-5
Victoria	-560	-10
Tasmania	-22	-8
Group	*-826*	*-8*

Postwar performance

Land value rating states

Change from 1947 to 1959	Change in Acres	%
Queensland	1,224	76
New South Wales	313	5
West Australia	2,545	71
Group	*4,082*	*3*

Improved value rating states

South Australia	262	7
Victoria	-311	-6
Tasmania	-22	-6
Group	*-61*	*-1*

Source: Geoffrey A. Forster, 'Australia', in Robert V. Andelson, *Land-Value Taxation Around the World*, Oxford: Blackwells, 2000, 3rd edn., p.403.

the rate of construction of dwellings in the private sector, adjusted for the number of marriages, the states which taxed dwellings lagged behind those that exempted dwellings.

Given its use of the land tax, we expect Australia to provide insights into the counter-cyclical characteristics of this fiscal policy.

The earliest land booms were in the 1830s and 1850s. These did not feature in the form of the modern business cycle, however, until the onset of capital formation and urban-based industrialisation between 1860 and 1890. It was during this period that Australia experienced its first 18-year cycle. Some remarkable conclusions can be offered on the strength of the historical evidence.

The first cycle (1876-94) featured the propensity to speculate based on property rights, financial institutions and attitudes that were imported from Britain. Speculation preoccupied frontiersmen in the late 1880s.[12] Banks all over the continent collapsed in 1893.

> Initially (between 1891 and 1892), non-banks and 'other' banks failed as a result of their financing of building and land trans- actions, reliance on short-term deposits, direct speculation in land, fraud, embezzlement and other unsound practices. The financial crisis spread to the note-issuing banks in 1893, leading to a widespread financial system collapse, which amplified and prolonged the economic downturn.[13]

Victoria, whose property tax was predominantly on the value of both land and buildings, suffered a deeper and more sustained depres- sion than New South Wales (NSW), which was markedly in favour of raising revenue from site values alone. NSW experienced a steady growth over the cycle (with intrusions from droughts). By contrast, there was 'a financial boom and collapse, occurring only in Victoria, which led that colony to a longer period of prosperity and a much sharper fall in output'.[14] The steady gains in NSW paid off, in the long run, for the expansion of Sydney.

The second cycle (1894-1912), however, was subjected to a powerful political 'shock'. Something remarkable happened in 1910 which undermined the property boom at what was supposed to be the Winner's Curse phase of the cycle. A federal land value tax was suc- cessfully introduced after extensive political debate on the virtues of optimising economic development and deterring land speculation. Following his lecture tour of Australia, Henry George helped to set aflame the demand for greater reliance on land rents as public revenue. This echoed events in the UK, with the difference that the Australian federal land tax was allowed to come into operation. It remained in place until 1952.

The land market did not destabilise the economy. The speculators were not able to extract large capital gains. Does this, then, qualify as a classic 18-year cycle? The possibility of a public charge on land values dampened speculation. Terry Dwyer of the Australian National University found that, in 1910-11, total land income at $63.7m comfortably exceeded total tax revenue ($44m, which was 6.49% of

GDP).[15] Thus, the scope for eliminating *all* non-rent taxes existed at the beginning of the 20th century.

The third cycle (1912-30) was not a business cycle as I defined it in Chapter 5. The benefits of the land tax's influence made themselves felt towards the end of this period. Australia did not escape the global depression, but the disruptive influence of land speculation was muted. In the nine years up to what would have been the end of the land-driven cycle, property prices grew at a similar rate to those of stocks and shares up to 1929. Remarkably,

> Property prices ... declined at a slower rate than stock prices ... there are no obvious signs of a domestic asset price bubble, and both bank and non-bank financial institutions acted prudently and survived the depression relatively unscathed.[16]

The 1929 depression in Australia was driven largely by events in Europe and North America, where land speculation did feature prominently in the 1920s. There is no explanation for the domestic stability in Australia other than that the speculators' expectations were undermined by the tax-take from the rent of land, which diminished the capital gains.

The fourth cycle (1930-48) was distorted by the onset of the Second World War. The munitions industry helped to buoy up the economy as it did in Britain and America. But in addition, the effects of the federal land tax continued until it was abolished in 1952. This coincided with the end of the decade-long adjustment of the world's leading economies back to 'normality', which historians date as 1955. The 1952 abolition, then, set Australia's fiscal policy on a pro-cyclical path once again.

The fifth cycle (1955-74) was doomed to conform to the classic profile of boom and bust. Sure enough, land speculation in the late 1960s pushed prices to a peak in 1974. Finance companies were among the victims. Prime Minister Gough Whitlam responded with rapid increases in interest rates in 1973 directly aimed at the property bubble. He declared: 'If as a consequence, the higher interest rates have the effect of curbing the speculative rush into land and property, that will be all too good'.[17] But the bubble was ready to burst anyway. It was not necessary to raise the cost of borrowing money to levels that penalised entrepreneurs who were not engaged in real estate speculation.

The bubble of the early 1970s would not have occurred if the federal government, instead of raising interest rates to penal levels, had announced in (say) 1971 that it would reintroduce the land tax and abolish income tax. Rent was sufficient as a fiscal base to finance a modern economy as well as deterring land speculation, as Dwyer's calculations demonstrate.

> It is interesting that, even with missing land values for subsoil assets or spectrum rights and with conservative valuations, the ratio of total [government] revenue to land values suggests considerable revenue potential, with land income (defined as including revaluations gains) almost equalling total taxes in 1972/73 and 1975/76.[18]

The sixth cycle (1974-92) featured a consistent reduction in the share of public revenue from the rent of land collected by state and municipal governments. That further encouraged the pursuit of capital gains from land. Regulatory restrictions on bank lending were ineffective: they were offset by the emergence of non-bank financial intermediaries that were willing to advance credit to the property market. The increase in house prices of about 40% in 1988 was unsustainable. The house of cards had a long way to fall. The predictable outcome:

> The 1990s saw the largest failures of the Australian financial system since the crash of the 1890s, and many authors have commented on the similarities of these two episodes of Australian economic history ... The boom in construction led to an oversupply of office space in the early 1990s, followed by a dramatic fall in property prices and a deep recession.[19]

It need not have turned out this way. With personal income tax revenue at $41.8bn, and total land income at $65.6bn, a restructured public finance would have deterred speculation in residential property and diverted cash and credit into capital formation in other sectors without prejudicing the construction industry at all. A sustainable, balanced economy would have delivered high wage jobs for the migrants who continued to flock into the continent.

The seventh cycle (1992-2010) displays all the characteristics of the 18-year cycle in the UK. The run-down of revenue from land values reached the point where the income from municipal and state site-value taxes were derisory compared with the capital gains that could be achieved from speculation. In NSW, during the first half of the cycle (1993-2003), land values increased by about $361bn. The land-based taxes collected £44bn of this, an 88% retention of 'unearned income' by landowners.[20] Not surprisingly, a benign fiscal environment encouraged the accelerated increase in prices. Graph 13:1 shows the take-off in property deals from 1996 with NSW leading the way.[21]

GRAPH 13.1

Total Real Estate Sale Prices:
Five major Australian states

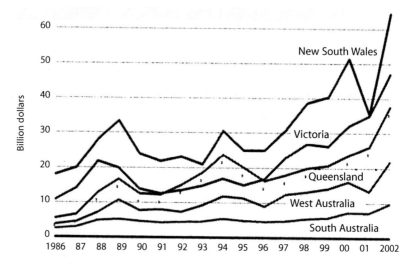

The transactions correlate closely with the growth of GDP, with the downturn in property deals preceding the recessions (Graph 13:2). The exception is the period from 1996. Record low interest rates made it possible for people to borrow heavily to buy property and use debt to buoy up the economy. But since low interest rates translate into higher land prices, the benign monetary environment would haunt the government and financiers as real estate prices reached unsupportable levels.

Booms and busts in Australia respond to the same incentives observed in the UK and USA. In the early part of the construction cycle, heading for the mid-cycle recessions of the early 1980s and 2001-2, the boom was led by residential land speculation, with house prices increasing at up to 20% a year. Then, as the cycle heads for its peak, the commercial and industrial sectors kick in. The commercial property bubbles in the early 1970s and late 1980s created the over-supplied market with buildings that entrepreneurs would not occupy. The political price was paid by the Whitlam, Fraser and other governments that were in power when the property market crashed.

This was not a historically inevitable outcome. From 1979 onwards, the rent of land exceeded tax revenue from both individual and company incomes. Rents were sufficient to cover a large part of

GRAPH 13.2

Real Estate Sale Value Growth and GDP Growth: Australia

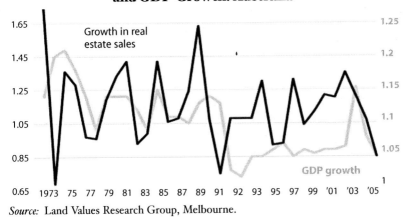

Source: Land Values Research Group, Melbourne.

public expenditure. In 1998/9 they were $133-141bn, compared with total Australian tax revenue of $177.9bn.[22] The gap would have been eliminated if we take into account that a restructured public finance would have reduced many people's dependency on state welfare. But optimum public and private pricing policies were not in place. *So the low rate of rent collection prevented public charges on site values from exercising their counter-cyclical influence. Large capital gains were available to attract the speculators.*

The RBA liked to believe that its increase in interest rates to 5.25% at the end of 2003 explained the easing off of house prices in Sydney and Melbourne. In fact, this was no more than a breath-catching pause in the trend that would gather speed through the Winner's Curse phase in 2007/8.

Meanwhile, an enquiry by the Productivity Commission concluded that houses were not affordable to many people because of government tax policies that bolstered property speculation. The Federal Government, however, refused to review tax policies that affected house prices (such as the decision to halve capital gains tax).

§3 The Politics of Failure

CENTRAL BANKERS believe that their monetary strategies help to stabilise volatile asset markets. But as two Australian economists have observed: 'Heavy-handed regulation does not necessarily prevent bubbles'.[23]

Regulatory action cannot prevent booms and busts because credit is constantly re-invented to outwit the regulators. An example was the secondary banks of the 1970s, many of which were bankrupted, some of which were rescued in 'lifeboat' operations by taxpayers. Today, central bankers rely on increasingly sophisticated analytical tools for stress testing the banks. Spain's techniques have attracted the admiration of Australian economists.[24] But the overheated market in real estate in Spain was fuelled, to a major extent, by money that did not originate within the domestic banking system. In 2003, according to Barclays Bank, 40% of all new houses built on the Spanish coasts were bought by Britons, the impact of which was a 21% rise in house prices in the year – triple the traditional price growth of 6-7%.[25]

The sophisticated approach to penalising hoarding is to require occupiers to pay an annual charge that corresponds to the benefits that they derive from their locations. They receive the community services that they want (why else would they be living or working in the locations of their choice?), and would pay for that benefit in the same way that they do when they buy groceries from a supermarket: an exchange of money for goods and services of equal value.

There is no excuse for the political failure of countries like Spain. They have access to the theoretical, historical and (by referring to Denmark, which employs a municipal land tax) the empirical evidence that points governments in the direction of remedial policies. But in Australia, one could expect more from political leaders, given that country's 150 years of trial-and-error experience with land taxation. Federal governments know that they need to restore the collection of rental revenues on a larger scale, to neutralise land speculation. The need to do so goes beyond purely economic considerations. The political failures of 20th century fiscal policy generated pathological consequences that reach deep into the hearts and minds of the families that are the building blocks of a nation that is still in the making.

The room for manoeuvre is enormous, given the very low rate of collection of rents to fund shared services. The dividends that would flow from a rational financial system are huge (see Chapter 14). Australia ought to have a head-start in the democratisation of public finance. Mysteriously, however, the people who pay the taxes do not even know how much revenue is tapped out of the land of Australia. According to the Productivity Commission, 'comprehensive data on total taxation revenue collected from property in Australia are not available'.[26] We do know that this revenue is a pathetically small proportion of the total. In 2002-3, property taxes as a share of total revenue available to each state and territory varied from 1.5% in the Northern Territory and 3.3% in Tasmania to 9.5% in Victoria and 11.1% in New South Wales.[27]

Federal fees from spectrum licenses are concealed under obscure headings in the nation's accounts. Rental revenue from petroleum is included in company income tax records. Even so, we can gain an impression of the political failure to treat resource rents with respect by considering the taxes on immovable property. These yielded $9.5bn in 2002 out of total taxation at federal, state and municipal levels of $216.9bn, or 4.38%.

The way in which dysfunctional political philosophy affects public policy is illustrated by the self-censorship among the people who administer the advisory and regulatory institutions of the state. The analysts know what the problem is, and yet they wilfully restrain themselves from enlivening democratic debate with deep analysis. Such was the case in Australia when the alarm bells rang over house prices in the 1990s.

Ian Macfarlane, the Governor of the RBA, identified credit and rising house prices as the single most important policy issue. These represented 'the one internal imbalance that could have put at risk the continuation of the long economic expansion that has been so beneficial to the Australian community'. This appears to suggest the need for forensic action directed at the source of the problem. Otherwise, in the next boom, they would be faced with a problem that was succinctly described by the Governor: 'The blandishments of the banks, brokers and other commercial agents plying them with offers of seemingly generous quantities of credit'.[28]

In the light of this diagnosis, were house prices the appropriate *target* for remedial action? The central bank was anxious to allay people's presumed fears. Its Deputy Governor assured the nation that, while they *were* worried about the housing market and people's borrowing behaviour, 'the concern was not out of a desire to *target* house prices ...' (emphasis in original).[29] House prices were the fly in the economic ointment, and yet the central bank, which oversees the credit facilities of the nation, was *not* targeting them! House prices would be left to live a life of their own. This was an unconscionable neglect of the kind that leaves us in no doubt where responsibility lies for the booms and busts in the market economy: with a palsied political system. The consequence is a social pathology that can be traced directly to the tax policies favoured by government. It appears that

civil society will need to take a grip of the problem if the people of
Australia are to be rescued from the wilful neglect of their elected
representatives and public officials.[30]

§4 The Pathology of Taxation

THE DEVELOPMENT model that treats land rents as public revenue
served Australia well in its formative decades. Had the colonial authorities consolidated and extended this fiscal policy into a permanent tool
for enterprise and equity, as was done in Hong Kong, the ceiling on
productivity would have been raised above the levels that were
achieved. Settlers from the earliest times to the present would have
enjoyed an efficient economy that did not divide people on the basis
of the distribution of assets. Those who wished to work would have
enjoyed tax-free wages, higher savings and a greater accumulation of
wealth. The community's infrastructure and common services could
have been adequately financed out of the rent of land and the other
rich resources bequeathed by nature. Instead, the gap between the
working poor and the idle rich grew inexorably, and the housing
market contributed to this process.

The trends continued up to the end of the 20th century. Real
average house prices in Australia have increased by an annual 2.3%
since 1970. This compares with an average increase of about 1% a year
in real household disposable income.[31] One consequence has been the
reduction in land occupied by new homes. The state of health as well
as the wealth of the state is compromised. The Productivity
Commission acknowledged that there is a clear link between home
ownership, social stability, people's health and education.[32] The
failure to make possible the security of affordable shelter for everyone
manifests itself in the pathological state in which families and their
neighbourhoods find themselves. In England and Wales, for example,
George Miller has calculated that about 50,000 people die prema-
turely every year from causes that may be traced back to the impact of
perverse taxes.[33] Those causes include unaffordable housing.

In Australia in the 1990's, the halving of the interest rate contributed to social stress by doubling the value of the mortgage debt
that was potentially available to people, as well as nearly doubling the
price of a home that could be 'afforded'. Thus, what ought to have
been a benign regime of stable money value, with low interest rates,
turns into a nightmare for people who wanted to marry, start a family
and settle down to a contented life. Instead, the prospects are for an

GRAPH 13:3

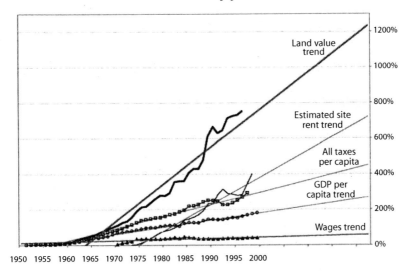

1950 1955 1960 1965 1970 1975 1980 1985 1990 1995 2000

Source: Tony O'Brien, 'The Wealth Poverty Gap', *Geo*philos, Autumn 2000, p.65.

ever-deepening rift between those who have accumulated wealth, and the indebtedness of those who are excluded. The trends are revealed in Graph 13:3. This confirms the worst fears of the classical economists. They believed that the monopoly power vested in those who possess land would result in a growing share of the nation's income falling without effort into the pockets of landowners, with a diminishing share received by people who rely on wages for their subsistence. This is Australia's fate. This outcome is disguised by (i) tax policies, which conceal the true level of net-of-tax incomes; (ii) the subsidies that are distributed to cushion the effects on fiscal victims; and (iii) the paucity of information on rents.

The pathological impact of government policies is rooted in the conjunction of property rights and public finance. While acknowledging that politicians are, on the whole, sincere in wanting to improve the condition of their electorates, it is also undeniable that the conventional taxes which they favour are self-defeating. The only way they can deal with this problem is by the selective amnesia that afflicts politics in the realm of land-related policy.

● In July 2000, the Australian government introduced a 10% Goods and Services Tax (GST). This increased the cost of constructing new homes, putting them beyond the reach of even more people.

To compensate for the damage it inflicted, the government introduced the First Home Owner Scheme (FHOS), available to anybody, no matter how rich they were, to purchase any house they wanted, including properties from the existing stock which were not penalised by the GST.

By this measure, government injected $4.3bn into the housing market just as it was reaching its mid-cycle peak. The effect was to increase demand from more than 500,000 first home buyers, many of whom would have bought their houses even without the subvention from taxpayers.[34] These measures (both GST and FHOS) distorted the market and contributed directly to the 'slump that followed when many other house buyers brought forward the purchase or construction of new dwellings into the first half of 2000 to avoid GST'. Dwelling commencements fell by 30%, in the second half of 2000, the largest decline since 1975.[35] Undeterred, government responded with the Commonwealth Additional Grant (CAG), which provided an extra $7,000 to those FHOS recipients who were buying a newly constructed dwelling. This additional taxpayer-funded subsidy intensified the implosion of communities, a process that was compounded by other tax measures.

- The Productivity Commission recommended that the government should consider measures to avoid the damage of imposing any property-related 'tax on tax', as when stamp duties are applied to sales that are already subject to GST. Collecting stamp duty more than once as a property changes hands reduces efficiency and raises prices above the levels that many people can afford.
- Changes to the capital gains tax in 1999 encouraged people to channel money into property at a time when prices were rising strongly.
- The high marginal tax on incomes encouraged people to invest in housing to reduce their liability. The top rate is applied at a relatively low level ($62,501) by international standards. Some of that burden can be eliminated by investing in loss-making property. According to the RBA, 'properties are commonly marketed on the assumption that they don't earn positive taxable income for a considerable period'.[36]
- Despite its concern about house prices, Australia's government subsidises new infrastructure even though this 'would primarily benefit land owners or developers rather than home purchasers', according to the Productivity Commission.[37]

The economics of property were understood. For example: tax reductions increase the price of land.[38] The Productivity Commission noted that the reverse happens when taxes are increased – 'over the longer term, higher taxes will see developers paying less for raw land than otherwise'.[39] But this route to lower land prices has a damaging effect on the economy as a whole, through the distortions that taxes cause to people's incentives to work, save and invest. The benign way to achieve lower selling prices is to invite people to pay for the services that they receive, which means they would pay less to owners when they negotiated the terms for occupying land.

- Despite recognising that house prices – 'and especially the value of the land on which they are sited'[40] – fluctuate considerably over time, government continues to reward investment in houses by not taxing capital gains. This windfall gain stems from not requiring home owners to pay a charge that corresponds to the benefits that they receive in the locations they occupy. Home-owners are free-riders on the backs of tax payers (that the two may be one and the same does not mitigate the perverse outcomes). They enjoy the exemption of their principal residence from capital gains tax, which results in over-investment in housing. This encourages a high rate of home ownership, which reduces the mobility of labour and the productivity of capital.

- Taxes redistribute income from tenants to freeholders. The tax base excludes land income which can be imputed to owner-occupied residential land. At the same time, tax revenue from people who do not own land is spent on infrastructure, which raises the value of other people's sites. To compensate for anomalies that arise from this maldistribution of income and assets, government promulgates higher marginal tax rates, allegedly to subsidise low-income families who are hurt by the original tax policies.

- As the share of taxes as a proportion of GDP rises, the best 'hedge' against the tax-and-inflation eroded value of disposable incomes is to buy land and hold it vacant. This reduces turnover of sites, which reduces urban productivity, causes ecological damage through sprawl and increases the need for higher taxes to fund under-used infrastructure.

The cumulative impact of pathological taxes needs a monetary measure, if people are to grasp their full significance. Some estimates for the rich countries can now be offered (Chapter 14). These ought to motivate people into wresting the initiative from politicians. Has the time come to dry the crocodile tears (over, for example, unaffordable housing) and deliver meaningful reforms?

REFERENCES

1   Productivity Commission, *First Home Ownership*, Melbourne, Report No. 28, 2004, p.154. The Reserve Bank of Australia concurred, stating that 'there is not much evidence to suggest that the growth in house prices has been due to a persistent shortage of supply of houses relative to underlying demand for new housing'. Reserve Bank of Australia, Submission to Productivity Commission Inquiry on First Home Ownership, November 2003, pp.2, 29.
2   G.J. Thompson, 'The Many Faces of Risk in Banking', Reserve Bank of Australia *Bulletin*, July, 1997, p.1.
3   I.J. Macfarlane, 'The Changing Nature of Economic Crises', Reserve Bank of Australia *Bulletin*, December 1997, p.18.
4   *Ibid.*
5   *Ibid*, p.19.
6   Thompson, *op. cit.* p.12.
7   'Recent Developments in Housing: Prices, Finance and Investor Attitudes', Reserve Bank of Australia *Bulletin*, July 2002, p.4.
8   *First Home Ownership, op. cit.*, p.7.
9   Dan Andrews, 'City Sizes, House Prices and Wealth', Reserve Bank of Australia *Bulletin*, December 2001, p.3.
10 'Recent Developments in Housing', *op. cit.*, p.1.
11 G.R. Stevens, 'Economic Conditions and Prospects: June 2004', Reserve Bank of Australia *Bulletin*, June 2004, p.19.
12 Harrison, *The Power in the Land, op. cit.*, p.231.
13 Jeffrey Carmichael and Neil Esho, 'Asset Price Bubbles and Prudential Regulation', Australian Prudential Regulation Authority, Working Paper 2001–03, p.9.
14 Bryan Haig, 'New estimates of Australian GDP: 1861-1948/49', *Australian Econ. His. Rev.*, Vol. 41(1), 2001, p.22.
15 Terry Dwyer, 'The Taxable Capacity of Australian Land and Resources', *Australian Tax Forum*, Vol. 18, No. 1, 2003, p.62.
16 Carmichael and Esho, *op. cit.*, p.10.
17 *Ibid*, p.11.
18 Dwyer, *op. cit.*, p.33.
19 Carmichael and Esho, *op. cit.*, p.12.
20 Frank Stilwell and Kirrily Jordan, 'Land Tax in Australia: Principles, Problems and Policies', in Laurent John, *Henry George's Legacy in Economic Thought*, Cheltenham: Edward Elgar, forthcoming.
21 The decline in New South Wales transactions for 2001, back to the level of Victoria's sales, is reported by Bryan Kavanagh of the Land Values Research Group, Melbourne, to be attributable to rogue data. Personal communication.
22 *Op. cit.*, p.67.
23 Carmichael and Esho, *op. cit.*, p.13.
24 *Ibid.*, pp.19, 22, 29. They acknowledged (p.22) that 'stress testing ... offers little by way of structured guidance for control of bubbles'.
25 Jon Boone, 'Ice-cream kiosk is hot property at £95,000', *Financial Times*, July 15, 2004.
26 Productivity Commission, *op. cit.*, p.15.
27 *Ibid.*

28 Macfarlane, *op. cit.*, pp.11, 12.
29 Stevens, *op. cit.*, p.18.
30 A valuable alternative source of information may be found on the website of the Melbourne-based Land Values Research Group, (www.earthsharing.org.au/taxcom.html). See, e.g., their 'What is the potential site and resource rent yield in Australia?'
31 *Ibid.*, p.38.
32 *Ibid.*, p.2.
33 George J. Miller, *Dying for Justice*, London: Centre for Land Policy Studies, 2003.
34 Productivity Commission, *op. cit.*, p.xxxii.
35 *Ibid.*, p.71.
36 RBA Submission to Productivity Commission, *op. cit.*, p.42.
37 Productivity Commission, *op. cit.*, p.xxx. The Commission added that government (i.e., taxpayer) subsidies are 'capitalised into the price of housing land' (p.164).
38 *Ibid.*, pp.86-7.
39 *Ibid.*, p.89.
40 *Ibid.*, p.xiv.

14

Dividends from Democratised Finance

§1 A New Social Contract

THE DEMOCRATIC challenge for the 21st century is to construct a
new role for the Tax State. That is a complex task. It entails changes
to personal status and to the character of our communities.

For progress to be made in the direction of personal freedom and
social renaissance, the language of political discourse itself will have to
be revised. Only then will it be possible to negotiate new terms for
funding public services. That entails a rewriting of the Social
Contract.

Is radical change in the way that we raise the public's revenue possible? It may be that we do not have much choice. Enormous pressures
are building that prescribe a new philosophy of personal and civic
responsibility. The signals that are alerting us to the shift may be
traced in the way that governments are groping towards a new
vocabulary of taxation. The outline of a new political grammar is just
perceptible, and it implies a departure from old ways of administering
the common wealth. The notion of the market is being used to
reshape attitudes. The exercise cannot proceed far, on the present
basis, however, because politicians are constrained by obsolete doctrines. They are attempting to blend market concepts with welfare
statism. Even so, this exercise is an acknowledgment that a fresh
approach is needed.

Encouraging advances are being made. In Britain, Tony Blair's New
Labour government adopted terms like *choice* and *prices*. Their appli-
cation is particularly striking in the sphere of transport policy. Alistair
Darling, the transport secretary, through a White Paper[1] and in his
speech to the House of Commons on July 20, 2004, declared that the
British government wanted to replace *taxes* with road *prices*. Motorists
would pay variable charges based on where they were driving, for how
long, and whether at peak or off-peak times. These are rents of the
highway.

Australia's fiscal experiments challenge the conventional view that people should pay sums that politicians think they can afford, irrespective of the level of services that the payers want to use. This is a shift in substance. The change is reflected in language: a drift away from the crude concepts of taxation in favour of 'ensuring that developer charges for infrastructure relate appropriately to the benefits provided to home buyers in new housing developments'.[2] These charges are payments for services accessed at particular locations: rental payments.

Two good reasons for levying them are the need to reduce infrastructure costs and to protect the environment.[3] But care needs to be taken, for

> the scarcity value of land in those cities will inevitably rise. Unless there are offsetting increases in housing density, affordability will be adversely affected.[4]

Enforced increases in the densities of the space that people occupy are not the healthy remedy. The rational strategy is to siphon off the enhanced rents of land for investment in the shared services of communities. By this means spatial discipline (conservation through better use of urban land) is complemented by cultural expansion to the enrichment of all citizens.

In Australia, the 'user pays' principle is acknowledged to promote efficient location decisions by home buyers, 'reducing the need for regulatory constraints directed at the same objective'.[5] An example is the hypothecated transport levy of $15,000 per lot in four new development areas in New South Wales.

> The government has justified the levy on the basis that it would extract what otherwise would be windfall gains to existing owners of raw land from extension of the urban rail system.[6]

The levy is a crude approach. If, for a particular site, the benefits are less than $15,000, the levy includes a tax element which distorts incentives. On the other hand, if an occupier was willing to pay more than $15,000 for the transport amenity, because of the locational attributes of his site (say, the close – or, for some, the distant – proximity to the railway station), that additional sum represents a windfall gain. The owner capitalises that implicit subsidy (courtesy of those who paid for the railway) into an increase in the price of land, which he pockets when the time comes to sell and move on.

Even so, the levy, based on the philosophy of obliging people to pay for the services that they want to use, begins to articulate a new social contract. It extends personal obligations in relation to the provision of shared services. For this approach to be consolidated into a progressive restructuring of all taxes, the public needs to be engaged in a thorough debate on the implications. What, for example, are the principles behind the British transport secretary's claim that property owners should contribute a 'fair' share towards the £10bn Crossrail that would link Heathrow with London's East End? We need a definition of 'fair' so that we can determine who should pay, how much they should pay, and whether via government or market institutions. These issues need to be explored outside the socialist paradigm, if the class-based taxes are to be replaced by a democratised public finance. The prize is a radically new kind of society that would emerge spontaneously, organically.

Some sceptics might claim that the dividends are not large enough to warrant such a break with present conventions, so why bother to incur the political risks of initiating the change? A good reason is the general dissatisfaction with current policies. People are discontent because they do not see the connection with what they are personally getting for the money they are forced to yield out of their earnings. They believe they are paying too much for what they receive. They suspect that others are getting more than them in public goods and services. Discontent is compounded by the knowledge that some rich people escape without paying anything into the public purse for the benefits they receive. This dissatisfaction justifies a critical review of the philosophy of public finance.

Over the 20th century, taxes evolved on the socialist principle that people should pay just because they happen to receive a certain income, rather than paying sums proportionate to the services which they choose and use. Governments decide how much you can afford to pay; how you will pay it, and on what to spend the money. One outcome is the criminalisation of people who earn their incomes. Tax dodging by the self-employed is a thriving activity that costs the British Treasury about £40bn in lost revenue every year.[7]

But it would be a mistake to treat this tax philosophy as *originating* out of socialism. The seeds were sown by the monarchs and aristocracy who privatised the social income. That left no choice but to pay for public services by socialising people's private incomes. This inverts the principles on which people base decisions in their day-to-day lives. As Mason Gaffney puts it, fiscal bias 'socialises a large share of personal effort while eliminating the public equity in the land resources of the nation'.[8]

This delivers outcomes that we do not tolerate in other spheres of our lives. For example, the price we receive when we sell land is the measure of the value of the services we use *without paying for them*. This is free riding on other people's backs. Windfall gains are a covert redistribution of income that was never democratically sanctioned by the losers. It represents an imbalance in rights and responsibilities that we reject as inappropriate except for those who choose to risk their money in the casino.

The force of this thesis is not diminished in its moral and economic significance just because many landowners (such as those who own their residential plots) are also taxpayers. As contributors to the exchequer they are subsidising themselves! This may seem humorous, but the circuitous routes that are taken to pay for shared services come at a huge price for all of us, especially for those who do not own a plot of land. This illustrates the pathology of taxation. As free-riders (landowners), many of us are riding on our own tax-paying backs. We have no one to blame but ourselves if we allow this state of affairs to continue.

If we defrayed the full cost of the services that we want to enjoy through the locations we occupy, there would be no rental income of land left to capitalise into selling prices. The outcome would be a simpler, morally healthier, economically efficient public finance in which property owners would sell untaxed improvements on the land (buildings, and other undepreciated assets on or in the land). This would replace the bizarre merry-go-round in which many of us are simultaneously both windfall winners and income losers.

Adoption of the new fiscal arrangements could not be executed overnight. Shock therapy, which the West inflicted on the former Soviet economies, would not be a wise approach. But would people contemplate such a dramatic change, no matter how sensitively implemented, if the outcome was the loss of the capital value of their land? I believe people would endorse the policy if they were provided with a full account of all the implications. With such an education behind them, we may reasonably assume that rational people would opt for the change that enriches them, and does not discriminate against the interests of others. The compensating reductions in the tax burden on earnings would more than offset the payments they made for the locational benefits they received. This is the dividend that arises from fiscal reform.

§2   The Pay-Off

ECONOMISTS USE the term 'excess burden' to describe the distortions inflicted by conventional taxes. This burden delivers *deadweight
losses*. Finance ministers never disclose the scale of those losses.

Concealed in the specialist academic literature, wrapped in jargon,
are a few numbers that offer hints on the losses. Two American economists decided to remedy this constraint on the democratic discourse
by offering estimates for the G7 countries that people could understand. Professors Nic Tideman and Florenz Plassmann asked: if a
government scrapped the taxes that damage the economy and invited
people to pay rents that were proportionate to the value of the services that they used, how would the economy be affected? The answer,
using 1993 national income data, appears in Table 14:1. Nearly $7 tril-
lion ($7,000bn) in goods and services was lost to those seven countries
alone because of the negative impact of conventional taxes. This is
a measure of the gain, if the governments were to switch to rent-as-
public-revenue.

TABLE 14:1

G7: Gain in Output and *Per Capita* Income
under the Public Rent Policy (1993)

	Net domestic product $ bn	NDP per capita $
USA	1,602	6,902
Canada	275	9,142
France	879	15,166
Germany	1,018	12,406
Italy	815	14,128
Japan	1,535	12,284
UK	716	12,133
Total	*6,840*	

Source: Nicolaus Tideman and Florenz Plassmann, Ch. 6, *The Losses of Nations* (ed.:
Fred Harrison), London: Othila Press, 1998.

For illustrative purposes, a breakdown of the numbers for the UK,
applied to financial estimates in Gordon Brown's budget for 2000, was
undertaken by Ronald Banks. As a former foreign exchange dealer,
Banks knew the nation's money system from the inside. He translated

the bald estimates provided by the economists into numbers that people could understand. The bottom line was that the £1 trillion British economy could have produced an additional £880bn under the reformed system of public revenue. This was about £15,000 more for each man, woman and child.[9] Even allowing for over-estimates (which were probably not serious, because Tideman and Plassmann had used conservative assumptions) it is clear that there was more than sufficient potential income for Britain to afford all the services that people wanted. This additional income would be delivered because people would raise productivity in response to the Treasury's modernisation of its revenue policies.

Today, government spending, which ought to raise the nation's productivity and people's contentment, has the perverse opposite effect. Taxes narrow, rather than expand, the financial base from which government draws revenue. This effect is intuitively appreciated by the public, but latent dissatisfaction is smothered in the veil of ignorance: governments will not allow themselves to be held to account over their revenue-raising methods.

Consider this transition as if a government decided to phase in the transformation over 10 years. This is the lifetime of two full administrations in Britain.

The initial deletion of bad taxes would be directed in favour of the people who are most vulnerable to the fiscal brutality of the Tax State. Removing income and payroll taxes would immediately lead to a switch from capital intensive production to skill-based people-centred ways of creating wealth and providing services. This begins to render obsolete a range of social services and expenditures that no longer need to be financed out of the public's budget. The volume of welfare services would shrink spontaneously in response to the reduced needs of those on the lowest incomes. People would, in short, be less dependent on the incomes of others. The Tax State's involvement in people's lives would diminish from Year 1. With less need for revenue, the graduated switch to rent-based sources of revenue would not pose a problem for government. Meanwhile, it becomes possible to phase out the public sector jobs that were no longer required to administer the disappearing underclass.

As the virtuous switch from taxes to rents proceeds, *so the absolute size of the nation's income increases*. Take the case of the UK. With output valued at £1 trillion, rent would be approximately 33% of this,[10] so Britain could spend £333bn on the public's services. Now, according to the calculations by Tideman, Plassmann and Banks at the end of our 10-year transitional period that economy would have increased to £1.8

trillion. This increase is not based on five-loaves-and-three-fishes miracles, but on the more efficient use of land and capital and the labour services of employees. One-third of *that* new economy would be £600bn, much more than the tax revenue collected today. So, in Year 1, as the economy breached the artificial ceiling imposed by the Tax State, the value of output would rise above the historic trends. No one who was genuinely in need of the help of others would be deprived of benefits on which he or she relied for survival.

But as the switch progressed deep into the transition period and people's earnings and prospects rose above what they could have expected on the basis of past trends, *the character of the public sector itself would change*. Most immediately, the Tax State would no longer exercise its patronising grip on people's lives. People would take more control over their affairs. One outcome would be the devolution of political power from central institutions to individuals and to their city and neighbourhood communities.

The time would quickly come when government found that it was running a surplus on its budget. What would people do with that value? The investment shortfalls of the past would need to be remedied, in infrastructure such as transportation. But people would also have the option of declaring an annual cash dividend for all citizens. This was the decision in Alaska, which had to decide what to do with the windfalls from oil-rents. Part of the surplus is now invested in the Alaska Permanent Fund to provide for the common future – to take care of social needs when the petroleum reserves run out. And part of the oil-rent is distributed as an annual cash dividend to all citizens. In 2000 the dividend was $1,963, which was the highest payout since 1982.[11]

This formula for restoring people's ancient rights to the benefits from land is the market-based alternative that competes with the socialist proposal of nationalisation. It would equalise the benefits that flow from land without appropriating existing possessory rights.

Strategies based on the allocation of plots of land to the underclass will not provide a solution on the scale that we need to rebalance the system itself. One advocate of the piecemeal approach is Ferdinand Mount, a former adviser to the Thatcher government. He is concerned about the moral and cultural welfare of the underclass. In his view, access to plots would nurture a sense of proprietorship. Mount is angry at the maldistribution of land in Britain and the widening income gap between rich and poor.

> Land ownership in Britain is much more concentrated than in
> any other major country I can think of. It is not simply that so

many of the great estates have survived to a remarkable degree
unparalleled anywhere else. The squires also have many more
acres than smaller proprietors elsewhere. And the average size
of farms is bigger too.[12]

One flaw in Mount's prescription is that he assumes that a permanent remedy lies in the reallocation of a little land to a few more
people today. This is the error made by reformers in the former Soviet
countries: they did not realise that what ultimately mattered was not
the physical possession of the land itself, but the appropriation of the
flow of rental income from the land.

The privatisation of social housing and the leasing of plots at low
rents would not unpick the injustices of the past. We need a broadly-
based policy that delivers equity in the distribution of income and
access to employment opportunities. We need to neutralise the way
the tax laws redistribute income from the working poor to the owners
of land. If the middle classes are concerned for the welfare of the
underdogs who are ghettoised on council estates, the most effective
step would be to champion tax reform. This would be for *everyone's*
benefit – including the welfare of *their* middle-class children who will
one day need to buy their way into the housing market.

§3 Routes to Disaster

THE PREDATORY character of taxes may be traced through the
impact of public spending in New Labour's second term. Money was
made available to raise investment in schools and hospitals. The aim
was laudable, but the means were fatal. For by investing taxpayers'
money in schools and hospitals, the locations within the catchment
areas became more attractive. The net income – the additional value
produced by the increase in productivity – was transferred to the
owners of land. This effect is concealed by the accounting conventions
of the Treasury. It may be illustrated by considering the Blair government's 10-year transport investment plan.

In July 2000 the government announced that £180bn would be
channelled into roads and railways. Table 14:2 (column 6) offers an
impression of the order of magnitude of the losses.[13] The government
proposed to spend about £123bn out of the public purse. This, according to Deputy Prime Minister Prescott, was 'a realistic and business-
like' approach.[14] Prescott failed to disclose to Parliament that such
expenditure would constrain output, over the decade, by something

like £400bn – the deadweight loss attributable to the government's tax tools.

A full audit of government revenue and expenditure would compute the effects on the land market. Column 5 in Table 14:2 suggests an uplift in land values of over £180bn. This is an extremely unrealistic low estimate. We know from worldwide experience over the past 200 years, as well as methodical academic studies, that investment of £180bn in improved transportation would raise land values to something closer to £400bn. The uncertainty over the precise increase stems from the failure of government to factor into its cost-benefit analyses the way in which the net gains from its investments are capitalised into land values.

TABLE 14:2

Ten-Year Transport Plan
Investment and Expenditure: 2002-11 (£bn outturn prices)[1]
Estimated uplift in Land Values and Lost Output[2]

	Public investment	Private investment	Public resource spend	Total	Land value uplift[3]	Deadweight losses to national income[4]
	(1)	(2)	(3)	(4)	(5)	(6)
Strategic road	13.6	2.6	5.0	21.3	23.4	58.9
Railways	14.7	34.3	11.3	60.4	66.4	82.3
Local transport	19.3	9.0	30.6	58.9	64.8	158.0
London	7.5	10.4	7.4	25.3	27.8	47.2
Other transport	0.7	n/a	1.5	1.5	2.4	7.0
Unallocated[5]	9.0	n/a	n/a	9.0	—	44.3
Charging income	n/a	n/a	2.7	2.7	—	—
Total	*64.7*	*56.3*	*58.6*	*179.7*	*184.8* [400?]	*398*

1 '£180bn Ten year investment plan to deliver top class transport system', London: Department of Transport News Release, July 20, 2000, p.3.
2 Estimates by Ronald Banks and the Centre for Land Policy Studies, London.
3 Derived from cols. 1-3, employing a ratio of 1.1:1.
4 Derived from cols. 1 and 3. A ratio of £3.167 deadweight loss for every £1 raised by conventional taxes is employed, based on the tax burden and national income data published in the Budget Estimates for 2001. The methodology is described in Ronald Banks, *Double-Cross: Gordon Brown, the Treasury and the hidden costs of taxes*, London: Centre for Land Policy Studies, 2002.
5 This revenue will be raised by conventional taxes, but we do not know how it will be spent. Therefore, we have estimated the deadweight loss, but we assume (unrealistically) no uplift in land values.

Thus, Gordon Brown's fiscal philosophy entails a hidden price tag. The CBI estimated that, between 1997 and 2005, the chancellor increased taxes that cost businesses about £50bn. This reduction in corporate profitability prejudiced investment plans. But that was not the spin presented to the House of Commons on December 10, 2002, by Transport Secretary Alistair Darling. He claimed that the Blair government's financial plans were 'measured and balanced'. He had applied these two tests to his Department's investment of £5.5bn in a major road building programme that was intended to reduce congestion. He told the Commons:

> Our roads and railways are facing increasing demands on them. We are one of the largest economies in the world. In the last five years we have got 1.5m more people into work. People are better off and travel more often.

The claim that public expenditure policies were measured and balanced cannot be substantiated. *Measured* policies would take into account all the financial consequences. The impact of the £5.5bn of taxpayers' money on the land market, for example, would be at least £6bn, and more likely £12bn or more in windfall gains for a privileged sector of the population. This is how much the price of land would be raised because of the increased efficiency in the movement of people and their products around the nation. Academic studies have computed the uplift in *additional* value of at least £1.1 for every £1 invested in transport (for those projects that are commercially viable).[15] The payback from such investment, however, can be considerably greater. In London, a ratio of 4:1 was the estimate calculated by property restorer Don Riley as the net gain from investment in the extension of the Jubilee Line Underground. A £3.5bn investment turned into a £14bn windfall for landowners.[16] On this basis, the £5.5bn highway investment would deliver windfall gains for landowners of something like £20bn. But in addition to the impact on land values, deadweight losses must also be taken into account. The £5.5bn would deliver losses of over £17bn. This is the estimate of goods and services that would have been produced if the Treasury had used the most efficient policies for raising revenue.[17] The losses are attributable not to *how much* revenue the government raises, but to *how* it raises money to fund projects.

What of the claim that the government's approach delivered a *balanced* outcome? Its financial policies undermine both its transport plans and wider social objectives. The beneficiaries of the capital gains would be the families that owned their homes. *Land values would escalate during the rest of the decade, and the transport programme would be a major conduit for distributing asset values away from taxpayers and tenants in favour of the owners of property.* This is neither fair nor efficient. There is no semblance of balance to this outcome. Transport financing would give an added twist to the upward spiral in house prices, making homes even less affordable to teachers and nurses. Public spending would also encourage hoarders to hang on to their sites in the expectation of ever larger capital gains.

Another outcome is the preservation of the boom-bust cycle which blocks investment in both public and private services. We saw this in the case of the construction industry (Chapter 7 §3). For the UK as a whole, the cumulative shortfall in public investment between 1992 and 2002 was of the order of £65bn. This calculation by Dr Rana Roy assumed a constant level of new public investment (in real terms) over the decade, and comparing the total (£159bn) with the actual cumulative net public investment (£93bn).[18]

The tools for straightening out these shambles in public policy were championed by Lloyd George and Philip Snowden. They ought to have commended themselves to the Blair government, for the financial benefits were not difficult to calculate. The benefits arising out of these reforms within one sector alone (transport) were estimated for Europe's transport ministers. Table 14:3 gives the results for Britain.

TABLE 14:3

Revenue Gains from Optimal Transport Pricing: Britain 2000

Revenues	€ billion per annum
Reference scenario revenues for all inland transport modes	59.84
Optimal revenues for all inland transport modes (including additional parking charges)	98.79
Net change in revenues	38.95

Source: European Conference of Ministers of Transport, *Reforming Transport Taxes*, Paris: OECD Publications, 2003, p.34, Table 1.

If prices were based on the fair and efficient principles that we have outlined, in Britain alone there would be an annual increase in revenue of €39bn (£24bn).[19] Rana Roy, the economist who investigated the consequences of the fiscal shift, concluded:

> Thus, a pricing system designed to maximise welfare rather than revenues delivers *total* revenues of €99bn *per annum* – and

additional revenues of €39bn *after* retiring €60bn of sub-opti-
mal taxes currently imposed on the transport sector.[20]

Without these optimum financial policies, the economy is subjected to the syndrome of one step forward in the period of growth,
and one step backwards in response to a recession: we are back to
where we started. But when people are relieved of taxes and invited
to pay for the benefits they receive – which includes the right to con-
gest the roads – total income increases. We can afford to catch up with
the investment needed in capital equipment; we can retire the bad
taxes, enjoy higher living standards and – thanks to the reduction in
the risk of unemployment – lower the levels of stress in the workplace.

Optimum pricing policies re-balance the economy, with lower
indebtedness and more investment in those services that remain the
legitimate obligation of the community. Such an outcome requires the
leadership of a tough chancellor to deliver. Unfortunately, the best that
Gordon Brown could offer was public consultations on what looked
like a standard tax on development land at the point when planning
permission was granted. Such a policy was repeatedly tried and tested,
with negative results, by Labour governments after 1947.[21]

§4 The End of Predatory Politics?

HISTORICALLY, there was justification for denouncing the aristocracy for privatising the rents that were traditionally reserved to
finance the services of the realm.

In the 20th century, the working class tried to reclaim a direct share
of rent, not by redistributing property, but through the public purse.
The attempt failed, so people turned to socialism for solutions. But
the ideological tool-kit of Marx and the 19th century English socialists
was not effective: rent as social revenue is possible only in a democratised community. This yields what looks like a philosophical paradox:
socialised rent requires the institutions of the free market to protect
the liberties of the individual. The USSR was not able to adopt the
No. 1 item in the list of 10 reforms that appear in the Communist
Manifesto (rent was to be used to pay for public services[22]) because of
the authoritarian character of the command economy. So the Soviet
Union had to assume the character of the Tax State to extract its revenue from people's wages. This was the most bizarre case of the pathology of taxation in the 20th century. Russia's revolutionary proletariat
escaped the clutches of the capitalists to end up exploiting themselves
because they could not devise a democratic form of public finance!

We may rationalise conventional taxes by viewing the Tax State of the 20th century as the tool of the Common Man. In its Welfare State form, the Tax State was a social device that could be used to equalise political power. Until the First World War, that power was monopolised by land-owners. Although the aristocracy was forced to relinquish parliamentary power, it retained control over the community's natural source of revenue. So the working class had to come to terms with this reality. This delivered a perverse outcome: using the agencies of the state to redistribute income, to *indirectly* appropriate a stake in rent, but in doing so turning the predatory power of the Tax State on themselves.

Action to compensate the majority of people was necessary, because property in the age of democracy still reflected the conditions of late feudalism. During the depression years of the 1930s, for example, 1% of people aged 25 and over in England and Wales owned 55% of the total property in private hands.[23] But the price for enhancing the collective power of the working class was the extension of the property and power of the state. This made it possible to narrow the gap in living standards by providing people with benefits, or claims on the incomes of others, rather than enabling them to acquire their own property. It locked people permanently into the state of dependency on others, for a pre-condition for increasing one's income was the possession of property. 'Thus, the inequality of the distribution of property may make the distribution of incomes still more unequal,' concluded Campion in a path-breaking study of property and its distribution in the years before the Second World War.

Welfarism, with the Tax State as the mediator of people's fate, continued to the end of the century. How will we fare in the 21st century? In an age that claims to be committed to human rights, we have paradoxically imprisoned ourselves within a legal and institutional framework in which we abuse ourselves by condoning coercive taxes. Today, however, the Tax State has exhausted its historic purpose. Creative initiatives are needed to evolve a new role for the state, a partnership role to complement the activities of people working in their communities. It is probable that leadership will have to be provided by those who have acquired a stake in the land – home owners.

The painfully secured gains of the past century will be unpacked as the centre of gravity of the world's wealth-creating capacity is transferred eastwards. The rational response to this prospect is the one over which home owners can now exercise influence through the democratic process: the democratisation of the public's finances. Home owners need to embark on an imaginative journey into the future, to visualise the improvements to the quality of their lives that would flow from an increase in the productivity of the economy. If they fail to rise to this challenge, they lose the right to complain about abusive taxes and the unaffordability of homes for their children; they must remain silent about stressful conditions in their places of employment, and the other collateral consequences of tax-induced crises, those that surface through the psychology of the individual and the dislocations in neighbourhoods.

Can the economic revolution of the 21st century be a peaceful one that unifies rather than divides people? By asserting democratic control over the way revenues are raised, we expand the options for greater control over the way in which those rents can be spent. Whether non-government agencies should oversee the allocation of revenue is a matter to be determined by communities in the light of their evolving needs. The changes would be organic, flowing from the bottom up in response to the self-selecting lifestyles of people who had taken control over – and responsibility for – new ways of living. By this means we give everyone a stake in their country. Much of what now passes for anti-social behaviour would disappear.

The authoritarian state would be a victim of the Great Tax Revolt. No longer would it decide whether you have the ability to pay what *it* deems necessary to spend. Instead, we would decide, individually and as members of a community, on the basis of the services that we wish to access through the locations in which we choose to live and work. This is the sole mechanism for democratising the public's finances; which bequeaths the freedom of choice to us all.

The alternative is a sclerotic Tax State whose coercive institutions will have to resort to ever harsher, intrusive measures. In countries that are open to the global economy, it will become increasingly difficult to raise revenue from mobile labour and capital. Unless the revenue base is shifted onto resources that are immobile the Tax State will become increasingly desperate and despotic. Out of self-preservation, it will reinvent itself – some combining as super-states to achieve a longer reach – and the lights of liberty will flicker as dreams of the past. This danger of an Orwellian society may already be upon us. In Britain, the Information Commissioner, Richard Thomas, who is answerable to Parliament, warns of a growing danger of East German Stasi-style snooping by the state.[24] With databases proliferating and closed circuit TV cameras spying on us, the authorities have at their disposal the tools for controlling our lives. 'I don't think people have woken up to what lies behind this,' warns Thomas.

The aggregation of political power, and the tectonic shifts of economic activity, make tax reform an imperative for survival. The precondition for both peace and prosperity is a public finance that removes ancient injustices. Otherwise, we know what is in store for us.

- Pension funds will not support people who thought they could enjoy post-employment rest.
- The cost of living will rise, as cheap energy – petroleum – dries up in the years to 2050.[25]
- Manufacturing industries will transfer to the new epicentres of production in the east.
- Europe will be vulnerable to external shocks as China locks herself into the boom-bust cycles driven by land speculation.[26]
- The tax revenues of North America will migrate outwards as the borderless world enables corporations to relocate in tax havens.

Without the productivity gains from democratic finance, Western civilisation will contract under the financial strains imposed by global competition. Europe faced a similar situation at the beginning of the 20th century, when new forms of transportation expanded international trade and disrupted the dominance of Britain, Germany and France over world markets. A century ago, there was a safety net: the colonies could be plundered to make up for the emerging economic deficits. To protect their claims over this safety-net, Europe embarked on the Great War. But we now live in the post-colonial era. There are no colonies for the Tax State to plunder to assuage the frustrations of the under-class.

We have now arrived at the final territorial frontier. But there is one route open to the future: we can go backwards. Each community can re-colonise its own social space. That would deliver enormous material, aesthetic and spiritual rewards. This is a large claim, one that will be elaborated at length elsewhere.[27] For present purposes, we may conclude that the reform would terminate the land-led booms and busts. Working people would be able to afford decent homes for their families, and enjoy a degree of security in employment that has not existed for two centuries. By re-democratising the public's finances, the injustices that were incubated in feudalism would be removed. From then on, people's destinies would finally be in their own hands.

REFERENCES

1   *The Future of Transport*, London: HMSO, July, 2004.
2   Productivity Commission, *op. cit.*, p.xii.
3   *Ibid*, p.xxv.
4   *Ibid.*
5   *Ibid*, p.157.
6   *Ibid*, p.163.
7   According to one estimate, reported in the *Economic Journal* (2000), Britain's tax-free black economy is of the order of 10% of GDP – more than £100bn. This costs the exchequer £40bn. While some people are pleased that others are able to escape paying taxes, they do not appreciate the increased burden that consequently falls on those who cannot escape the clutches of the taxman. Charlotte Moore, 'Brown eyes £100bn black economy', *The Guardian*, July 26, 2004.
8   Mason Gaffney, 'Taxes, Capital and Jobs', *Geophilos*, Spring 2003, on which I draw for some of the insights into the waste of liquid capital at the top end of the business cycle.
9   Ronald Banks, *Double-cross: Gordon Brown, the Treasury and the Hidden Cost of Taxes*, London: Centre for Land Policy Studies, 2002.
10 Ronald Banks, *Costing the Earth*, London: Shepheard-Walwyn, 1989. On rents in all their forms as a sufficient revenue base for public spending, see Mason Gaffney, 'An Inventory of Rent-yielding Resources', Appendix 1, *The Losses of Nations*, *op. cit.*
11 Alanna Hartzok, 'The Alaska model of Governance: Resource rents for public investment and citizen dividends', *Geophilos* Spring 2002, No 2(1). The first dividend payout, in 1982, was $1,000. In 2003, it was $1,107.
12 Ferdinand Mount, *Mind the Gap*, London: Short Books, 2004.
13 Harrison, *Wheels of Fortune*, forthcoming.
14 DTLR Press Release, July 20,2000, p.1.
15 This is the minimum payback, as repeatedly emphasised by Nobel prize-winning economist William Vickrey in his studies on transport and urban economics. For a jargon-free exposition of his conclusions on rent as the suitable source of public revenue, see Vickrey's four chapters in Kenneth C. Wenzer (ed.), *Land-Value Taxation*, New York: M.E. Sharpe/London: Shepheard-Walwyn, 1999.
16 Don Riley, *Taken for a Ride*, London: Centre for Land Policy Studies, 2001.
17 The methodology is described in Banks, *op. cit.*
18 Rana Roy, *Not By Spending Alone: the Case for a Comprehensive Tax Review*, London: Railway Forum, June 2004, p.6, Table 3.
19 European Conference of Ministers of Transport, *Reforming Transport Taxes*, Paris: OECD Publications, 2003, p.34, Table 1.
20 Roy, *Not By Spending Alone, op. cit.*, p.13.
21 V.H. Blundell, 'Flawed Land Acts 1947-1976', in Nicolaus Tideman, *Land and Taxation*, London: Shepheard-Walwyn, 1994.
22 Karl Marx and Friedrich Engels, *The Communist Manifesto*, Introduction by A.J.P. Taylor, Harmondsworth: Penguin, 1967, p.104.
23 H. Campion, *Public and Private Property in Great Britain*, London: Oxford University Press, 1939, p.120.
24 Richard Ford, 'Beware rise of Big Brother state, warns data watchdog', *The Times*, August 16, 2004.
25 World reserves provide enough oil to last for another 41 years at current rates of consumption, according to BP's 2004 statistical review of world energy. James Boxell, 'World oil reserves up 10%, says BP', *Financial Times*, June 16, 2004.
26 The peasant clearances of China, in the 21st century, were not so much from the rural as from the urban centres. The mass of unemployed people were also rootless, as property speculators demolished residential areas for the land that was

wanted for skyscrapers. The State Council attempted to rein in the 'growth in property investment that has sparked fears of real estate bubbles in urban areas and possible overheating in the wider economy', but the Peking regime was issuing its proclamations against the overwhelming pursuit of power that would deliver the privatisation of rent: 'Clearances are often backed by the police and strong-arm tactics are used, such as shutting off water and electricity.' Mure Dickie, 'Beijing opposes homes demolition', *Financial Times*, June 16, 2004.

27 It is the author's intention to do so in *The Pathology of Capitalism*.

PART V

The Reckoning

15

'

2007:
From Peak to Downwave

§1 The Alchemy of Debt

BANKS NO longer lend money. They sell 'products'. Subliminally, this is calculated to create the illusion that, like manufacturers, they sell something solid. Money-lenders have a psychic need to feel they are adding to the wealth of nations. So when house prices began to escalate in the 1990s, people were encouraged to believe (as *Time* was to declare): 'The boom created wealth throughout the economy'.[1]

Families, after all, appeared to be getting wealthier without having to expend energy. As the price of their homes rose, they borrowed their way into previously out-of-reach lifestyles. New cars in driveways and dream holidays reassured them that homes were wealth-creating machines. In fact, their dwellings were depreciating with wear and tear. The rise in prices was attributable to the locational value of the plots beneath their homes.

This was the economics of real estate that the policy-makers had suffused with metaphysics, so that now not even they appeared to understand the nature of value. One of them was Alan Greenspan, who claimed that 'Even in a digital age, bricks and mortar (or plywood and Sheetrock) are what stabilize us and make us feel at home'.[2] In the virtual world occupied by conventional economists, land lurked invisible, below the statistical radar screen, a load-bearing debt that would one day buckle...

It was largely on the back of these debts that bankers expanded the money supply. They created credit by using real estate mortgages as collateral. Debt was treated as an asset to lever more debt into the economy. At each step, financiers took their fees and bonuses – which were frequently invested in real estate as they sought some of the windfall gains that were showering onto the property markets. Eventually, the whirlpool in the financial sector would have to spin out of control as financiers, using homeowners as tools, milked their own credit-creating machine.

The merry-go-round would keep spinning for as long as families at the bottom of the credit chain kept paying the instalments on their mortgages. But as rising prices squeezed incomes to the limit, and central bankers piled on the agony by raising interest rates, defaults were inevitable. In the US, the Federal Reserve raised rates five times in quick succession. People found themselves unable to fund their personal collateralized debt obligations (mortgages). So the banks began to foreclose. In 2007, at least 2m borrowers were set to default.

§2 Delusion: Sub-prime Borrowers

FINANCIERS discovered that their attempt to capture some of the capital gains from real estate had backfired. Their technique for sharing in the real estate bonanza was achieved without having to buy and sell property. They invented 'products' which packaged other people's property debts, but these contained the seeds of their own destruction.

Formerly, if a borrower defaulted, the bank foreclosed ... and if there were too many such sour deals, the bank itself might be bankrupted. Now, however, the debts were being circulated in the world's money markets. So investors who had purchased these financial instruments in Germany could find themselves at the losing end of repossessed homes in Denver or Miami.[3]

Commentators sought comfort in the thought that the problem was confined to people on the lowest incomes who could no longer finance their mortgages. They were branded as 'sub-prime' borrowers. But even middle income people found themselves at the financial precipice. They had 'traded up' in the residential market in pursuit of capital gains. No matter how high their income, if they had borrowed to the hilt, formerly creditworthy people would also be unceremoniously ejected from their homes once they defaulted.

- In the US, an estimated $680bn worth of mortgages were due to have their rates adjusted – upwards. So the foreclosures, which doubled to 179,599 in June 2007, would be dwarfed in 2008. The ultimate price of the reckless lending would put more than 2.5m Americans at risk of foreclosure.
- In the UK, 2m households are on fixed-rate mortgage deals which they signed when rates were as low as 4.2%. About 800,000 of

these are due to end in 2008 – and they would have to pay around 5.5%. Defaulting – and losing their homes – could be the only option for many families.

Where will it all end? Economic pundits sought comfort in a magic mantra – the world economy was 'fundamentally sound'. But the seeds were already sown. As US house prices led the way, prices in Spain, France and Ireland also turned down (Table 15:1).

TABLE 15:1

Average House Price Growth: Eurozone

	France	Germany	Ireland	Italy	Spain
2003	11.8	-1.2	15.9	10.2	17.6
2004	15.2	-0.8	11.6	10.4	17.4
2005	15.3	-0.1	11.8	8.1	14.0
2006	12.1	0.5	13.4	6.7	10.4
2007*	6.6	0.7	0.8	4.3	4.4

*Forecast   *Source:* Barclays Capital

§3 The Correction

CENTRAL BANKERS struggled with the panic that swept the stock exchanges in August 2007. This was a 'correction', but they were blind to what would follow. If there had been dishonesty in assessing the credit worthiness of borrowers – did that not count as an 'external' shock which they could not be expected to have anticipated? Did this not exonerate them?

Families cut back on credit-card spending. Wal-Mart, among others, blamed poor trading results on sagging consumer confidence. The Ford and Chrysler motor companies appealed to the Federal Reserve to cut interest rates. Free market doctrines were brushed aside in the search for taxpayer-funded bail-outs, to stem the bankruptcy of mortgage companies. Countrywide Financial received a $2bn (£1bn) lifeline from Bank of America.

In Europe, debt levels were above 100% of GDP in the property hot-spots of Ireland, Spain, Denmark and the Netherlands. In Britain, the debt carried by consumers was £1,345bn. The debt-driven illusion of feeling wealthy had inflamed the 'buy now, pay later' culture. The self-fulfilling prophecy was behind every step up the debt ladder: as house prices rose, more was borrowed to buy electronic goods from Asia.

FIGURE 15:1

Land, House and Building Costs (UK 1983-2007)

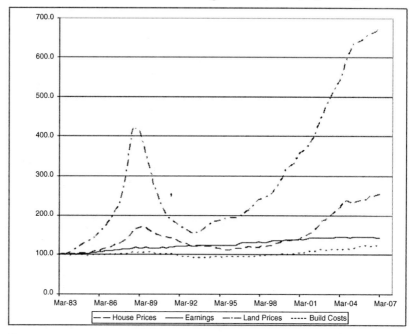

Sources:

House Prices: Halifax UK house price index, non-seasonally adjusted (http://www. hbosplc.com/economy/NationalPressRelease.asp).

Average Earnings: Office of National Statistics, Average Earnings Index 196301- 200704 (whole economy, seasonally adjusted, including bonuses).

Land Prices: Valuation Office Agency, Residential Building Land Index (England and Wales excluding London) (http://www.voa.gov.uk/publications/property_ market_report/pmr-jan-07/residential.htm).

Build Costs: BCIS (Building Cost Information Service) House Rebuilding Cost Index.

All series rebased to March 1983 = 100 and adjusted for inflation using the Office of National Statistics Retail Price Index.

Central bankers around the world had focused their efforts on controlling inflation. Diligently, however, they turned Nelsonian blind eyes on the one asset that would have alerted them to the looming disaster: land. Its value escalated way above the price of houses, or of the cost of the labour and materials used to construct dwellings. Fig. 15:1 tells the story for the UK since 1983. Wages rose in an orderly way up to the boom/bust of 1988-92, as they did during the following cycle. Land prices, however, were excluded from retail price calculations, and so, unconstrained by anti-inflationary public policy, rose fourfold from 1983 to 1989. Land prices then plunged until 1993, dooming the UK economy. They then recovered to rise sevenfold, immune to government attempts at fine-tuning the economy with monetary policy. But, if 2007 is the year of reckoning for the UK, land prices were already plunging in the US, Spain and southern Ireland.

Governments and central bankers were asleep, their macroeconomic instruments set on auto pilot. Gordon Brown, for example, informed the House of Commons in his 2007 budget speech that

> by holding firm to our commitment to maintain discipline in public sector pay, we will not only secure our 2% inflation target but create the conditions for maintaining the low interest and mortgage rates that since 1997 have been half the 11 per cent average of the previous twenty years. And we will never return to the old boom and bust.

Once again – even under a Labour government – it was workers' pay that had to be 'disciplined'. But with the rude awakening, the blame game would begin.

§4 The Policy Panic

IN WASHINGTON DC, the Democrat-controlled Congress panicked. Barney Frank, chairman of the House Financial Services Committee, announced plans to regulate the 'unregulated entities, and an essentially uncontrolled secondary market into which those originators sold their products'.[4] The legislators were once again trying to pull the wool over people's eyes. Joining them was Alan Greenspan, the guru of the financial markets who could not claim to be ignorant of how public policy had led innocent households into the debt trap. For, in discussing how home-ownership in the US had increased markedly, he claimed in his memoirs (on page 230) that

> The gains were especially dramatic among Hispanics and blacks, as increasing affluence as well as government encouragement of subprime mortgage programs enabled many members of minority groups to become first-time home buyers. This expansion of ownership gave more people a stake in the future of our country and boded well for the cohesion of the nation.

Greenspan approved, but the program would actually tear communities apart as properties were repossessed and left unsold, to blight the value of the homes of neighbours.

The financial crisis was no more than a slight variation on the old theme. Towards the end of the previous property cycle, for example, it was the (regulated) savings and loan institutions that were the epicentre of the 1980s crisis. In the cycle before that one in the UK – terminating in the early 1970s – the crisis surfaced around the so-called 'secondary banks' which triggered credit seizure in the City of London. Neither regulation nor monetary policy is the solution to the structural flaw in the capitalist economy.

For the roots of the speculative bubble in the new millennium, we have to return to the story of Alan Greenspan (Ch. 4 above). Under his chairmanship, the Federal Reserve lowered interest rates to 1%. Ever more borrowers could sink deeper into debt to buy properties that would otherwise have been beyond their financial reach. The economy grew, but not through investment in wealth-creating enterprises (Americans *dis*-saved). Growth was fuelled by debt. Exotic financial instruments were invented to ensnare a wider range of households. And Greenspan encouraged the shift to lower variable rate mortgages without alerting borrowers to the prospect that interest rates could not remain at 1% forever.

The bubble inflated, with more than half of the increase in output and employment over the first six years since 2000 anchored in the economics of land speculation. Greenspan retired, lionised by Gordon Brown, who had similarly allowed debt to expand in Britain to create the illusion of continuous growth during his 10 years at the Treasury.

Both Greenspan and Brown walked away from the economic levers just in time. Greenspan launched himself as a highly paid pundit on the speakers' circuit. Brown became Britain's Prime Minister. And as congressmen agonised over what kind of regulatory mechanism might forestall the next property crash (round about 2025), an estimated $3 trillion was wiped off the value of shares in the bourses around the world.

Buy-to-let speculators in Britain continued to purchase off-plan properties in the second half of 2007, holding prices beyond the reach of first time buyers. Compounding the agony, mortgage-lending companies like Northern Rock – the Newcastle-based lender was a victim of the US sub-prime securities – raised interest rates for borrowers. Would there be a full-scale US-style housing crash in the UK? In the quest to increase the supply of affordable dwellings, the British government created a think-tank which reassuringly announced in its first report:

> Predictions of a housing market crash do not reflect market fundamentals – **demand for housing, driven by economic and population growth, continues to outstrip available supply.**[5]

But repossessions were rising and builders were reducing the construction of new dwellings. Fundamentally speaking, someone was dead wrong. Central bankers were in a quandary. If they cut interest rates, to help mortgage companies, this would encourage a further rise in property prices and lead to an even steeper drop from the precipice. If they raised interest rates, to counter inflation, this would damage the enterprises that created the real wealth – and give another twist to the downward spiral. The credit crisis of 2006 proved that central bankers had not learnt the lessons of the Great Depression.

- In Britain, the *débâcle* that triggered the run on the Northern Rock led to criticism of Mervyn King, the Governor of the Bank of England, by MPs. He admitted under questioning that the regulatory architecture was flawed.

The bank's chief economist, Charles Bean, admitted that they did not have an adequate working grasp of the nature of 'money' and the Bank of England was 'therefore considering refining our definition of broad money (M4), so as to provide a measure that is more likely to reflect its use in economic transactions'.[6]

- In America, Alan Greenspan washed his hands of the crisis. And yet, he had lulled low-income people into complacency. He admits: 'I would tell audiences that we were facing not a bubble but a froth – lots of small, local bubbles that never grew to a scale that could threaten the health of the overall economy.'[7]

The froth overflowed and *did* threaten the health of the US economy, according to alarmed economists at the International Monetary Fund. Greenspan, as a privileged insider, had tracked all the warning signals. So he ought not to have been in doubt about what was fermenting beneath the froth. There was, for example, the growing gap between rich and poor: 'Two-tier economies are common in developing countries, but not since the 1920s have Americans experienced such inequality of income'.[8]

Big question marks hung over the property boom in Asia. Double
digit growth rates in India and China fostered speculation in real
estate. Particularly dangerous for the global economy are the savings
accumulated by China. Her factories' profits have saturated the
Shanghai stock exchange. The frugal Chinese accumulated savings
estimated at $2.3 trillion (£1.4 trillion). There is one obvious outlet for
this liquidity. A Shanghai-based economist forecast that the outflow of
hundreds of billions of dollars would be in the direction of 'Residential
land in Hong Kong and Vancouver, farmland in Africa and natural
resources in Asia'.[9] So flush with cash is China, thanks to the willingness of the US to collapse into debt, that the hot money would have
two effects. By outbidding others for land and natural resources, the
Chinese would solidify the global dimensions to the depression of
2010. And as markets crash, the cash-rich Chinese would become the
bottom feeders, amassing control over the raw materials and properties in strategic locations around the world to give them the competitive edge over Europe and North America in the upturn in 2012.

As the IMF warned that the 2007 credit crunch in the financial
markets would damage the global economy, policy-makers were confronted with the realisation that monetary policy had failed. Now, tax
policy was once again on the political agenda. But would governments
have the courage to challenge the privileged relationship between real
estate and politics? To lay the foundations for the upswing of the next
business cycle, the correct strategy is to cut interest rates and make a
bonfire of the special concessions that favoured land owners. The
early signs were not good. In the UK, for example, David Cameron, as
leader of the opposition, promised that a future Conservative government would relieve first-time buyers of the cost of stamp duty. Far
from making homes affordable, however, this would increase prices at
the bottom end of the housing market and set the scene for the next
explosion in land prices after the depression of 2010.

REFERENCES

1 Barbara Kiviat, 'Real estate's fault line', *Time*, August 27, 2007, p.30.
2 Alan Greenspan, *The Age of Turbulence*, London: Allen Lane, 2007, p.230.
3 In Germany, Sachsen LB, a public bank, was rescued by regional savings banks after
   it was unable to provide the €17.3bn ($23.5bn) credit facility it had pledged to an
   investment fund it operated. It had invested heavily in US sub-prime mortgages.
   Even in China, two banks between them held more than $11bn in securities backed
   by US sub-prime mortgages.
4 Barney Frank, 'A (sub)prime argument for more regulation', *Financial Times*, August
   20, 2007.

5   National Housing and Planning Advice Unit, *Affordability Matters*, London, 2007, p.22. Emphasis in original. The chairman of the NHPAU was Prof. Stephen Nickell, Warden of Nuffield College, Oxford, and a former member of the Bank of England's Monetary Policy Committee. He was emphatic. In an interview with the *Daily Telegraph* (Edmund Conway, 'The ex-MPC dove who misses "the fun" of setting interest rates', August 27, 2007), Nickell declared: '[T]here won't be a crash. It would take a recession – unemployment rising by half a million; what we saw in 1990'.

6   Charles Bean, Foreword, *Bank of England Quarterly Bulletin* 2007 (Vol. 47:3).

7   Greenspan, *op. cit.*, p.231.

8   *Ibid.*, p.232.

9   Stephen Green, 'Get ready for the next big China effect', *Financial Times*, August 21, 2007.

Index

Absorption, Economic Law of, 50
Afghanistan, 54, 64, 159
Age of Turbulence, The, x
Ahern, Bertie, 126
Akamai Technologies, 47
Alaska, 252
Aloha Petroleum, 44
Al-Qaeda, 64
Amazon.com, 46
Ambrose, Peter, xvii
AOL Europe, 39
ARM Holdings, 46
Arrow, Kenneth, 50
ASDA, 41
Asian Tigers, 122, 137, 159, 171, 176, 268, 272
Association of British Insurers, 12
Attitude Network, 46-7
Australia, 93
— banks and, 226, 229-30, 233, 238, 239
— construction and, 229, 231-2, 235, 236
— cycles:
    18-year, 28, 235
    1956-74, 238
    1974-92, 226, 227, 236
    1992-2010, 227, 231, 235, 236, 242
— debts of households, 230, 236, 240
— demography, 95, 226, 229
— First Home Owner Scheme, 242
— house prices and, xii, 18, 125, 226, 228, 230, 235, 239, 240
— investment properties, 230
— land booms, 105, 112, 123, 232-7
— land supply, 229
— land value, 228, 235
— land value taxation, 231-5, 238, 240
— speculation and, 230, 233-4, 236, 238
  See also: Australia, Reserve Bank of;
  Productivity Commission (Australia)
Australia, Reserve Bank of, 227, 237, 242

Australian Prudential Regulatory
  Authority, 227
Austria, 33

Balls, Ed, 12
Bank for International Settlements, 69, 168, 170
Bank of America, 267
Bank of England, xv, 29, 45, 102, 112, 130
— house prices and, xviii, 8-9, 10, 14, 15, 18, 19, 144, 196, 197, 212
— independence of, 8, 187-8, 202, 203
— interest rates and, 132, 133, 194, 200-1
— land prices and, 191
— monetary policy committee of, 17, 36, 185, 187, 212-13
— Northern Rock and, ix, 271
Banker's Magazine, The, 112
Bankgesellschaft Berlin, 169
Banks
— crises and, ix-xii, 58, 139, 182-3, 265-71 *passim*
— land, credit and, ix-xi, 88, 90, 169, 175-6, 196, 265-71 *passim*
— profits from real estate and, 29, 215
  See also: Business cycles; Land;
  Northern Rock
Banks, Ronald, 250-1
Barber, Anthony, 6-8, 132
Barclays Bank, 238
Barker, Kate, 15, 17, 22, 25, 131-2, 210
Barnes, Yolanda, 190
Barton, Mark, 48
Bean, Charles, 271
Belgium, 13, 33
Bell, Marian, 17
Berkeley Group, 197
Bertelsmann, 39
Birmingham, 32, 69, 82, 86, 100, 103, 199
Blair, Cheri, 8

Blair, Tony
— British model promoted by, 159
— EU reforms and, 210
— Gordon Brown as rival of, 4, 7, 27,
— government of, xv, 31, 41, 194, 214,
  246, 255, 256
— House of Lords and, 3
— New Labour and, 28
— politics and, 218
— property purchased by, 8
— property rights and, 166
— Third Way doctrine and, 208, 211
Blaug, Mark, 150
BMW, 192
Boom bust, xii, 65, 69, 119, 143, 162, 211
— financial revolution and, 83
— government responsibility for, xvii,
  80, 131, 144, 156, 160, 163, 195, 217,
  237, 239, 241
— law of nature, 128-9, 185-6
— markets and, 85, 89
— myths and, 39, 155-60
— planning and, 25
— property cycles, xv, 19, 28, 29, 56, 57,
  67, 82, 116, 129, 202
— remedies, xv, xvi, 4, 8, 85, 107, 127,
  150, 159, 195, 198, 214-18, 231, 237, 238,
  260
— 1973-4 and, 6-7, 108, 132, 136, 140,
  170, 202
— 1988-9 and, 6, 7, 19, 27, 31, 34-5, 127,
  170, 202, 223, 269
  See also: Depression; Property cycles;
  Recessions, Enema Theory of
Braybrook, Edward, 29-30
Brisbane, 227, 228
Britain
— credit crunch in, x, 271
— debt, 267-8, 270
— GDP, 168, 250
— homelessness in, 163
— housing market, xi, xii, 270
— population, 95, 228
— productivity in, 21
— railways and, 104-5, 112, 253-4
— recessions, 28, 130, 266-7, 269, 270
— savings, 12, 26
— wealth in, 228
  See also: Boom bust; Housing; Land
British Antarctic Survey, xiii
British Chambers of Commerce, 192
British Columbia, 173-5

British Telecom, 93
Brittan, Sir Samuel, 146
Brown, Gordon
— as Prime Minister, 270
— Bank of England and, 8, 199, 202
— Brown's boom bust, 6, 134, 145
— budget (2000), 250
— budget (2003), 4
— budget (2004), 3, 9-10, 27, 36
— budget (2007), 269
— business cycle (1992-2010), 3-6, 7, 9,
  14-15, 27-8, 31, 35-6, 186-7, 195-6, 199
— criticised, xiv-xv, 9, 11, 27, 28, 219,
  255
— debt and, 270
— electro-magnetic spectrum and, 92
— euro and, 4
— fosters property speculation, xvii, 10,
  11, 219
— house price instability and, 4, 10-11,
  210, 218
— housing and, 163, 218-19
— in opposition, 91
— magic mantra, 184, 185, 187, 189, 199,
  218
— People's Budget and, 221
— planning system and, 22
— political ambition of, 4, 7, 27, 202
— recession of 2001 and, 9, 27, 202,
  212
— record of 200 years and, 5, 21
— savings and, 12
— unearned increment in land and, 28,
  131, 257
  See also: Inflation; Taxation; Treasury
Buchanan, James, 50
Building industry (UK), 21, 73, 88, 106,
  116, 130-2, 147, 189, 195, 209
— costs of, 96, 197, 268
— 14-year construction cycles, 56,
  87-93, 95-7, 100, 103, 109-10, 217
— 18-year cycles, 86-96, 100, 108, 129
Building societies, 29, 97, 105, 199
Burns, Lord, 146-7
Bush, George, 180
Bush, George W., xi, xii, 44, 58, 63-5,
  180, 207, 214
Business cycles, 188
— first global, 58, 169
— land hypothesis, 76-7, 129-30
— mid-cycle recessions, 109-15
— patterns in, 25, 28

Business cycles—*contd*
— 18-year cycles, x-xi, xii, 73-5, 78-80,
   95, 97, 100, 109, 115, 133, 145, 169, 218,
   269, 270, 272
   See also: Banks
Business Week, xiii

Cahill, Kevin, 140
California, xi, 39, 52, 146
Cameron, David, 272
Campion, H., 258
Canada, xii, 125, 228, 250
Canning, Charles, 103
Capital, 41, 85, 88, 90, 94, 104, 124, 142,
   213, 217, 235, 243, 251, 266
Capital Economics, 15
Capitalism, xiii, xvi, 6, 21, 28, 29, 35, 40,
   65, 88, 97, 136, 140, 146, 150, 170, 182,
   201, 203, 208, 217, 270
Centre for Economic and Business
   Research, 15, 16
Chamberlain, Austen, 220-1
Chamberlain, Neville, 222-3
Chaos Makers, The, 185
Charles II, 83
Chicago, 86, 181
China, xii, 201, 211, 214, 260, 272
Chrysler motor company 267
Church Stretton, 49
Churchill, Winston S., 114, 219
Citigroup, 15
City Index, 55
City of London, x, xii, 5, 39, 45, 93, 107,
   111, 112, 122, 161, 270
Clapham, John, 76, 113
Clay, Christopher, 80
Clinton, Bill, 156-60, 166, 170, 179, 180,
   207
Coleridge, Samuel Taylor, 103
Comfort, Steven, 42
Commercial Investment Real Estate
   Institute, 171
Competition and Credit Control
   (UK), 7
Confederation of British Industry, 21,
   185, 200, 255
Conference Board, 177
Congdon, Tim, 16, 19
Construction industry: *see* Building
   industry
Construction Products Association,
   132-3

Consumer Federation of America, 183
Convention of Scottish Local
   Authorities, 195
Co-operative Permanent Building
   Society, 32
Cotis, Jean-Philippe, 14
Countrywide Financial, 267
Crossrail, 248
Crown land, 79, 81
Cunningham, W., 29
Cyberspace, 163, 194

Darling, Alistair, 246, 255
Darwin, Charles, 49
Deadweight losses, 250, 254-5
Debt, x-xi, xviii, 10-12, 14, 55, 181-2,
   265-6, 267, 269, 270, 272
Denmark, 13, 32, 33, 238, 267
Depression (1929), ix, xi, 110, 130, 202-3,
   258, 271
Depression (2010), ix, 28, 109, 145, 156,
   185, 197, 203, 272
Deutsche Bank, 16
Development Land Tax (UK), 25
Disraeli, B., 111
Dizard, John 51
Dot.com bubble, 34, 38, 41, 42, 43, 45-8,
   52, 55, 58, 123, 162, 175, 176, 181, 203,
   207
   See also: New Economy
Downs, Anthony, 172
Dreiman, Shelly, 57, 59
Dublin Transportation Office, 126
Dudley, 111
Dwyer, Terry, 233, 235
Dye, Tony, 14, 15, 16

East India Company, 120
Economic and Social Research Council,
   92, 208
Economics, x, 140, 141, 157, 208, 221-2
— Classical, 40, 131, 158, 241
— Models, 17, 21, 135, 139, 146-7, 161,
   163, 191
— Theory, xiii, 55, 60, 65, 66, 85, 96,
   136, 150, 175, 265, 267, 270, 271-2
Economist, The, 15, 18
eGroup, 42
Eichel, Hans, 210
Electro-magnetic spectrum, 42-53, 92-3,
   166
Elizabeth I, 79

Elizabeth II, 66, 69
Empty Homes Agency, 198
Enclosures, 84, 114
Enron, 43, 44, 68
Enterprise zone, 52
European Union, 192, 202, 210-11
Evans, Linda, 200
Excite@home, 52

Fannie Mae, 57
Farman, Joseph, xiii
Fastow, Andrew, 44
Federal Housing Finance Board, 178
Federal Reserve Board (USA), x, xvi, 202-3, 266, 267, 270
Financial Services Authority, 11, 196
Financial Times, The, 16, 51, 93, 187, 212
Finland, 13, 139
FIRE sector, 182
First Home Owner Scheme: *see* Australia
Forbes, 176
Ford motor company, 267
Forrester Research, 200
FPDSavills, 34, 109, 189-90
France, 4, 13, 85, 110, 121, 125, 147, 168, 208, 209, 211, 228, 250, 260, 267
Frank, Barney, 269
Freddie Mac, 57
Free-riders, 147-50, 243, 249
Freeserve, 46
Fukuyama, Francis, 112

Gaffney, Mason, 22, 88, 248
Galbraith, John, 130-1
Games Domain, 46
Gates, Bill, 47, 48, 194
Gazumping, 89
General Motors, 46
George, David Lloyd, 114, 218, 219, 223, 256
George, Henry, 114, 221, 233
George, Sir Edward, 161, 192, 194
Germany, xi, 4, 10, 13, 32, 33, 107, 125, 132, 168-9, 208-10, 228, 229, 250, 260, 266, 267
Glasgow, 96, 111, 114
Goldman Sachs, 15, 16, 43
Greenspan, Alan
— criticised, x, xii, xiv, 160
— dot.com bubble and, 55-6, 123, 175, 203, 207
— financial crises and, 60, 66-9, 269-70, 271

Greenspan, Alan—*contd*
— Gordon Brown and, 202, 270
— house prices and, 33, 59, 179, 265
— knighthood, 66-9
— land market and, 56, 66-7
— metaphysical language of, 56, 66, 136-9
— monetary policy, 60-1
— oil prices and, 65
— sub-prime mortgages and, 269-70, 271
— 1990s boom and, 54, 180
— 2001 recession and, 56, 67-8, 177
  See also: New Economy
Gross, Bill, xi
Groupthink, 140, 214-15, 222, 224, 241
Guardian, The, 22
Gwartney, Ted, 173

Half Moon Bay, CA, 38
Halifax Building Society, 16, 32, 105
Hammond, J.L. & Barbara, 147-9
Hanson, Esau, 105
Harken Energy, 44
Heath, Edward, 7
Henry VIII, 77, 222
Hitler, Adolf, 222
Hobsbawm, Eric, 113
Honda, 219
Hong Kong, 240, 272
Hope, Dennis M., 166
House Financial Services (USA), 269
House of Commons
— Treasury Committee, 35-6, 193, 199
— Environment Committee, 41
House of Lords, 3, 113-15, 212, 220
House of Representatives (USA), 43
House Rebuilding Cost Index, 268
Housing
— capital gains and, 6, 25, 59, 84, 179
— consumption and, 8
— debt, xvii, 267-8
— distinguished from land, 31, 269
— inflation and, 26
— mortgages and, 8, 88, 193, 266-7
— prices (Australia), xii
— prices (Canada), xii
— prices (Europe), 125-6, 267, 269
— prices (UK), xi-xii, 10-11, 18, 26, 33, 55, 89, 116-17, 128, 155, 188, 190, 193, 196, 265, 268-9, 270-1, 272
— prices (USA), ix, x-xi, xii, 267, 270

Housing—*contd*
— stop-go cycles, 4-6, 8, 10, 18, 23, 84, 89-91, 108-9, 203
— taxes, 39
— vacant dwellings, 84, 198
— 1930s boom in, 107, 223
See also: Building industry
Housing and Town Planning Act (1908), 23
Housing and Urban Development (USA), 61-3, 178
Houston, 24, 59
Houston Chronicle, 24
Hoyt, Homer, 86-7
Hudson, George, 104, 105-6
Hudson, Michael, 88, 138, 182
Hussein, Saddam, 63-4, 214

Income tax: *see* William Pitt
Independent Labour Party, 222
India, xii, 211, 272
Industrial Revolution, xv, 69, 82-3, 100, 149-50
Inflation, xiii, 161, 168, 188, 268-9, 271
— Alan Greenspan and, 60
— defined, 8, 10, 187, 189, 202
— Gordon Brown's targets, 8, 11, 26, 36, 192-3, 199, 201, 212, 269
— recessions attributed to, 26, 27, 188
— 19th century, 26
— 1980s, 7, 268-9
Information Age, 40, 50, 51, 52, 158
Infrastructure, 90, 110, 124, 146, 198, 240, 252
— land values and:
       Australia, 242, 243, 247
       Ireland, 125-6
       Spain, 125-7
       UK, 104, 209, 219, 253-7
       USA, 45
Institute of Fiscal Studies, 223
Interest rates, ix, 96, 191-2, 197, 202, 236, 266, 267, 269, 270-1, 272
— 5%, 77-8, 83, 87, 97, 100, 105, 199-201
Internal Revenue Service, 41
International Monetary Fund, 14, 15, 18, 55, 136, 271
Internet, 39, 42, 45, 48-58, 158-9, 162, 194
Iran, 64
Iraq, 63-5, 196

Ireland, 13, 18, 125-6, 209, 267, 269
Italy, 13, 85, 125, 164, 228, 250, 267

Janis, Irving, 214
Japan, 10, 28, 57, 85, 93, 95, 125, 140, 159, 168-70, 194, 228, 229, 250
Jarrow, 106, 113
Jenkins, Roy, 113-14, 221-2
Johnson, Melanie, 188
Johnson, Peter, 197
Johnston, Thomas, 101 *passim*

Kennedy, John F., 214
Ketley, Richard, 32, 82-3
Keynes, John Maynard, 10, 88, 93-5, 135-6, 138, 139, 140-4
Keynesianism, 10
King, Mervyn
— criticism of, 271
— house prices and, xviii, 201, 212-13
— money defined by, 19
— recessions analysed by, 130
Klein, Lawrence, 50
Knight Frank, 116-17
Knight Ridder Information, 48
Korean War, 136
Kosovo, 159
Krugman, Paul, 44
Kuwait, 64
Kuznets, Simon, 84

Lamont, Norman, 128-9
Land, 21, 83, 85, 114, 140, 159
— capital gains, 81, 92, 109, 127, 139, 143, 164, 175, 197, 209, 215, 219, 223, 233, 235, 237, 243
— cycles in, 34
— defined, 22, 40-1, 42, 142, 164, 191
— income redistribution and, xviii, 82, 85, 87, 88, 111, 124, 147, 162, 164, 182, 195, 241, 249, 253
— interest rates, 212-13
— macroeconomic impact of, 34, 57, 67, 81, 84, 87-8, 90, 97, 103, 150, 178, 190
— market, 29, 34, 40, 50, 56, 67, 77-82, 86, 255
— monopoly power of, 40, 132, 219-20, 241, 258
— owners, xvi, 29, 39, 48, 104, 114-15, 135, 138, 143, 163, 190, 194, 197, 220-2, 249, 252, 255
— prices, 265, 268-9, 272

Land—*contd*
— speculation, 7, 17, 19, 24, 31, 34, 45,
  58-9, 68, 69, 79, 80-1, 89-91, 93, 95,
  103, 110, 112, 114-15, 117, 127, 131-4,
  141, 143, 146-7, 157, 171, 183, 195, 217,
  222, 234, 236, 270, 272
— taxation, 113-14, 140, 148-9, 213, 216,
  222, 231-7, 240, 243, 247-8, 250-3
— values, 31, 33-5, 86, 89, 109, 113, 120,
  138, 140, 144, 173-4, 177, 189-90,
  191-3, 197-8, 217, 249, 254
  See also: Australia; Rent; USA
Land Clauses Consolidation Act (1845),
  104
Land Registry, 195
Land Values, 114
Land Values (Assessment and Rating)
  Bill, 114
Law, John, 121
Lawson, Nigel, 6, 7, 8, 19, 34, 35, 91-2,
  128-9, 133, 223
Lay, Kenneth, 43
Leeds, 112
Lenard, Dennis, 130
Letchworth, 32
Lewis, J. Parry, 73-7, 79, 84, 96, 102,
  106-7, 110, 116
Liberal Party, 114-15, 220
Lisbon Accord, 210
Liverpool, 102-3, 112, 114, 165
Lomax, Rachel, 213
London, x, 73-4, 114, 117, 192, 198
Los Angeles, 24
Losses of Nations, The, 224
Louisiana, 121
Loveridge, Danny, 127
Luxembourg, 33

Macfarlane, Ian, 227, 239
Manchester, 110, 112, 114
Manchester City Council, 41
Marsh & McLennan, 51
Marshall, Alfred, 216
Marx, Karl, 40, 52, 105, 135, 146, 212, 216,
  257
McCarthy, Jonathan, 183
McDonald's, 41
Melbourne, 228, 229, 237
Merthyr Tydfil, 16
Mexico, 137
Microsoft, 47
Miller, George, 78, 240

Miller, Marcus, 180
Monaco, 164
Monetarism, 19
Monetary policy, xiv-xvi, 26, 161, 213-16,
  237-8, 269, 270, 272
— Anthony Barber and, 7
— consumption, effects on, xviii,
— Nigel Lawson, 128-9
Morgan Stanley, 183
Mount Ferdinand, 252-3
Muellbauer, John, 7

Napier, Iain, 22
Napoleonic Wars, 26
NASA, xiii, 67, 176
National Audit Office, 36
National Bureau of Economic Research,
  54
National Institute of Economic and
  Social Research, 15, 16
Neath, 16
Netherlands, 13, 18, 33, 119-20, 125, 230,
  267
New Economy, xv, 172, 177
— as myth, 155-60, 164
— cost-cutting productivity and, 51
— debt and, 182
— resource rents and, 68, 170, 194
— virtual reality and, 38-49, 175
  See also: Dot.com bubble; Alan
  Greenspan
New Jersey, 24
New Labour, 5, 28 12, 35, 187, 188, 196,
  208, 253
New Statesman, xvi, 27
New York, 42, 50, 93
New Zealand, 50
Newton, Isaac, 119, 128, 129
Nickell, Stephen, 8
Northern Rock, ix-x, 270, 271
Norway, 139, 165

O'Donnell, Gus, 163
Office of Federal Housing Enterprise
  Oversight, 57-8
Oil rents, 63-4, 108, 140, 143, 165, 223-4, 252
Oklahoma land rush, xvii
OPEC, 64, 108, 124
Oregon, 23
Organisation for Economic Cooperation
  and Development, 14, 15, 67, 85, 172,
  196, 210

Oswald, Andrew, 16

Pacific Investment Management
    Company, xi
Palm, 52
Patten, Chris, 211
Paul, Ron, 60-1
Peach, Richard W., 183
Pensions
— UK, xi, xvii, 12, 44, 260
— USA, xi, 55, 67, 68
People's Budget (1909-10), 3, 113-15,
    218-21
Perkins, Tony, 176
Peston, Robert, 8
Pidgley, Tony, 197
Pitt, William, 147-8
Planning (UK), 23, 124, 195
Planning system, 21-5, 27, 226
Plassmann, Florenz, 250-1
Plating, K. & S., 200
Port Talbot, 16
Portland (Oregon), 24, 59
Portugal, 33, 209
Power in the Land, The, 28, 108, 129,
    224
Prescott, John, 198, 253
Price, Seymour J., 32
Productivity Commission (Australia),
    226, 229, 237, 238, 240, 242-3
Public property, theory of, 165-7, 198,
    217, 258

Quantum Fund, 45
Quick Save, 41

Ramsey, Lord de, 125
Real estate investment trusts, 171
Recessions, Enema Theory of, 130-2
Rent
— electro-magnetic spectrum, 93
— feudalism and, 40
— formation of, 163-7, 246
— growing share of GDP, 40, 52, 162,
    241
— of resources, 124, 143
— pressure gauge, 55, 106, 137, 172-3,
    186, 253
— securitisation and, 43-4, 121-3, 175
— social revenue, 81, 82, 216-17, 222,
    235-9, 248, 257
— theory of, 135, 190, 223

Rhode Island, 59
Ricardo, David, 135, 138
Riley, Don, 255
Roach, Stephen, 183
Roy, Rana, 256
Ruffley, David, 36
Russell, Lord, 107
Russia, xii, 159, 171, 221, 229, 257

Sacrifice ratio, xiv
Sage, 46
San Fernando Valley, 38
    See also: Silicon Valley
Sarkozy, Nicolas, 211
Savings and loans associations, 29, 97,
    139, 270
Schmidt, Andreas, 39-40
Scotland, 195
Seager, Ashley, 65
Securitisation, 43, 121-2
Shanghai Stock Exchange, 272
Shannon, H.A., 73
Shaw, George Bernard, 135
Shelter, 130
Shropshire, 49, 83
Silicon Valley, 38, 42, 52, 176
Simonian, Haig, 169
Slavery, 121, 165
Smith, Adam, 82, 135, 147, 148
Snowden, Philip, 221-4, 256
Socialism, 208, 248, 252, 257
Soros, George, 45
South Sea Bubble, 119-20
Soviet Union, 170, 253, 257
Spain, 13, 18, 125-7, 139, 164, 209, 230,
    238, 267, 269
Spitzer, Eliot, 51
Stagecoach, 193
Stamp duty, 193-4
Stanworth, Dave, 46-7
Stelzer, Irwin, xiv
Stevens, Glenn, 230-1
Stringer, Graham, 41
Sub-prime mortgages, ix, 266-7, 269, 270
Summers, Lawrence H., 160-2
Sunday Times, The, 194-5
Sweden, 13, 33, 57, 131, 137, 139
Sydney, 227-9, 233, 237
Sykes, Sir Richard, 12

Taliban, 64
Tax State, 40, 207, 246, 251-2, 258-60

Taxation
— democratisation of, 208
— Gordon Brown, 189
— land values and, 126, 164, 272
— losses arising from, 156, 193, 211
— production costs and, 51, 144, 149
— recessions and, 116, 186, 192-3
— redistributes income from poor to
  rich, xviii, 113, 243
— rent and, 216-18, 240-4
— socially divisive, xvi
— urban sprawl and (USA), 178
  See also: Deadweight losses;
  Free-riders; Land; People's Budget;
  William Pitt
Taylor, Jay, 61
Taylor Woodrow, 22
Temperance Permanent Building Society,
  32
Tenants in Common Associations, xvii
Terminating societies, 30, 32, 82-4, 87, 97
Texas, 23
Thailand, 57
Thames Gateway, 198
Thatcher, Margaret, 7, 19, 25 28, 31, 128,
  129, 146, 193, 196, 210, 252
Thomas, Richard, 259
Thompson, Graeme, 227
Tideman, Nicolaus, 250-1
Time, 265
Time Warner, 39
Times, The, 16
Titanic Guidance System, Doctrine of,
  160, 186, 187
Toon, Roger, 49-50
Town and Country Planning Act (1947),
  23
Treasury
— building industry and, 130, 197, 198
— electro-magnetic spectrum and, 92
— First World War and, 107
— Gordon Brown and, 185, 187, 270
— inflation and, 188
— model of economy, 36, 191, 194, 201
— tax policy and, 203, 224, 248, 251, 255
— 1992 recession, 28, 128-9, 223
  See also: People's Budget; Philip
  Snowden
Tricks, Henry, 15, 17

UK: *see* Britain
United Nations, 190

Uriconium, 49
USA, 95, 162, 168, 179-80, 228, 229, 250
— consumer debts, 59, 60, 61, 62, 90,
  177-9, 183
— homeless, 38, 53,
— house prices and, xii, 18, 33, 59, 125,
  178, 183
— housing crisis, ix, xii, 61-3, 178, 183
— housing cycle (1976-89), 27
— housing cycle (1994-2010), 27, 56-7,
  171-2, 178, 179
— land prices, 38, 57, 58, 90, 138
— land speculation in, 111, 142, 167
— monetary policy and, 60, 175-7,
  203
— productivity of, 162, 170, 171, 182,
  207, 208
— railways (19th-century), 43-5, 50
— recessions and, 28, 54, 56, 137, 139,
  170, 177, 212
— slavery and, 165
— vacancy rates, 52
— virtual reality and, 36, 39, 42, 66, 68,
  160
— 18-year cycles and, 86, 145
  See also: Dot.com bubble; New
  Economy; Pensions; Planning;
  Taxation
Usury, 29, 78, 100

Verdict, 186
Vodaphone, 93

Wadhwani, Sushil, 185
Wages, 89, 97, 113, 147, 168, 176, 188, 193,
  199, 215, 235, 240, 268-9
— settlements, in 1971 (UK), 7
— rents and, 51, 116, 148-9
Wagner, Dan, 48
Wales, 16, 192, 196, 197, 240
Wall Street, x, xii, 39, 41, 63, 88, 122, 155,
  157, 161, 168, 171, 176, 177, 180, 181, 221
Wal-Mart, 41, 267
War, 63, 73-6, 81, 106, 110
Warenne, William of, 194-5
Washington, DC, 59, 86, 269
Watling Street, 49
Wealth effect, 183
Webb, Sidney and Beatrice, 102
Weber, Bernard, 96
Whitewater land deal, 157
Whitlam, Gough, 234, 236

Wilcox, Steve, xvii
Wilkinson, Ellen, 106
Wimpey, George, 197
Winner's Curse, xi, 89-93, 128, 139, 145, 173, 177, 197, 213, 227, 231, 233, 237
Wolf, Martin, 15, 16
Wolff, Edward, 176
Woodall, Pam, 18
Woodward, Llewellyn, 115
World Bank, 136, 190

World Economic Forum, 159
World Trade Center, 54
World Trade Organisation, 168
World War I, 26, 107, 136, 169, 258, 260
World War II, 107, 169, 234
World wide web, 42
Wright, Whitaker, 124

Yahoo!, 46
Youings, Joyce, 77-9, 81